Praise for *Deadly Election*

Betsy Hartmann has written an elegant mystery story, a political thriller that confronts the darkest imponderables of our post-9/11 world. *Deadly Election* is that rare thing: a thoughtful page-turner.

> —Kai Bird, co-author with Martin J. Sherwin of the Pulitzer Prize-winning biography, *American Prometheus: The Triumph and Tragedy of J. Robert Oppenheimer*

Betsy Hartmann has done something extraordinary: created a virtual reality version of the Bush administration that is both utterly convincing and even more bone-chillingly scary than the real thing. Like Richard Condon did in *The Manchurian Candidate*, she's grasped something that few other writers have: there are times when only a distorting mirror gives us back a true image of ourselves.

> —Anthony Giardina, author of *White Guys* and *Recent History*

The Republicans fear they're going to lose the coming election so they hatch a Machiavellian plot to have it postponed. Can they pull it off?

In Betsy Hartmann's gripping novel, *Deadly Election*, we're swept up by the intrigues of a cunning and treacherous political game. Every time we think we see our way clearly to the bottom of things, the story takes a dazzling new turn. Hartmann has her finger on the pulse of behind-the-scenes Washington, and she's given her characters such depth and verve it's easy to forget we're reading fiction.

Deadly Election is more than an electrifying thriller. It's an insightful investigation into the human condition—what makes some of the most promising people turn evil, and what turns some unlikely people into heroes. This is a dangerous book, and should be required reading for anyone who takes our democracy for granted.

> —Corinne Demas, professor of English at Mount Holyoke College and author of *Eleven Stories High: Growing up in Stuyvesant Town, 1948-1968*

Deadly Election is a seductive thriller that leads us into the beating heart of present day American politics. I turned the pages for the brisk plotting and lively characters, then found myself caught by Hartmann's profound and chilling understanding of the grave danger faced when fear of terrorism is used as cover for savage political ambition. This is a novel that is a pleasure to read quickly, and which needs to be read urgently.

    —Roger King, author of *A Girl from Zanzibar*, winner of the BABRA award for best novel.

Betsy Hartmann has taken our darkest fears of the Bush administration and carried them one terrifying step further: she's written a highly plausible thriller about a government conspiracy to postpone the 2008 elections. An electrifying novel that's not to be missed!

    —Michael Klare, author of *Blood and Oil*

DEADLY
ELECTION

DEADLY ELECTION

ELECTION

Betsy Hartmann

WRP

White River Press
White River Junction, Vermont

DEADLY ELECTION

Betsy Hartmann

published January 2008 by White River Press
by arrangement with the author

front cover design by Jamie Hartmann-Boyce

text design by Sonja Hakala, White River Press

White River Press
PO Box 4624
White River Junction, Vermont 05001
www.whiteriverpress.com

ISBN: 978-0-9792451-4-5

Library of Congress Cataloging-in-Publication Data

Hartmann, Betsy.
Deadly election / Betsy Hartmann. — 1st American pbk. ed.
p. cm.
ISBN 978-0-9792451-4-5 (pbk. : alk. paper)
1. Presidents—United States—Election—Fiction.
2. Dictatorship—Fiction. I. Title.
PS3608.A7875D43 2007
813'.6--dc22
2007031344

In memory of my father, Thomas B. Hartmann, who taught me that
political decisions are moral choices and
to value integrity above ambition.

Also by Betsy Hartmann

The Truth about Fire, a novel

Reproductive Rights and Wrongs:
The Global Politics of Population Control

A Quiet Violence: View from a Bangladesh Village
(co-authored with James K. Boyce)

Making Threats: Biofears and Environmental Anxieties
(co-edited with Banu Subramaniam and Charles Zerner)

Acknowledgments

I am deeply grateful to my many friends, colleagues, and family members who offered valuable support and suggestions on the manuscript throughout the writing process. I would like to offer special thanks to members of my writing group, Mordicai Gerstein, Joann Kobin and Marisa Labozzetta, for keeping me on course; to Jim Boyce and Molly Wolf for their careful editing; to Jamie Hartmann-Boyce for designing the front cover; and to Linda Roghaar and Sonja Hakala at White River Press for shepherding the manuscript into print and out into the world.

prologue

At the still unnamed military prison in the middle of the Nevada desert, the interrogators always kept a stainless steel pitcher of ice water on the table. If Salim Mohammed answered their questions satisfactorily, he would get a glass of water. If not, he would go thirsty until they let him back into his cell. That could be hours from now, hours in which they let the desert heat continue to suck him dry. His throat was already parched. Today they had chained him to a post in the courtyard in the midday sun. "Niggers don't get sunburned," the guard had taunted him. "They just burn in hell."

This was hell and he was burning. He watched a bead of water slide down the outside of the pitcher, making a trail he wanted to follow with his tongue. Today's interrogator was new, older and fatter with a slouch he kept fighting by pushing his rear against the back of the chair. His voice had a dull, monotonous tone, not like Mr. Angry, who ranted and raved, or Mr. Kind, who had come only a few times. Mr. Kind was tall and thin and leaned forward as he paced the room. He tried to wheedle information out of Salim, giving him water when he asked for it. What would he call this new interrogator? Mr. Nobody?

Mr. Nobody asked the same questions and Salim gave the same answers. No, he wasn't aware that the Islamic charity the Raleigh mosque supported was a terrorist organization. No, he hadn't channeled money through the mosque's accounts to terrorist cells in the United States.

Mr. Nobody poured himself a glass of water and brought it slowly to his lips. "If you continue being uncooperative, Mr. Jones," he said, refusing to use Salim's Muslim name, "we're going to send you out of the country for interrogation. To a prison which isn't nearly as nice as this one. To Egypt or Saudi Arabia maybe. You've heard about what they do to prisoners there?"

Salim's mouth was so dry it hurt to speak. "You can't do that."

"Yes, we can. You're no longer a citizen."

"The Supreme Court is hearing my case in two weeks."

Mr. Nobody shook his head incredulously. "You really believe the Supreme Court is going to be sympathetic to your case? You're a terrorist, Mr. Jones, and this country has no room for terrorists."

Salim felt faint. If they didn't give him water soon, he was going to die of thirst. Maybe that's what they wanted; maybe Mr. Nobody was the last in line, the executioner. The room started to spin, so he closed his eyes and dropped his head, hallucinating his mother singing him an old gospel tune:

> *Wade in the water.*
> *Wade in the water, children.*
> *Wade in the water.*
> *God's gonna trouble the water.*

On the edge of consciousness, he heard Mr. Nobody shouting and then the door opened and he heard the voice of Mr. Kind. "What the hell do you think you're doing?" Mr. Kind exclaimed. "Get him some water, fast. He's no use to us dead."

part one

1

Justice Matthew Pomeroy sat in the passenger seat of his wife's car, trying not to brake with his foot as she darted in and out of the heavy traffic on Connecticut Avenue. Although she lacked confidence in almost every other aspect of her life, Dora drove like a New York cabbie. He was grateful to have her as a chauffeur. Ever since his high school accident, he didn't trust himself behind the wheel. He'd been drunk the night he swerved off the road and hit a tree, but the police never tested him because his father was the District Attorney. Thank God he'd just dropped her off at her parents' house; otherwise she would have died. He spent two months in a body cast considering that, considering everything. He figured he was handed a light sentence for a reason, and that reason became his life's work.

He enjoyed good health in the intervening decades, but several years ago his heart started acting up and this morning his blood pressure reading was the highest ever. They were on their way to see his cardiologist, Dr. Levinson, who was known in Washington as a man of discretion, well versed at keeping the coronary secrets of the rich and powerful.

Stopped at a red light, Dora started to make a list out loud for their daughter's wedding. "We have to pick up the invitations on the way back," she said, "and remind me to call around about florists. David's parents are going to pay for the flowers, but I said I'd find a florist for them. And then I need to call Jessie and figure out when she's coming home next…"

Matt half-listened, the rest of his mind focusing on a case the Court was deciding next week. It was a challenge to one of the more controversial provisions of the first Citizen Defense Act, or CDA as it was known now. The plaintiff Salim Mohammed, an African-American convert to Islam, had been stripped of his citizenship and incarcerated indefinitely because the Justice Department claimed he belonged to a terrorist cell. It was the first time the government had stripped someone of citizenship under the act. Once again, Matt's would be the swing vote, and the responsibility weighed heavily on his shoulders. He knew if the first CDA was judged unconstitutional, it would have an impact on the enlargement of the act now before the Senate.

"I wish Jessie would come home more often," Dora was saying. "Atlanta's not that far away and I could really use some help. They're always going to David's family on the weekend."

"That's because it's only an hour from Atlanta."

"The plane ride here isn't much more than an hour."

"Dear, there's a big difference between getting in a car and getting on a plane."

"I know," she sighed. "I just miss her."

Jessie was their only child. Dora had tried hard to keep the umbilical cord attached, even through Jessie's twenties, but their daughter had finally severed it. Secretly, he was glad, though he would never say so. He watched his daughter's ascent in the competitive medical research world with the same pride with which he'd watched her take her first steps as a toddler. The Centers for Disease Control was the perfect place for her. And David was OK. A Roman Catholic, but not a strict one, with a good job as a tenured business professor at Emory. It could be a lot worse.

Dora pulled into a narrow space in the parking lot at the doctor's office. Matt opened the door, careful not to scratch the car next to them. It was harder lifting himself from the seat than it should have been. He felt like he had gained a few pounds, quite a few in fact, but he hadn't. He breathed heavily as they climbed the stairs to the second-floor office. Dora wanted to come into the examination room with him, but he insisted that she stay in the waiting room. He didn't recognize the nurse who took his blood pressure. She looked barely out of high school and smiled too brightly as she wrote down his numbers. "How is it?" he asked.

"170 over 105."

"Not so good."

"No," she said, still smiling. "Too high."

"Well, hello, Matt," Dr. Levinson greeted him as he entered the room. He was one of the few people outside the justice's family and close friends who called him by his first name. The doctor had seen him naked and poked and prodded him in private places too many times to stand on ceremony. He was from a different generation too, a product of the sixties. He was bald now, but on his desk there was a photograph of him fresh out of medical school with long black hair and a beard, ministering to children on an Indian reservation. Along with the stethoscope around his neck he wore a string of turquoise beads. Now his only jewelry was a simple gold wedding band. He picked up Matt's chart. "Been under a lot of stress lately?"

"The usual."

"A little more than usual?"

"Maybe," Matt acceded reluctantly. "We're deciding a big case next week."

"I read about it. If I was in your position, my blood pressure would go up too. I'm going to increase your medication, but I want you to check your blood pressure twice a day, once in the morning and once in the evening, and phone in the numbers twice a week to the office. The medicine should help, but I think you need to do more to manage the stress. Are you exercising?"

"Sometimes."

"How often?"

"A couple times a week."

"That's not enough—every day, like it or not. And," he added, "watch the sodium intake."

"OK."

The doctor paused and looked earnestly at him, too earnestly. "The country needs you, Matt."

Comments like that were precisely what made his blood pressure rise, but he couldn't bring himself to tell the doctor. He suspected Dr. Levinson was a liberal, and he was the liberals' last hope on the Court because even though he was a Republican, he had a reputation for independence and for voting his conscience. He took the new prescription and shook the doctor's hand. "Remember to call in your numbers," Dr. Levinson instructed as he showed him to the door.

A different set of numbers worried the President's chief advisor, Lyndon

Tottman. The latest polling data showed the President losing his lead and running neck and neck with Democratic candidate Bill Hartley. And as if that wasn't enough bad news for the day, Lyndon had just learned that the Saudis had withdrawn billions of their dollar holdings from American banks and converted them into Euros deposited in French and German banks. The dollar was plummeting.

He was in an emergency meeting now with the President, Treasury Secretary Brad Ames and Federal Reserve Chairman Phil Douglas. Lyndon didn't like Phil; he was a holdover from the last administration, a skilled technocrat but without the sense of mission the President expected from his team. When his term was up, they would let him go.

The President turned to get the go-ahead from Lyndon, as he always did, as though he was scared to start anything by himself. Lyndon was an African-American in his early forties, named after Lyndon Johnson by parents who made good in the Great Society, rising through the Texas state civil service from lowly clerical positions to senior management. Now they were dead, and Lyndon was born again. God had blessed him not only with a sharp mind but the kind of physical energy that allows you to get by just fine on a few hours of sleep. He nodded at the President. "Shoot," the President said.

Brad fired the first salvo. "Mr. President," he began, "we've got a crisis on our hands."

The President leaned forward over his vast expanse of desk. "I know— Lyndon told me. What did the Saudis want to do that for?"

"They're punishing us for going into Syria," Lyndon said straightforwardly. "They warned us there would be consequences. Well, we can come up with a few consequences of our own."

"No, I don't think it's that," Phil interjected, his face nervously twitching like a lab rat getting electric shocks. "Sooner or later it was going to happen. The dollar's weak and getting weaker. If I were the Saudis, I'd probably do the same thing."

"That's unpatriotic of you, Phil," Lyndon quipped.

"I'm not talking about patriotism here," Phil replied, still twitching. "The financial markets don't give a damn about patriotism. The real question is who's next after the Saudis. How bad does it get and what do we do about it?"

"Well, what can we do about it?" the President asked.

"The first thing we need to do is to restore confidence. We've got to raise interest rates so foreign investors get a better return on their dollars."

"But that will drive the economy further into recession," Brad countered.

"That's the price we have to pay."

"I can't pay that price," the President responded. "Any more bad news on that score and my approval rate dips below 60 percent and that's not where I want to be, only eight months out from the election. If we don't play this right, Hartley's going to seize on it. Did you see his last campaign ad? There's a clip of me standing by an abandoned factory, with his voiceover saying, 'It's the economy, stupid.'"

"I understand your concern, Mr. President, but if we don't raise interest rates, we risk a major run on the dollar," Phil told him.

Lyndon leaned back in his chair, stretching his legs. "What the President is suggesting, gentlemen, is that we need to pick our pain carefully. Americans care more about jobs than about whether the dollar is going up or down. Besides, we can blame this one on the Saudis. Who likes the Saudis?"

"And what do we do when the Japanese start pulling out?" Phil asked with a touch of anger in his usually well-modulated voice. "Blame the Japanese?"

Lyndon shrugged. "Why not? A new yellow peril."

"I hope you're kidding." Phil paused, looking directly at the President. "If we don't raise interest rates, we're courting economic disaster, and ultimately that's going to affect the polls too. There's no way you can get around it."

"I've got a solution," Brad said with a flush on his pallid cheeks. Behind his back people called him Casper the Ghost. He looked almost albino, as though he never stepped outdoors. "We raise the interest rate a few decimal points and announce that we're considering a further hike. Whether we do that or not is another question, but at least it buys us some time and restores confidence in the short term without deepening the recession too much. And then we come up with a tax cut proposal for the little guy—not much, but enough to show we care and to make up for the fact that gas prices are rising."

"I like that," the President said.

"But we can't afford a tax cut," Phil cautioned.

"Just a little tax cut for the little guy," Lyndon chimed in. "We'll get to work on it." With that, he made eye contact with the President, signaling it was time to bring the meeting to a close.

———

Lisa looked nervously at her watch. Even if there was no traffic, she was already late for picking up Sam. Senator Barrett had scheduled their meeting for

3:00, but it was after five now and she still hadn't showed up in the office. "What should I do?" she asked Marla, the senator's executive secretary. "I have to leave, but the Senator is going to be really pissed off. She wanted me to brief her on the new Citizen Defense Act."

Reluctantly, Marla looked up from her computer. She was in her sixties, jaded but generous, with a penchant for plaid jackets that didn't quite match her skirts. An e-Bay addict, she was currently engaged in a bidding war for a Hummel figurine, a boy with a fish. "Can you believe it's up to $150 dollars now?" she said to Lisa, pointing at her screen. "I don't know whether to top that or not."

"What should I do, Marla?" Lisa asked again, this time more desperately. "You know her better than me."

Marla shrugged. "What can I say? She's always pissed off—it's just a matter of degree. If you leave now, wear some heavy armor tomorrow and I'll try to provide some reinforcements."

"Thanks," Lisa said as she returned to her desk to pick up her jacket and briefcase. She walked briskly down the corridor to the elevator, but when the door opened, Senator Barrett stepped out. She was a big, broad-shouldered woman in her late fifties who had followed the law of the political jungle so long that she was starting to look like one of its beasts. Lisa imagined her as a tiger on her better days, a hyena on her worse. A permanent scowl was etched into the wrinkle lines on her face. "Where are you going?" she asked Lisa. "I thought we were meeting."

"I have to pick up my son."

"That bill is over 600 pages long and we're voting on it the day after tomorrow. I need you to brief me on it."

"I realize that," Lisa responded, "but we were supposed to meet at three."

The senator glared at her. "I need you to be flexible, Lisa. Washington runs on different time than Minneapolis. Didn't I tell you that when I hired you?"

Lisa felt her face flush, but she managed to control her voice. "Yes. I'm sorry," she said. "I'll brief you first thing tomorrow morning."

"All right, but don't let this happen again."

———

Nick was looking at his watch when Sam finally hit a three-pointer. 6:15. Fifteen minutes late. "Did you see that, Mr. Connor?"

"That was great," Nick lied. "See if you can do it again."

Except for the janitor cleaning the locker room, they were alone in the school. All the other after-school kids had been picked up more or less on time, but Sam's mother was late again, even though last week she paid over $50 in late fees. A dollar a minute was the charge during the first half hour, rising to two in the second. Nick was pissed off. He had only two hours between this job and the next at the fitness club and she was eating into his time, taking him and her son for granted. One more infringement and he was going to tell the principal that Sam had to leave the program. He was a nice enough kid even though he sucked at sports, being a little too fat and way too cautious. Nick looked at his watch again. 6:20. He wouldn't have time to make dinner.

The basketball hit the rim and bounced back toward him. He caught it and passed to Sam who tried a two-pointer this time, without success. "Just keep working at it," Nick advised. "That's what it takes. Got a hoop at home?"

Sam shook his head. "We live in an apartment."

Nick was surprised. Most kids who went to the prestigious Ryder School in Chevy Chase lived in big houses, not like the kids at Jefferson Elementary in Southwest D.C., where he used to work. There were homeless kids in that school and the basketball hoops had no netting. They laid him off because they did away with gym classes in the last round of budget cuts.

He was looking at his watch when Lisa came in. "I hit a three, Mom," Sam shouted as he ran over to her, still young enough to want a hug.

"I'm so sorry I'm late," she apologized to Nick.

"Almost twenty-five minutes."

"I'll pay," she responded quickly.

"That's not the point. I need to have a word with you, Ms. Derby—alone."

"Sam, why don't you go get in the car," she said, tousling his hair. "I'll be there in a second." The boy left reluctantly, with one parting shot, an air ball that arced gracelessly and hit the floor with more of a thud than a bounce.

"This can't go on, Ms. Derby," Nick began. "You might not believe this, but I have a life. In fact, I have another job I need to get to by 7:30 in Bethesda. And have you ever thought about how your son feels when you're late every day? I watch him watching the other kids leave with their parents."

"I'm sorry I'm late," she bristled, "but I'm a single mother and I have the kind of job that demands I stay late some times. I pay the fees. And please don't pretend to know how my son feels. That's not your job."

"Oh, yes, it is." He looked hard at her, like he might look at one of the kids acting up. "One more time and we'll ask Sam to leave the program."

"You can't do that."

"It's in the contract you signed, Ms. Derby. The school reserves the right to expel students from the after-school program if their parents are habitually late. I suggest with the money you spend on late fees you hire someone to pick him up. Other parents do that."

"So he can come home to an empty house? He's only eight years old."

"You can hire people to take him to their home and you can pick him up from there. Ronald Jacobs's mother does that."

"She does?"

There was something in her clueless response that reminded him of Sam, and he softened toward her despite himself. She needed help, he could see that. Like most of the other women who sent their children to Ryder, she was a Washington professional, dressed for success in a sleek beige pantsuit, but she didn't carry the act off as well as the others. Her haircut was ragged, her leather purse scuffed. Her lip was quivering, but he pretended not to notice. "Why don't you try calling Mrs. Jacobs?"

"I will," she said. She paused, looking at him for the first time as if he were anything other than an enforcer. "Thanks for the suggestion."

As she turned to leave, he picked up his clipboard from the bleachers, jotting down $20 instead of $25 in late charges.

In Maidenhead Beach, North Carolina, Faith Jones closed up the fish store at six and walked over to the beach, as she did almost every evening when the weather was fair. It was her only moment of peace all day. Since her husband Paul died five years ago, she had managed the store by herself, buying from the fishermen and selling to the tourists, and now that Jackson was in prison, she had her daughter-in-law Samira and grandson Ali to worry about too. They'd moved in with her when they were evicted from their house in Raleigh after Jackson's arrest. Faith refused to think of her son as Salim Mohammed. He was christened Jackson after her favorite uncle, and Jackson he would forever be in her eyes and the eyes of the Lord.

She kicked off her shoes and walked along the wet sand at the water's edge. It was low tide and sand crabs were scurrying around like nervous nellies. Usually she got a kick out of watching them, but this evening she was too preoccupied with Jackson's case to pay them much heed. She picked up a shell, turned it over in her hand, then tossed it in the direction of a gull feeding off a fish carcass. The bird went screeching off into the air.

She wished she could screech and fly away too, fly all the way to that military prison in Nevada where they were holding her Jackson in solitary. The prison was so new it didn't even have a name. She wondered if he had a window in his cell and could see the sky. It wasn't so long ago that he would have been running ahead of her on the beach, teasing her to chase him, dashing into the water and swatting at a breaking wave right before he ducked under. When the weather got warmer, Ali could do that if his mother let him. Samira dressed in a long black robe and was scared of the sea. She was a city girl, born and raised in Raleigh. She couldn't even clean a fish.

Faith's hands always smelled of fish, no matter how much perfumed soap or lotion she used. Maybe that's why Ali shied away from her. She wanted to sit him on her lap and rub his fuzzy head, but like a timid puppy, he wouldn't come close unless she offered him a treat. He liked gingerbread cookies. She'd have to make some more. Maybe they could decorate them together. The poor boy. Over fifty men had come that night to arrest his father with a helicopter overhead. Samira said she couldn't tell whether they were cops or soldiers since they were dressed in black. If they'd asked, Jackson would have given himself up voluntarily, but they just knocked down the door and ran up the stairs pointing their guns. Ali saw it all. He saw them push his father to the floor and manacle his hands. Sometimes at night Faith heard Samira comforting him after a nightmare.

Faith looked out over the sea. The spring sky was streaked with pinks and oranges and the water was blue gold, her favorite color. She wondered if Jackson could see and hear the ocean when he closed his eyes at night in the desert. She hoped so. She hoped her son at least found some peace in his dreams.

2

Lyndon arrived before the President had finished breakfast and sat down at the table with him and Trudy. The First Lady was younger than the President by about five years and played Southern regal to his Kentucky homespun. In high school, she was prom queen and star of the musical, and at Florida State she sang the National Anthem before football games. She could still belt it out. A year ago she sang to cheering troops on their way to Syria. Now they were starting to come home, in body bags.

The more he tried, the less Lyndon liked her. Unlike the President, she couldn't seem to get past his race. She was Old South and it made him uncomfortable. But maybe it helped the President politically that she played to the closet racist vote. She poured Lyndon some coffee, but didn't pass the cream even though she knew he took it. When he asked for it, she feigned surprise.

He hoped she would skip out on the Bible reading this morning. She was skin-deep religious, or rather her skin was her religion. Gossip columnists claimed she had a daily facial. He could believe it. Her skin was perfect and so was her hair, flaxen and shiny like one of those American Girl dolls his cousin's daughter collected. He fought an urge to muss it up.

Luckily, she had to leave for an appearance at a children's hospital, so the President and Lyndon could retreat to the den alone. Every morning the ritual was the same. Lyndon took the straight-backed chair, the President the couch. They turned on a single lamp with a single bulb. Boozers and losers in their late twenties, they had met in a twelve-step program. Bible reading was now their shared step thirteen.

Lyndon opened the Bible to Genesis 22 and began to read:

> *And they reached the place that God had told to him and Abraham built an altar there, and he arranged the wood, and he bound his son Isaac, and he laid him on the altar on top of the wood. Then Abraham reached out his hand and he took the knife to kill his son. But the angel of Yahweh called to him from the heavens and said, "Abraham! Abraham! Lay not your hands on the boy! And do not do anything to him, for now I know that you fear God, because you have not withheld your son, your only son, from me."*

He paused to check that the President was still listening, then cleared his throat and continued:

> *And Abraham lifted his eyes and he looked and see! a ram caught in the thicket by his horns! And so Abraham took the ram and he sacrificed him as a burnt offering instead of his son. And the angel of Yahweh called to Abraham a second time from the heavens, and he said, "I swear by myself that because you did this thing and did not withhold your son, your only son, surely I will bless you and your descendants shall possess the gates of their enemies, and through your offspring, all the nations of the earth will be blessed because you obeyed my voice.*

"So what does that mean for us today?" the President asked.

"I don't know," Lyndon deferred. "What do you think?"

"You know me, Lyndon. I'm too literal. I think about my own son when I hear that and it spooks me. What if God hadn't spoken up?"

"Then Abraham would have sacrificed him."

"Would that have been the right thing to do?"

"In this case, I don't think it's a question of right or wrong. It's the willingness to sacrifice that matters and gets rewarded. Abraham's descendents will possess the gates of their enemies. If we're willing to sacrifice, we too will possess those gates."

The President scratched his head. "Sacrifice what?"

"Whatever it takes."

"I wouldn't sacrifice my son."

"I'm talking metaphorically. Abraham grabbed the ram by its horns when given the chance. We just have to be ready. It's all about readiness."

"I see," the President nodded, though Lyndon could tell he didn't. Lyndon liked to leave him a little confused. It was better that way.

Back in his office he skimmed the daily press summary. He knew he should concentrate on the financial crisis, but instead his own words echoed in his mind. It's all about readiness. The new version of the CDA was going to pass easily, the pundits predicted. This close to the election the Democrats couldn't afford to look soft on national security, especially after the latest outrage, the bombing of an American tourist bus in Mexico. Whether it was political or narco terrorism didn't matter. The attack was close to home.

While the passage of the second CDA was critical, his strategy could all unravel if the Supreme Court ruled against them in the Mohammed case. It was the Court, not Congress, that could be the problem. Lyndon was willing to act, but he needed one last piece of information before setting Operation Daybreak in motion. When would he get it? How much longer could he hold the knife above the altar?

When the gym phone rang at 6:01, Nick ran over to pick it up. "Mr. Connor, this is Lisa Derby."

"Where are you?" he asked curtly.

"Still in my office in D.C., in the Dirksen Building."

"Do you know what time it is?"

"I don't know what to do, Mr. Connor. I called the woman Ronnie Jacobs's mother uses, but she can't start picking up Sam until next week. I tried to leave on time, but my boss wouldn't let me. She threatened to fire me. I don't know what to do." She stifled what sounded like a sob. "Please tell me what to do."

He resented the way she was trying to place the burden on his shoulders. Something about him made him easy prey for women in distress—but she was in distress, so what was he going to do? "Mr. Connor," Sam shouted. "I bet my mom's waiting outside. I'll go see."

"No, stay here, Sam. I'm talking to her." He paused. "Ms. Derby, this can't happen again."

"It won't."

"Do you have any friends where I can drop him off?"

"We just moved here. I really don't know anyone. That's the problem—there's no one who can help me."

"All right, listen. I'm going to take him to my place and you can pick him up there. I live in Silver Spring."

"So do we."

"It's 64 Beech St. Do you know Beech?"

"I'll find it."

"Why don't you speak to Sam and let him know what's happening."

"Thanks so much, Mr. Connor. This will never happen again, I promise."

After calling Sam to the phone, Nick collected his belongings. He didn't have to work at the fitness club tonight, thank God, because who knows when she'd show up. One evening at Jefferson Elementary, a mother never showed and he ended up calling the cops. It took hours before they figured out what had happened. It turned out the immigration police had picked her up in a raid on a laundry service and she was deported to Mexico without even having the chance to say goodbye to her daughter. The school found some relatives the girl could stay with in Baltimore. That was the last he saw of her. Natalia Mendez was her name, a nice kid. There was something wrong about separating a parent and child like that. Something wrong, too, about Sam's mom getting fired if she left the office on time to pick up her son. Of course, maybe she was lying and she was late for some other reason, like meeting a lover. She was a piece of work; that much was clear.

Nick could tell that Sam was thrilled to ride in his car, an old Chrysler with red leather seats that he'd inherited from his father. At the house he poured Sam a glass of orange juice and put a frozen pizza in the oven. He wanted a beer, but didn't feel comfortable drinking alone in front of the kid. He was serving up the pizza when Lisa arrived. Even though it was past sunset, she was wearing dark glasses and didn't take them off even when she stepped inside the entryway. She thanked him profusely and told Sam it was time to go. "But we're having pizza, Mom," he pleaded.

Then Nick did what he'd sworn he wouldn't do. He invited her in to share the pizza. She took off her sunglasses and he offered her a beer. He found it unnerving to be sitting across the table from her, outside the safe boundaries of the school, but she seemed at ease, eating her pizza in big bites and draining her glass with relish. She showed no signs of wanting to leave and when Sam asked if he could watch TV, she let him.

Nick poured two more beers. She took off her suit jacket and hung it on the back of her chair, then pushed up the sleeves of her black turtleneck as if preparing for a serious game of cards or a hand wrestle. She had beautiful wrists, he noticed, slender but not fragile-looking. Her fingers weren't long, but they had a lively grace about them he associated with a musician's hands. No wedding ring, just a sapphire band on the other hand. He didn't want to notice these things. "So who do you work for?" he asked.

"Senator Barrett, from Minnesota. I come from Minnesota."

"The senator people love to hate."

She nodded. "Yup, that's her. Senator Big Mouth, the President calls her. If she was a man, he'd never say that."

"Do you like her?"

"I like her politics." She paused as if unsure how much to tell him. "But no, I don't like her personally, especially after today. She yelled at me for needing to pick up Sam. I don't think I'm going to last there."

"What do you do for her?"

She put her hands around her beer glass as if to cool them. "I'm a legislative analyst. My specialty is privacy and civil liberties—same as hers."

"How long have you been working for her?"

"Only three months. A professor of mine from law school is a friend of hers and he recommended me. I was working in a law firm in Minneapolis, which was even worse than this job in terms of Sam. I never saw him. I thought no matter how difficult Senator Barrett was, it couldn't be as bad. I knew I'd never make partner no matter how hard I tried. Besides," she paused again, "I wanted to get away from Minnesota."

"Why?"

She shrugged. "Lots of reasons. It would take all night to tell you." She blushed and quickly asked, "How about you? Are you from this area?"

He shook his head. "No, I grew up in Ohio—Columbus."

"So what brought you here?"

He debated what to say and decided on the short version. "I followed my fiancée. I served in the army during the Gulf War. When I got out, she'd moved here for a job. I developed health problems and the relationship didn't last."

"What kind of health problems?"

Did he want her sympathy? Sympathy was so short-lived, broken as easily as a promise, but she was leaning forward, encouraging him, and it had been a long time since a woman had done that. "I got sick after I got back," he began. "Chronic fatigue, lots of bad headaches and muscle pain—Gulf War Syndrome, I guess. I couldn't concentrate on anything. I don't blame her for leaving, but I do blame the VA for telling me it was all in my head. I finally went to a private doctor who started treating me and that's when I got better. I went back to school a couple of years ago and got a teaching degree in phys ed, but the jobs are all drying up with budget cuts. I took the job with the after-school program at Ryder after I got laid off the last time. I'm looking around, but there's not much out there."

"Maybe something else will open up at Ryder."

"Maybe, but private schools don't pay very well." He took a sip of beer. "Of course beggars can't be choosers."

She looked over in the direction of the living room where Sam was curled up on the couch, asleep. "I'd better get him home," she said. "He needs to take a bath and do his homework. Thanks so much, Mr. Connor. You saved me today. Next week it will all be straightened out."

"Call me Nick," he ventured.

She laughed. "OK. And call me Lisa."

After they left, Nick sat at the table, nursing the rest of his beer, sorry that next week someone else would pick up Sam.

———

At 10:00 PM Dora switched off her bedside light, pulled up the covers and turned away from Matt in familiar reproach. One of the small tensions in their marriage was her need for an hour more of sleep at night. While she resented it, Matt treasured the time between ten and eleven when she was lightly snoring and his mind was free to wander and gestate new ideas. Sometimes when he was lucky, he woke up in the morning with them fully born. That was his real legal genius. Logic was a craft anyone could learn; the more nebulous musing was what made him an artist of the law.

Tonight no ideas came to him. He felt too anxious, but about what he didn't know. Perhaps it was his blood pressure, though that seemed more a symptom than a cause. It was the same feeling he had as a little boy, when he heard noises in the night and turned on the closet light and laid awake, on guard, his ears straining for every sound.

Taking care not to stir Dora, he eased himself out of bed and went downstairs to the front hall where he checked the controls on the burglar alarm. It was set. He looked through the window to the street outside. There were a few parked cars, but that wasn't unusual. The Meads were probably holding another one of their excruciating dinner parties. After Lena's bout with cancer, they had turned into nutritional fanatics and wanted to cure everyone with their taste-free vegan recipes.

He poured himself a glass of water in the kitchen and then took it into the den where he switched on the TV, surfing channels until he hit on an interview with Republican whip Stewart Goodell. "How do you respond to Senator Barrett's accusation that the administration is rushing the second Citizen Defense Act through Congress before the Supreme Court rules on the constitutionality of the first one?" the interviewer asked. She was a perky redhead, unusual in this day of either the ubiquitous blond or the dark-haired Asian newscaster.

"They are two very different pieces of legislation," Goodell replied. "Whatever the Supreme Court rules in the Mohammed case should have no bearing at all on the new legislation. The first act was designed to prevent further terrorist attacks on the United States. The second is designed to give the government the necessary tools to deal effectively should a terrorist strike occur."

"Do you think another strike is imminent?"

Goodell gave her a patronizing smile. "The administration is doing the best to prevent that, of course. But we have to be prepared, especially after what happened in Mexico."

The redhead turned slightly so the camera could catch her in profile. "Democratic presidential candidate Bill Hartley said yesterday that the administration is so preoccupied with the war in Syria that it's not paying enough attention to the failing economy. What do you say to that?"

"Well, all I can say is that if Mr. Hartley has a problem doing more than one thing at a time, he shouldn't be running for President. We Republicans don't have that problem. We're multi-taskers. We're taking care of national security and we're taking care of the economy."

"Thank you, Senator Goodell."

"My pleasure, Anita."

Matt muted the volume during the car ad that followed. It wasn't true that there was no connection between the first and second Citizen Defense Acts, he thought. If the Supreme Court ruled next week that stripping Mohammed's citizenship was unconstitutional, it would have all kinds of political ramifications. The administration was smart to try to ram the second bill through beforehand. They knew he could swing the Court either way.

Which way would he rule? Certainly, citizenship was a privilege, but it was also a birthright if you were born on American soil. Salim Mohammed's given name at birth was Jackson Jones. He was born just down the coast from Wilmington, North Carolina, where Matt grew up. In prison on a small drug charge, Mohammed converted to Islam and joined a mosque in Raleigh when he got out. According to the Justice Department, the relief fund he ran was knowingly channeling money to Syrian terrorists. If that was true, he deserved a hefty prison sentence, but did he deserve to lose his citizenship and the legal rights it conferred? Was there a compelling reason to undo over two hundred years of legal precedent?

Matt doubted it. He'd lived long enough to realize that there would always be wars and there would always be enemies. He was a religious man; he believed in heaven and hell and was doing his best to avoid the latter. But unlike some of the men around the President, he didn't believe that history was on an inevitable path toward the apocalypse. The darkness in the world would lift and then settle again. History was like the weather, cyclical and changeable, but how could he use that argument in a legal decision?

Among his fellow justices, Reynolds, Williams, McDormand, and Lane would uphold stripping Mohammed's citizenship because they believed extreme times warranted extreme measures and they had no compunction about weakening civil liberties. Merritt, Lovins, and Jenkins would make their usual liberal counter-arguments. Fox, a libertarian who hated Big Government, would vote with them on this one. Matt's would be the swing vote, and each side was looking to sway him.

He was used to being in this position, so why did it frighten him now? Why was he turning off the lights and pulling back the curtain to see if someone was lurking outside? It was childish. The chill he felt was silly too, but still he couldn't stop shivering. He went to the kitchen and put his glass in the sink. It was 11:00, but Jessie would still be up. He dialed her number in Atlanta and she answered the phone after a few rings. "What's up, Dad?" she asked.

"Just checking to see how you are."

"I'm fine—a little stressed, but what else is new?"

"Your job or the wedding?"

"Both."

"Your mother's really working hard."

"I know, and it makes me feel guilty."

"Oh, don't worry, she loves it, but she'd really like it if you could come up for a day or two."

"I'm just so busy right now, Dad."

He took a moment to respond. "I'd like to see you too."

"How are you doing?" she asked, her voice expressing more concern. "I keep reading your name in the paper."

"It's going to be a tough decision, Jessie."

"You'll do the right thing. You always do."

"I'm not so sure of that any more." He could solicit her opinion—he had taught her over the years to be an intelligent legal observer—but it wasn't advice he wanted. What did he want? "How's David?" he asked.

"Up to his neck in student papers, but otherwise OK. Look, Dad, I could come up this weekend if you really want me to."

"Oh, you don't have to."

"I know I don't have to, but would you like me to?"

"Yes," he said quickly before he had time to waver.

"I could come Friday night after work and leave Sunday afternoon."

"That sounds good. Could David come too?"

"I don't think so. He'll be happy to have a quiet weekend to finish up the papers. I'll call tomorrow when I figure out the flights."

"Your mother will be delighted."

He thought of waking Dora to tell her, but she was sleeping soundly when he got back in bed. He snuggled close, breathing in the familiar smells of her body. The idea of Jessie's visit quelled his anxiety enough that he fell asleep, but his dreams were fractured and violent, like clips of different action movies spliced together. When he woke in the morning, his blood pressure reading was the highest yet.

3

Motherhood hadn't come naturally to Lisa, the way her mother told her it would. She had had a hard delivery, ending in a C-section, failed at breastfeeding, and suffered postpartum depression, although in retrospect the latter probably had more to do more with her marriage than her hormones. She loved her son, yes, but constantly chafed against the constraints he imposed. Today, as she dropped him off at school, she spoke with a slow, patient voice but could hear another shriller one in her head. "You're getting picked up with Ronnie Jacobs today," she reminded him, "and I'll come get you at Mrs. Cummings's house as soon as I get out of work." The other voice told him to hurry the hell up and get out of the car. Senator Barrett was speaking on the Senate floor in three hours and wanted to go over the speech with her one more time.

"I don't like Mrs. Cummings," Sam complained, scrunched up against the door.

"But you only met her once and she seemed perfectly nice."

"Why can't I go home with Mr. Connor instead?"

She looked at her watch, her irritation mounting. Sam had a hard time with transitions, and God knows, she had put him through enough of them, but she was getting tired of his sulking. "I already told you he has another job in the evening," she said.

"But you could pay him so he could leave that job and take care of me."

"It's not that simple, Sam," she replied, wishing it was. She would miss seeing Nick at the end of the day, she realized. "Now, go on—school starts in a few minutes." He didn't lean over for his customary kiss but instead got out of the car without saying good-by. She watched him walk alone into the school, passing by the other kids congregating on the sidewalk in clusters of friends. No one had befriended him since he started at Ryder in January. Maybe getting picked up with Ronnie Jacobs would help. She sure hoped so. She didn't know how much longer she could take being his only friend.

She drove to the Metro station, and on the train to the Capitol read the front section of the *Washington Post.* She expected to see a major article about today's vote on the second Citizen Defense Act, but there was only a short piece buried on the back page. It said that the bill was likely to pass the Senate by a huge bipartisan margin. The editorial page was silent too. Tomorrow, no doubt, commentators from opposing sides would wax eloquent about the bill, but after the fact, when it was too late, like holding a championship game after the trophy has already been awarded. The virtual news blackout made Senator Barrett's speech even more significant, and Lisa had drafted the most critical section.

Later that morning, sitting in the Senate gallery she watched her boss deliver the speech. It was not hard to admire the senator. She was a gifted orator, Minnesota state high school debate champion in the fifties when girls were supposed to keep their mouths shut. With her shoulders thrust back, she commanded the podium, all fire in a red-orange silk suit. She played to the TV cameras because there was no one else to look in the eye. The Republicans in the chamber were fidgeting and feigning lack of interest, while the Democrats, with a few exceptions, looked down at their laps like chastised pupils.

Lisa listened closely to the passage she had written. "The choice is clear," Senator Barrett proclaimed. "Do we want a democracy or do we want a dictatorship? Since the passage of the first Citizen Defense Act, we have witnessed an unprecedented extension of police powers. The fundamental rights to privacy, due process, and protection from cruel and unusual punishment are under attack as we speak. With the passage of this second bill, the House and Senate will hand the President a blank check to declare a state of emergency for whatever reason he wants and whenever he wants, to suspend or end democracy as we know it. Sure, he is supposed to have evidence of a substantial terrorist threat, but what does evidence mean any more? Who sets the standard? This provision, by the way, is buried in fine print on page 420 of this mammoth document, a document, I might add, that I received only a few days ago." She waved the thick stack of paper in front of the cameras. "Perhaps my fellow senators haven't had time to read it yet. That's what I'd like to believe. I'd like to believe that if they had found the time, they would be as outraged as I am, as outraged as the American public will be when they discover that their elected representatives have voted to dismantle the separation of powers that is the bedrock of our democracy. Let me be perfectly clear." She paused and looked fiercely out over the crowd.

"This bill will not just wound the Constitution," she trumpeted. "It will kill it in cold blood."

A few senators clapped at the conclusion of the speech—Delaney from Massachusetts, Eisman from New York, Martin from Iowa. Otherwise there was a palpable lack of reaction. Three hours later the bill passed by a 90–6 vote.

In the afternoon Lisa was called into the senator's office. Senator Barrett was standing by the window, a drink in hand, with her suit jacket off and her blouse untucked. "It was a great speech," Lisa complimented her.

"No, I don't think so," the senator replied. "Great speeches require an audience. I had no audience today."

"You'll have a huge audience this evening. Millions of people."

"I doubt it. I doubt they'll even show it on TV, except maybe on C-Span a month from now."

"They'll show it tonight."

"How can you be so sure?" There was an aggressive edge to the question, and Lisa steeled herself for the senator's wrath. Instead the senator motioned her to a chair and offered her a drink. "I've got bourbon and a bottle of Johnny Walker Black."

"No thanks."

The senator poured herself more Scotch before she sat down opposite Lisa. "I used to be an optimist like you," she said, stirring the ice with a finger. "You have to be an optimist to get into politics. But I can't sustain it any longer. A strange thing happened when I was giving that speech."

"What?"

"Those words of yours—about killing the Constitution."

"Yes?"

"Well, usually when I use words like that, I'm fully aware it's hyperbole and I'm just playing to the crowd. But it felt like an understatement today. I felt like using even stronger words like murder, butcher, slaughter. I felt like screaming at those complacent bastards, but then they'd just label me hysterical and that would be the grand finale of my political career. 'She's gone nuts,' they'd say. 'Completely bonkers. Senator Big Mouth has finally lost it.' And you know maybe I have." She gave Lisa a piercing look.

"I don't think so."

"But you're an optimist, so what do you know?"

"I know you said what needed to be said."

"Yes, but where does that get us? Nowhere. Ninety to six, can you believe it? That's even worse than the first one."

"But you can't just look at the vote," Lisa countered. "If the Supreme Court rules our way next week, the first act will start to unravel. And then this one will too. And then people will remember your speech and you'll have your audience."

"So you're advising patience?" The senator shook her head bemusedly. "Remarkable times when the young are telling the old to be patient." She set her drink on the table. "I want to believe you, but I can't. Don't worry," she quickly added, "keep doing what you're doing. You're good at it. No one else spotted the fine print on page 420. You've got hawk's eyes, my dear." She smiled ever so slightly. "Sorry I yelled at you the other day."

———

"Scott, hi, sorry to bother you on Sunday morning. I hope I didn't wake you up." Matt was speaking on his cell phone while Jessie drove. They were on their way to Great Falls Park on the Potomac, just father and daughter for a change. Blessedly, Dora had decided she couldn't skip church. "I wondered if you could contact the other clerks and set up a meeting for tomorrow morning," Matt continued. "I've made my decision." Matt listened impatiently to his reply. Night or day, his head clerk always had the same officious tone of voice and it was starting to get on his nerves. He would be glad when Scott's term was over.

After he hung up, he slid back his seat, stretched his legs and tried to relax. It was a fine mid-April day, sunny with high clouds and warm enough for just a sweater. They drove along the river on the parkway where the flowering trees were dripping with blossoms. In places, the white petals on the ground looked like snow. The river was moving fast from spring melt and he found himself longing to be out on a canoe, making distance with the sheer force of the current.

He knew better than to make much conversation with his daughter when she was driving. She wasn't a nervous driver like him, but all her concentration was fixed on the road. She must be like that in the lab, he thought: no room for slack or error. They'd given her a toy microscope on her seventh birthday, never guessing that within a few months, it would become more important than her dolls. In high school her passion for the sciences stoked her perfectionism—the perfectionism that almost consumed her when she developed anorexia. She was past that now, thank goodness, although she was still too thin, her face too haggard for her years. He hoped she and David wouldn't wait too long to have children. Perhaps it was old-fashioned of him to think so, but having children might help round her out, force her to spend less time on her job.

After parking the car, they took a trail to the falls. Jessie slowed her pace for him and he wondered if Dora had told her anything about his heart. His reading was better this morning, and he tried to persuade himself the crisis had passed. But his breathing was still heavy and he had to stop a couple of times to catch his breath. Jessie reached into her bag and pulled out a water bottle.

"Want a drink?"

"No thanks."

She took a few sips, and then they started back down the trail. A young couple passed them, the man carrying a sleeping baby in a backpack. It wasn't long until they reached the river, where they found a picnic table overlooking the falls. She spread out the lunch Dora had packed—turkey sandwiches, sliced carrots and celery, and a thermos of iced tea. She gave him the red plastic cup from the top, pouring her own tea into a paper one. The red cup made him nostalgic for the camping trips they'd taken as a young family, before his career ruled out long vacations. She must have read his mind because she told him she'd like to take him to the Smoky Mountains some time. "I'd like that," he said.

"We should do it in the spring when the rhododendrons are blooming."

She ate her sandwich too slowly, in small bites, as if eating were an obligation and not a pleasure, a residual effect of her eating disorder. By contrast, he ate too fast even though he wasn't really hungry. The carrots were woody, past their prime. She watched him closely as if any moment he might choke. He didn't like this new vigilance of hers.

"So it sounds like you've made your decision on the Mohammed case," she said.

He swallowed a chunk of carrot, though if she hadn't been there, he would have spit it out. "I think so," he replied. "I'm meeting with my clerks tomorrow morning to go over it."

"Can you tell me what you're going to do?"

A moment of silence hung between them. "If you swear not to tell anyone, even David."

"You know me, Dad. I've kept your secrets all my life."

He watched her hand wave a fly away from the thermos. "Has that been a heavy burden?"

"No. On the contrary, it's been a privilege."

"You're too kind."

"You're the one who's too kind."

The comment surprised him. "Kind" had never been an adjective people associated with him. He was known as a stern judge, fair but not empathetic. Perhaps she meant the way he handled Dora's foibles. In family therapy for her anorexia, Jessie once said she wished he protected her more from her mother's exasperating attentions. "You never say no to her," she complained. He didn't tell her it was part of the deal he made with God after the accident—to love Dora, no matter what. It was a matter of duty, not kindness, but it might look different through a child's eyes.

He listened to the falls for a moment, deciding what he could and couldn't tell his daughter. He knew these legal confidences were still important to her, and important to him, as proof of their bond. He took a sip of ice tea—too sweet, instant from a jar. "I'm going to vote against the government on this one," he finally revealed. "It's unconstitutional to strip the defendant of his citizenship. That's the legal grounds." He paused and then lowered his voice, though there was no one around to overhear them. "I have political grounds too."

"What are they?" she asked.

"I want to slow things down."

"What do you mean?"

"I don't like the way the administration rammed the second Citizen Defense Act through Congress."

"Neither do I," she said with conviction.

"There was no time for deliberation, and deliberation is what democracy's all about, or at least it used to be. I'm getting tired of this manufactured sense of urgency. Why strip this man Salim Mohammed of his citizenship? Why not try him in a proper court of law? Sure, it will take more time, there will be appeals, but it also means more time for the truth to come out. Ruling to restore Mohammed's citizenship is the right thing to do, and it will also apply the brakes. I'm going with the liberals on this one and Fox will join us."

"So you'll be the majority?"

"Yes. Do you approve?"

She nodded. "I was hoping that's what you'd do."

He felt a deep sense of relief, not because she approved—he expected that—but at his own candor. Saying it simply made it all seem so much simpler. Of course, this is what he would do. How could he decide any differently? The pressures and fears of the last few weeks seemed to melt away, loosening the vise around his heart. Maybe his blood pressure would come down now. He looked at his daughter. She was beautiful to him, though maybe not to others. Her chin was sharp and her eyes set a little too far apart, her curly dark hair cropped too short. He had liked it those last years in college when she wore it long, untidy, as if to signal her recovery. In a few months' time he would give her away in marriage. Even though he was a traditionalist, the idea struck him as oddly antiquated. What right had he to hand her over to another man, and what right had that man to receive her?

"Sometimes I wish everything would slow down," she said, but her hands were already purposefully collecting the trash, signaling that their time together was almost over.

Monday evening Lyndon couldn't shake his bad mood when he got home from work. Now the Chinese were threatening to convert their dollars to Euros and they had over $500 billion in reserves. Phil Douglas had been in a panic, almost apoplectic, when he met with the President in the afternoon. "Let's give them some trade concessions," the President had suggested.

"This isn't about petty trading, Mr. President," Phil barked back. "It's about interest rates."

The President didn't like Phil's insubordination. He didn't like it at all. After Phil left, he told Lyndon they should try to get rid of him. Put so much pressure on him it would force him to resign. Then replace him with someone with muscle who would stand up to all this foreign financial blackmail. But Lyndon knew that if Phil left, the Democrats would quickly capitalize on it. Hartley would woo him, and his pride would be wounded enough that he'd swallow the bait. Lyndon could see it now: an op-ed by the ex-Federal Reserve Chairman in the *Wall Street Journal*. The President has no economic policy. Hartley does. Cut to the chase: Vote for the Democrat.

If Phil left now, it would be a political disaster. Lyndon would have to find a

Bible reading for tomorrow morning to convince the President to mend his fences with Phil. Something from the Epistles, perhaps.

He flung his jacket on the couch and walked into the kitchen. The larder was bare except for some leftover chow mein. After his workout, he'd heat it in the microwave and the chicken would turn all rubbery. He regretted not accepting the dinner invitation at the British Embassy, but he had an important phone call scheduled for 8:00 PM.

I need a wife, he thought as he went into his bedroom to change. Someone who shops and cooks and spreads her legs. In his bygone drinking days, he'd been satisfied with high-class call girls who wore nice clothes and were regularly checked for venereal disease. Pity that they were no longer an option. The price of virtue was a perpetual hard-on, and he feared it might lead him into temptation. Work it off, Lyndon, he chastised himself as he pulled on a T-shirt and pair of athletic shorts. In the basement he had his own little gym, complete with treadmill, rowing machine, and weight bench. There was a wide-screen TV too. Lately, he pumped iron watching basketball. For the first time ever, the Wizards might make the play-offs. Maybe he would go to a game. The Secret Service wouldn't like it—he would be an easy target for terrorists—but it was good to be seen out in the world, mixing with the hoi polloi. You have to take a few risks.

Tonight he didn't turn on the TV. He didn't want to hear any voices except the ones in his own head. He got on the rowing machine and closed his eyes, imagining he was rowing against the current in thick, muddy water in the Texas hill country where his parents sent him to an exclusive boys' summer camp, one of the first to integrate. The director had realized ahead of his time that the future of power was multicolored, even in the Lone Star state. The other boys laughed at Lyndon's kinky hair, but his athletic prowess earned their respect. He won swimming and boating races and hit the bull's eye in archery. He stayed a straight shooter until Princeton where he fell into the debauchery of the dining clubs.

He opened his eyes to check his speed on the gauge and then closed them again, moving from the river in Texas to Princeton's Lake Carnegie. He rowed crew his freshman year, before his descent into drinking. The other boys on the team complained about early morning practices, but he liked to watch the dawn reflected on the lake, slicing through it with his oar as if he had the power to slice the sky. He had real power now; he didn't need to imagine it. Nothing left to prove. His parents would be proud of him if they were still alive. They wouldn't like the company he kept, but they would admire his earning the right to keep it.

He rowed for twenty minutes and then did the treadmill for another half an hour. After that he was too tired and hungry for the weights. He showered and ate the leftover Chinese on the cherry table in the formal dining room. According to the rules he set himself, eating dinner in the kitchen was strictly forbidden. He was studying the latest intelligence report on Iran when the phone rang at 8:00 on the dot. The voice was muffled, but he recognized it at once. "Hi, Lyndon," the man said. "Are you going to the Wizards game on Thursday?"

"Afraid not. I might go on Saturday though. How do you think they'll do against the Nets?"

"They're going to lose."

"That's bad news coming from a loyal fan."

"They suck at the free throw line. Mark my words—they're going to lose it on foul shots."

Lyndon hung up. That's all he needed to know. Operation Daybreak was a go. After the initial adrenaline rush, he felt strangely disembodied, watching his feet walk upstairs as if they belonged to someone else. He lay down on his bed and stared up at the ceiling. For one flicker of a second he considered calling the whole thing off, but he let it pass. He sat up, picked up the phone, called a number, and let the phone ring three times exactly.

A few hours later he took a long Jacuzzi in his white marble bathroom. It was his favorite room of the house, and he insisted the cleaners give it extra care. It was here, in the bath, that he sought both relief and absolution. Tonight for the first time he imagined Trudy sitting opposite him and he came with a fury that surprised him. He let the bath drain and then ran the water again, washing his body cleaner than his conscience.

Every morning before she went to work and every evening before she went to bed, Faith Jones prayed for her son. On Tuesday night, kneeling beside her bed like a devout little girl, she prayed that the Supreme Court would restore Jackson's citizenship on Friday and that he would be transferred from the military prison in Nevada to one closer to home where she could visit him. She had visited him every week when he was in prison in Raleigh on a two-year drug charge. It was then that he converted to Islam. Although she didn't approve, she had to admit she liked what the religion had done for him. It straightened him out, gave him a sense of purpose. One of his Muslim brothers convinced him to study book-keeping in prison, and it led to a job when he got out. He did all the accounts for the mosque, including charitable giving. It was his own records they used to try to prove he was aiding terrorists. But if he knew he was aiding terrorists, why would he keep such meticulous records about it?

She stopped praying to think about that again. It was a question no one had a good answer for, not even Richard Brown, Jackson's lawyer from the ACLU, who had an answer for almost everything. "You have to understand that the government doesn't really care whether your son is guilty or not of knowingly aiding and abetting terrorists," he told her when they first met. "They just want to establish the principle that they can strip someone like him of citizenship and then deny them due process. He's a sacrificial lamb."

"But why?" she asked. "Why Jackson? He isn't a danger to anyone."

Richard shrugged. That's one thing she didn't like about him—he shrugged too much, like someone who couldn't be bothered. But of course he was bothered, bothered enough to take on Jackson's case for free and fight it all the way to the Supreme Court. "Whether or not he poses a danger to the national security of the United States should be up to a court of law to decide—a bona fide court of law, not a sham military tribunal. That's how I'm going to argue the case. Frankly, I don't really care if your son is innocent or guilty. I hope for your and your family's sake he's innocent, but I don't lose sleep over it."

She did lose sleep over it though. When she returned to her praying, she rested her forehead against the mattress edge and prayed as hard as she could for his innocence.

Her mind was so concentrated that she didn't hear the door opening or realize her grandson Ali was standing right behind her until she said "amen" and turned her head. It was the closest Ali had come to her of his own free will. "What is it, child?" she asked gently as she stood up. One of her hips was stiff and it took a while to straighten her leg.

He didn't say anything, just stared at her with vacant eyes.

"Ali, honey, are you awake?"

He moved his head, but it was unclear whether it was a nod or a shake, and she realized he was sleepwalking. "Let's get you back to bed," she said, taking him by the arm. He didn't resist as she led him down the hall into the bedroom he shared with his mother Samira. Samira was asleep, breathing heavily. Faith brought Ali to his bed and whispered for him to lie down. She pulled the covers over him and sat for a few minutes on the edge of the bed. His eyes were still wide open. "Close your eyes now," she instructed like a hypnotist. She stroked his head until he fell back to sleep, breathing in the same rhythm as his mother.

Faith couldn't go to sleep after that. When she was little, her older cousin Dee told her that when you sleepwalk, it's because a restless ghost has crept inside you and is using your body to move around. Her mother claimed that was nonsense, but even now Faith wasn't so sure. She could feel a ghost lingering in her bedroom. Not her husband Paul—she was used to him. Sometimes he even lay down next to her in bed.

She was still awake when the police car pulled up to the house a few minutes before midnight. The doorbell rang, and she hurried into her housecoat before going downstairs. She opened the door to find Lieutenant Paige standing on the stoop. He was a regular customer of the fish store; she always put a half-pound of shrimp away for him on Fridays. "May I come in, Mrs. Jones?" he asked politely, too politely. "I'm afraid I have some bad news for you. Perhaps we could sit in the living room?"

There was something wrong about having a fat white cop sitting in her husband's favorite rocking chair, but that's the seat he chose and she felt powerless to say anything about it. He folded his hands in his lap. "I hate to bring you this news," he began, "but we were contacted by the military authorities and told to relay the information to you. I don't know why they didn't send one of their own people…"

"What information?" she asked, drawing the housecoat more closely around her to ward off a chill.

"Your son was found several hours ago hanging in his cell. Apparently, he was being treated for severe depression."

"Are you telling me my son's dead, Lieutenant Paige?"

He turned down his eyes. "Yes."

"And that he hanged himself?"

"Yes." He paused, looking up. "I'm repeating what they said to me. I'm so sorry, Mrs. Jones. Really, I am."

It was then she saw Samira standing in the entrance to the living room, her black robe draped around her shoulders. "What's happened?" she asked.

"Jackson's dead," Faith told her. "They lynched him in his cell."

4

Justice Matthew Pomeroy got up before dawn on Wednesday, eager to write in his journal before Dora woke up. Maybe someday an historian would read his account of the Salim Mohammed ruling and understand the small, painstaking steps by which law and precedent are crafted, like the model ships he built as a little boy. He still had one of them, a New England clipper ship, perched high on his bookshelf. Years of dust had turned the sails a dirty yellow, but he couldn't bear to part with it.

He listened to the gentle spring rain falling outside as he replayed the events of the last few days in his head. After Jessie left on Sunday, he started drafting his arguments for the restoration of Salim Mohammed's citizenship. On Monday morning he showed the draft to his clerks and spent the rest of the day refining it with the help of his head clerk Scott, whose priggishness made him an exacting editor. Scott had five Princeton ties which he wore consecutively Monday through Friday. By the end of the day, Matt was tired of orange and black.

Tuesday morning Matt presented the draft to Justice Lovins who was writing what would now be the majority decision. As usual, they went head to head. Lovins was using the Mohammed case to write a sweeping liberal interpretation of the Bill of Rights, which would open a Pandora's box of litigation. Matt threatened to write a separate concurrence if Lovins didn't pull back and restrict himself to the citizenship issue. Lovins refused, so Matt went back to his office to gather his wits.

That's when Chief Justice Reynolds called him to his chambers. Reynolds, who lately preferred to eat alone, had just finished lunch and a waiter was clearing the round table near his desk. Matt noticed fresh stains on the white tablecloth. The rumor circulating among the clerks was that Reynolds had Parkinson's disease and couldn't properly manage a knife and fork. Maybe the clerks were right, Matt thought. It would explain his hand tremors and his unsteady walk. Matt wished he could feel sympathy for the man, but he would be glad when Reynolds retired. He had reached the top not by dint of legal brilliance or the ability to forge consensus, but by clawing his way there on the backs of others.

That afternoon Reynolds made no pretense of affability. How could Matt go out on a limb like that and join with the civil libertarians? he charged. Where were his conservative values? His loyalty to the Constitution? Then he changed tack. If Matt switched sides, Reynolds said, he had the assurances of Williams, McDormand, and Lane that Matt's views would be taken into account in their opinion against Mohammed.

"But how can you take my views into account when we have a fundamental disagreement?" Matt challenged.

"We can get our clerks working on it. We can introduce language that sets very strict conditions under which the government can revoke citizenship—we can firm up the law, make it fairer, but not throw it out altogether."

"That doesn't help Mohammed."

"Well, it might help down the line if new evidence emerges that the government didn't meet those strict conditions when they revoked his citizenship."

"But how can that evidence emerge if he's not given a fair trial?"

"There are enough journalists sniffing around this case that if there's new evidence, they'll find it."

"You can't count on that."

Reynolds responded with his eagle look, as arrogant as ever despite the slight tremor on the left side of his face. "In case you haven't noticed, Matt, we're living in dangerous times. I'm not saying the government needs a free hand, but Lovins wants to cut off the arms of the anti-terrorism effort. Are you sure that's what you want for the country?" His frown worked its way into a thin crescent moon smile. "I'm sure we can work something out. What do you say?"

Absolutely not, Matt thought, but he refrained from saying it out loud. Unwittingly, Reynolds had just handed him a card he could play against Lovins, so Matt left things hanging. Back in his office, he called up Lovins and told him Reynolds was making him an offer he might not refuse if Lovins stuck with his sweeping decision. Then he called Fox, the conservative libertarian who was his best friend on the Court, and persuaded him that they should join forces in moderating Lovins. By the time Matt went home for dinner on Tuesday night, he had cemented the deal. The majority of Lovins, Merritt, Jenkins, Fox, and Pomeroy would rule that the section of the Citizen Defense Act that allowed the government to revoke the citizenship of a terrorism suspect was unconstitutional. Nothing more, nothing less.

That was justice at its most perfect, Matt thought as he began to write in his journal, that narrow wedge between nothing more and nothing less. The skill was in knowing how to cut it razor thin. That's the insight he would leave for posterity.

He had been writing for more than an hour when the phone rang. He picked it up fast so as not to wake Dora. It was Jessie and she sounded agitated. "I hope I haven't woken you up, Dad."

"No, I've been up since six. Is anything the matter?" he asked, for she never called so early.

"Have you heard the news?"

"What news?"

"Salim Mohammed committed suicide. I heard it on the radio."

"That can't be! We were about to rule in his favor."

"They say he hung himself—in his cell."

"It can't be."

"I'm sorry to be the one to tell you. Are you OK, Dad?"

No, of course not, he wanted to tell her, but he made some vague assurances that convinced her it was all right to hang up. He stared out the window, unsure of what to do next. If Salim Mohammed was dead, the decision Matt so ingeniously crafted had died along with him.

———

The TV camera zoomed in on Faith Jones. Although her eyes were red and swollen, she sat bolt upright on her living room couch as if it were a straight-backed pew. A shrouded Samira sat on one side of her, Ali on the other. "I'm a woman of faith," she declared to the young black woman reporter. "I'm a Christian and I believe in God and I obey His rules. I used to have faith in this country too, but not any more."

"Why not?" the reporter asked, moving the microphone closer.

"Because they killed my son."

"Who killed your son, Mrs. Jones?"

"The government. They lynched him in prison and pretended he committed suicide. I know my son and he would never kill himself. He had too much to live for—his wife and child sitting right here." As she gestured toward them, the camera caught a tear in her eye. "He loved his family so much he would never kill himself, never. The government killed him so he couldn't have his day in court. People need to wake up and do something or it's going to happen again and again until no black man is safe in this country."

"Do you agree, Mrs. Mohammed?" the reporter passed the microphone in front of Samira.

She nodded, but didn't say anything.

"Do you want to say something?" the reporter gently asked Ali.

"I want my daddy back," the boy said. "When's he coming back?"

Senator Barrett clicked off the TV. "They've been showing that clip all day on the news. What do you think?"

What did she want her to think? Lisa wondered. Ever since she helped the senator with her speech, her status had shifted from lowly aide to trusted confidante, but it made her more vulnerable, not less. "Always keep up your guard," Marla the secretary warned her. "She chews people up and then spits them out. Just learn as much as you can while she's chewing on you so you have something to take with you to your next job."

"What if the mother's right and they killed him?" Lisa ventured. "Do you really think that's possible?"

"Anything's possible with these guys. Convenient timing, wouldn't you say? Now there won't be any Supreme Court decision. The first Citizen Defense Act will stand until there's another challenge, but the earliest that could come would be the fall, since the Court breaks for the summer."

"And the press will forget the second act in the meantime."

"Exactly."

"But I can't believe they'd do it. It's too obvious."

"Obvious to us, but not to everyone else." The senator paused, twisting her gold wedding band like a magic ring. She was separated not divorced; she spent family holidays with her husband and they sent out a joint Christmas card. "Here's the point. Either they killed him, or they drove him to suicide. Who knows what they do in those military prisons, what kind of interrogation techniques they use. Both scenarios make the administration look bad. If they killed him, they're murderers, Pinochet style. If they drove him to suicide, they're not only immoral but incompetent because they let a potential intelligence source slip out of their hands. Maybe information died with Mohammed that could have prevented a terrorist attack. We'll never know."

"So what do we do with this?"

"What do you think?"

Another test, Lisa thought, and the senator expected the right answer from her star pupil. "Go to the press" was the easy answer, but the wrong one. You had to go to the press with more than just speculation. "You call for an independent Senate investigation," she said.

"Exactly," the senator smiled. "But in a few days, when all our ducks—or at least enough of them—are in a row. We need to dig around a bit first. I'm sending James down to North Carolina to meet the mother and I want you to meet with Mohammed's lawyer in New York tomorrow. Richard Brown's his name." She paused. "Draw up a list of questions and we'll go over it together before you go home. And keep quiet about it. We don't want anyone to get wind of this."

Lisa nodded, although she was already worrying about the arrangements. Could she get back from New York in time to pick up Sam? Maybe Mrs. Cummings could keep him longer. His birthday was coming on Saturday, too, and she'd promised him a roller skating party but hadn't invited anyone yet. She was thinking of inviting Nick.

"OK, then?" the senator broke her reverie.

"Yes," Lisa replied, "I'll get working on it."

"This time we'll get them," the senator said boldly as she walked Lisa to the door. "I feel it in my bones."

———

Lyndon didn't want to go, but he had no choice. That was the price of a political life. How could he turn down an invitation to watch the Wizards–Nets game on TV with the President and First Lady? Oh, but he didn't want to go. Even after four ibuprofen, his head felt like someone was beating on it with a sledgehammer. A dark quiet room was what he needed. He closed his eyes and rested his head on his desk. Why was he the only one in the administration with the wits to weather two crises at once?

Crisis number one: Salim Mohammed's death. In the morning he sorted out the spin for that. If the mother was going to play the race card, so would he. He called Marty Jordan in the Pentagon's PR office and told him to get ready to do his black grandfather act for the press. Marty played it just right, so sweet and sincere you could almost imagine him bouncing a baby on his knee. Mohammed was being treated for depression, Marty told an afternoon press conference, and his prison cell was under constant video surveillance. He took advantage of a brief power outage to hang himself. The prison authorities and the Defense Department deeply regretted his suicide. Had it not been for the power outage, it could have been prevented.

"Surely, the prison must have a back-up generator," Art Connelly, the pain-in-the-ass *L.A. Times* reporter, had challenged.

"Yes, but unfortunately, it takes a few minutes to switch on," Marty replied. "You can be assured we're now working out ways to improve the system so this doesn't happen again."

It was nicely done, the way Marty diverted attention to the electrical system, so the press would get all caught up in technical debates. It wouldn't last of course; sooner or later journalists would start asking serious questions. But it would buy some time.

And crisis number two: the Chinese threat to convert to euros and petulant Phil at the Federal Reserve. Lyndon forged a compromise. He convinced the President to let Phil raise the interest rate half a point, and meanwhile got some wheeling and dealing going with the Chinese, promising them a piece of the new oil pipeline in Central Asia if they agreed to hold onto their dollars. They were holding out for more—those clever bastards always did—so tomorrow he'd have to find something else to throw into the bargain. But at least, once again, he'd bought some time.

His genius was in buying time, he thought, but to buy time he sold himself into mental slavery. His brain was overworked, the neural networks shorting out. Zap. Bang. Boom. Bust. Smoke was probably coming out of his ears. And no real gratitude from anyone, including the President. Others might think the invitation to watch the game was the President's way of saying thanks, but they were wrong. The President needed him there because it was in front of the TV, watching sports, where he felt tempted to drink again. Lyndon, not Trudy, was his real enforcer.

That evening the President didn't even bother getting up from the couch to greet him. He was slumped in a corner, his feet resting on the coffee table, a toe showing through a hole in his sock. "Hi there, Lyndon," the President said. "Grab a soda and take a seat. The game's just started."

Lyndon sat in his customary seat, the padded brown rocker with matching footstool. Grampy's chair, they called it. Obviously it had sentimental value, although it was out of place in Trudy's floral décor. Trudy settled next to her husband who put his arm around her. She wore a conservative cashmere cardigan, but in the gap between the buttons Lyndon spied something purple and lacey underneath. He diverted his attention to the TV. The Nets star player stole the ball and headed down the court for an easy slam dunk. "They've got to find a way to stop him," the President said. "Otherwise it's all over."

"Oh, I don't know," Lyndon replied. "Sometimes he stops himself. He's hot and cold."

"Well, he's hot tonight."

At half time the Nets were up by twenty and the Wizards retreated downcast to the locker room. Trudy got up to check on their son Brendon and get some snacks. "Peanuts, boys," she asked, "or pretzels?"

"Doritos, honey."

"I'll see if we've got any."

"Sure would taste good with beer, wouldn't they, Lyndon?" the President said after she left the room.

He nodded. "Sure would, but let's don't go there."

"I've been going there too much these days."

Lyndon sat forward, his head starting to throb again. "You're not drinking, are you?"

"No, no, no," the President laughed, "don't worry about it. But I dream about it all the time. Do you ever dream about it?"

"Sometimes, especially when I'm under a lot of pressure. You're under a lot of pressure lately."

"I guess you're right. Lots of pressure, from all sides. Sometimes I feel like I'm a balloon people are throwing darts at, like in an amusement park."

"But they never manage to pop you."

"Who says one of them won't, one of these days."

"I'm doing my best to prevent that."

"I know you are." The President paused, knitting his brow. "I appreciate that. Just tell me one thing, Lyndon."

"Yes?"

"Did that black boy really hang himself?"

Lyndon nodded.

"That's a relief."

Lyndon nodded again. "We have to be prepared for lots of rumors though."

"Do you think Hartley's going to try to take advantage of the situation?"

"He'll wait and see. He can't afford to appear weak on terrorism. I'm more worried about Senator Barrett."

"What do you mean?"

"Knowing her, she's probably got something up her sleeve."

"Like what?"

Lyndon shrugged. "I wouldn't put it past her to call for some kind of investigation."

"Well, let her. If the boy hanged himself, there's nothing to hide."

"Right," Lyndon said, not wanting to pursue the matter any further. He pointed at the TV, where a Miller Lite commercial featured a crew of yuppie yahoos drinking it up at a bar. "That's why you can't stop thinking about beer," Lyndon said. "It's the commercials."

"You got a point there."

Trudy came back with a bowl of chips and set them on the end of the coffee table furthest from Lyndon. She wouldn't offer to pass them to him, he knew. He tried to convince himself it didn't matter. He didn't like Doritos anyway. When the next commercial came on, his eye followed an SUV longingly as it drove higher and higher up a rugged canyon. He imagined ripping off her sweater and taking her on the back seat, then pushing her out and driving away. She would cry for mercy and die of thirst.

The President picked up the bowl of Doritos and put it in his lap. "Want some, Lyndon?" he asked.

5

The last time Lisa was in New York City was the summer she flew out from Minneapolis to meet Kevin's family. Although the weather was hot and humid, the icy look on his mother's face chilled her to the bone. Law degree or not, a Midwest farm girl was not what his parents had in mind for a daughter-in-law. They did their best to make her uncomfortable. When Lisa started a conversation, they refused to continue it, leaving her words hanging in mid-air like dust that wouldn't settle. At dinner they gave her looks that made her feel like a cow chewing cud. She was an untouchable whose very presence polluted their luxury apartment on Central Park West. Only the doorman was kind to her.

She should have broken off the engagement then and there, but Kevin insisted his parents would come around. In the end he was the one who did the coming around—full circle back to their expectations. When Sam was two years old, Kevin left her for an old classmate from Yale, a blueblood born and raised on the Main Line outside Philadelphia. He moved with her out to L.A. where they both got jobs as corporate lawyers. They had two boys of their own now, which made Kevin care even less about Sam. He had him for a few weeks every summer and they traded off Christmas and Thanksgiving. He was a Disney Dad par excellence. Sam had been to Disneyland so many times that Mickey Mouse and Donald Duck had lost their magic.

Oh, if only Kevin's parents could see her now, she thought: Lisa, the farm girl, all spiffed up, riding in a speeding taxi, aide to a powerful senator, a person

of more importance to the world than their second-rate son whose latest client
was an energy giant hauled up on fraud and embezzlement charges. Their pre-
cious Kevin was the one shoveling shit, not her.

The taxi driver was forced to slow down as they entered southern Manhattan
where a multi-colored mix of humanity clogged the streets, bumping against each
other like a wild roll of marbles. She reached into her purse for a comb and ran
it through her hair. Maybe someday she would cut it short and severe, pretend to
be sophisticated like the woman she spied prancing out of a boutique like an
Arabian thoroughbred.

The taxi dropped her at the ACLU offices on Broad Street a few minutes
before her scheduled appointment with Richard Brown. He had been curt with
her on the phone and she hoped he was friendlier in person. He wasn't, at least
not at first. He kept her waiting in the reception area for almost half an hour, and
when he finally came to get her, he didn't bother to shake her hand. "We're going
out," he announced brusquely. In the elevator he stood in the corner next to the
control panel, staring silently at the buttons.

It was only on the street that he began to engage with her. He put his hand
on her back to guide her across a busy intersection and then led her to a sandwich shop where he asked for a table in the far back. The narrow walls were hung
with autographed pictures of baseball players, all from the Mets. "You don't dare
set your foot in here if you're a Yankees fan," he told her. The Formica-topped
tables and vinyl chairs looked like genuine artifacts from the fifties. "I know it's
only 11:30," he said as they sat down, "but I've been up since 5:00 and I need
some lunch." He was a big man, bordering on heavy, with shoulders bent into a
perpetual slouch. By the gray in his beard, she guessed he was in his forties,
though his hair was still thick and black. His skin was pock-marked from acne,
but the effect only served to augment his presence. He was a man with a presence, that was for sure. She felt small and slight by comparison.

When the waitress came, he didn't look at the menu, telling her he wanted
the regular—a Diet Coke and a Reuben sandwich. Lisa ordered an English
muffin and a cup of tea. "Getting something to eat is not the only reason I
brought you here," he explained after the waitress left.

"Oh?"

His eyes darted around the room and then settled back on her. "I don't think
it's safe to meet in my office any more. I think it's bugged." He unfolded his
napkin and smoothed it with his hand. "Do you think I'm paranoid?"

What was she supposed to say? she wondered. Was he testing her like Senator Barrett? "I don't know the situation well enough to judge," she responded.

"My colleagues think the stress is getting to me." He pointed at his head. "Making me go a little nuts."

"Just because you're paranoid doesn't mean they're not out to get you."

He smiled. "Right, my favorite saying. Look, Ms. Derby—or can I call you Lisa?"

"Lisa's fine."

"Look, Lisa," he leaned across the table, almost upsetting his glass of water, "I bet your office and phone are bugged too. We're in a new ball game and most people don't want to believe it—they want to play by the same old rules. They're naïve, but I can understand. I was naïve too. I thought the old rules would work in Salim Mohammed's case, and they almost did. That's why they hanged him—so they can make their own rules from now on."

"So you think they killed him?"

"Of course they killed him. We were about to win the case."

"How do you know that?" she challenged.

He paused and shrugged, his gaze straying to one of the photographs on the wall. She followed along. The player, whoever he was, was standing at bat, but she suspected he was posing for the shot. His expression was a little too solemn and determined, reminding her of a soldier's face in an army recruitment poster. "Look," Richard Brown replied at last, "Justice Pomeroy may be the swing vote on the Court, but he's not erratic. He's a conservative in the old sense of the word. He doesn't like to see things change. Stripping suspects of citizenship is way too radical for him. I'm positive he was going to vote with Fox and the liberals on this one. The decision would have been five to four in our favor."

With both elbows on the table, he leaned even closer, his face so near it violated her sense of personal space. She inched back her chair. "They say Mohammed was depressed," she observed.

"Sure, he was depressed. Wouldn't you be depressed if you were being held in solitary in a military prison in the middle of the desert?"

"When was the last time you saw him?"

"A month ago, for fifteen minutes. It was a photo-op. They took my picture as I stepped off the plane."

"I remember seeing it in the newspaper."

"Front page—designed to reassure the public that Mohammed had legal representation. Fifteen minutes, fifteen bloody minutes. What can you get done in that short a time?"

"What was he like?"

"Paranoid, I thought then. He was convinced they were going to kill him before we won the case. Now I know he was right."

"But you still can't prove it."

"Doubts can be raised."

The waitress came and set their food in front of them. "Tell me how," Lisa urged, spreading a packet of sorry-looking strawberry jam on her muffin.

"Tell me first if you're planning a Senate investigation."

"That may depend on what you tell me."

"Lisa, Lisa…" When he picked up his sandwich, the melted cheese squeezed out the sides. He took a big bite and chewed slowly, watching her. "How do I know I can trust you, Lisa, Lisa?"

The repetition of her name was too intimate, another violation of personal space. "Because I work for Senator Barrett, Mr. Brown," she said coolly.

"You can call me Richard," he replied. "I checked up on you. There are over a thousand entries under your name on Google—did you know that?"

"I don't make a habit of looking myself up online."

"Search-engine narcissism, a friend of mine calls it. I checked out the law firm you worked for in Minneapolis. It has a good reputation with the civil liberties crowd."

"Thanks," she retorted.

"But even if I decide to trust you, can I trust Senator Barrett?"

"Why not? She's the only one who spoke up against the CDA."

"She's a politician. It got her national coverage."

"Not much. In fact, a lot of people claim she's committing political suicide. She's up for re-election in November and the polls aren't looking too good."

He drained half a glass of Coke in one gulp. "Look, Lisa," he said her name less flippantly, "I'm glad you came to see me, but I'm not going to send you back to Senator Barrett with any promises. I need to make a few more inquiries before I figure out the best course of action. I'm going to be in D.C. next Thursday. Let's meet again then for lunch. Pick a place you've never been, a taxi ride away from your office."

"There's a sushi place in Dupont Circle—Osaka."

"OK, we'll meet there at 1:00 next Thursday. Don't contact me in the meantime. Just show up."

After lunch, he walked her to the nearest corner to get a taxi. "Heading back to La Guardia?" he asked.

She looked at her watch. "I think I might take a quick detour and see the World Trade Center memorial."

"They should have left it bare so people could fill it with their own memories," he said. "I saw the first tower come down before I started to run."

"I'm sorry."

"Don't be. I didn't lose anyone close to me. It's all we've lost since that concerns me." He nodded in the direction of a bank machine down the block. "See that guy in the blue parka at the end of the line?" She nodded. "I see him everywhere I go. Do you think I'm being paranoid?"

"Honestly, I don't know."

He hailed a taxi and opened the door for her. "Just look," he said, "our friend is getting a taxi too. I bet you'll see him at the memorial."

But he was wrong. It wasn't at the memorial that she saw the man with the blue parka again. It was the next day in Washington, when he followed her from the Metro station to work.

At five minutes to ten, the buzzer summoned Matt to conference. He gathered his papers on the Mohammed decision, though now they were of little use. Scott met him in the hall. "I thought you might need these," he said, handing him some notes on upcoming cases: child pornography on the internet, mandatory morning prayers in a Miami charter school, another fetal rights case from South Carolina. All important issues, but today they seemed minor by comparison, as tiny and insignificant as the tigers on Scott's Princeton tie.

Matt said thank you but nothing more. The usual irritation he felt with Scott was blossoming into full-scale dislike. Scott had taken Mohammed's death too easily in stride, treating Matt's concern with the patronizing indulgence young men on the make show to old men on the decline. The law can make you too logical, Matt thought, too linear, so that you move too rapidly from one case to the next. The best practitioners are those who take the time to spin out all the repercussions. Scott wasn't a spinner—his mind wasn't nimble enough to work the thread. Matt turned away and walked down the hall.

The oak-paneled conference room seemed gloomier than usual, the grand chandelier a poor substitute for natural light. Matt usually took pride in the impeccably polished nameplate on the back of his chair, but today he wished the brass was as tarnished as the world outside. Repercussions—he hoped there would be time to address them here in the inner sanctum of the high church of justice.

Chief Justice Reynolds made his entrance a few minutes late, stepping cautiously on the plush carpet as if it were slippery grass. His hand shook as he took his seat at the head of the table. As senior associate justice, Lovins had the honor of sitting at the other end. They glowered at each other as usual, and Matt was glad that the table stretched twelve feet between them.

"Ladies and gentlemen," Reynolds began, his voice still strong despite his frail body, "as you're all aware, we have a lot of decisions to make before the summer break and I don't want to take up too much time on the Mohammed matter. However, I think we need to reach some kind of agreement on how to proceed. I ask that we all exercise the utmost discretion in the coming days. The press is already clamoring to know what our ruling would have been, and the pressure is going to intensify. It's likely there will be similar cases in the future, and we have an obligation not to show our hand and prejudice the decisions of the lower courts." He looked around the table. "Are you in agreement with me on this?" Lovins cleared his throat. "Justice Lovins, do you wish to say something?"

"Yes." Lovins cleared his throat again. For a man with a quick mind, he had a slow, ponderous presentation. "With all due respect, I think it's premature to think that the Mohammed case is closed. An argument could be made that his citizenship should be restored even after his death, in which case the ball rolls back into our court." He stopped to consider his inadvertent pun. "Figuratively and literally."

Before Lovins could say anything else, Reynolds turned to the justice next in line of seniority, Eileen McDormand, who also happened to be his main ally on the Court. Matt didn't care much for her. She was hard-working and erudite, but she always bent to Reynolds's will in the end, even when her own logic led elsewhere. The other female justice on the Court, Nancy Merritt, was just the opposite, stubborn and so unwilling to compromise or concede defeat that the clerks called her General Custer behind her back. "Justice McDormand, do you want to speak?" Reynolds asked.

"Well," she said peering over her reading glasses, "I can see Justice Lovins's point. But even if the case were returned to this Court, there would be a significant delay. The Chief Justice is right—we mustn't show our hand. I suggest that we order our clerks to remain silent in no uncertain terms. Nothing about the Mohammed case is to leave this building."

Matt was next in line. "Do you have anything to add, Justice Pomeroy?"

That's how Reynolds would put it, Matt thought bitterly. "Did he have anything to add"—as if as if he were incapable of an original thought. The punishment for his defection was just beginning. His heart was beating too fast, his hands were moist. He felt an urge to break out of the mold and shock them all by placing the repercussions squarely on the table. "There's an invisible elephant in this room," he began, "and try as we might to tiptoe around it, we won't be able to avoid running into it sooner or later. Yes, I think it's appropriate to exercise discretion in the outside world, but here, in this room, we have the opportunity and the responsibility to voice our very gravest concerns. My concern, rightly or wrongly, is that the state may have taken Mohammed's life in order to preempt our decision. I have no evidence for this, but I believe we have to prepare ourselves in the eventuality that evidence does emerge. If that occurs, we will find ourselves at a critical juncture in our nation's judicial history. I would like us to be prepared to meet that challenge and so I suggest we take this meeting to acknowledge and examine the invisible elephant that treads among us."

"I beg to disagree," Reynolds almost shouted, his face reddening. "It's not our role in this room to jump to such wild conclusions."

"The justice is voicing a concern, not a conclusion," Lovins countered.

"He's making an extremely serious allegation with absolutely no evidence," Reynolds insisted. "This conference room is not the place for conspiracy theories. We need to move on. There are other urgent cases at hand. I suggest we start with a discussion of the Florida school prayer case."

An aide brought the news to Lyndon at 8:00 PM, just as he was preparing to leave the office. A suicide bomber in Damascus had blown up a popular fast food restaurant frequented by American soldiers. They were sorting through the carnage now. Preliminary estimates were twenty Americans dead, fifteen wounded.

Lyndon thanked the aide and closed the door. It was the biggest one-day death toll since December. He was sorry for the soldiers but grateful for the diversion the episode would provide. The blood and gore of Damascus would be splashed across the front pages, taking up space that otherwise would have been devoted to the Chinese negotiations. Someone, probably at Treasury, had leaked the news that the administration was bribing the Chinese not to sell dollars for euros. Now no one would give a damn. With any luck, Salim Mohammed's death would get pushed off the front page as well. The war might be unpopular, but nobody liked to see American GIs blown to bits.

Lucky today, but who knows about tomorrow, Lyndon thought as he got up from his desk. His knees were stiff—too long on the rowing machine last night. "Politics is a roller coaster," Maxwell, his political science professor at Princeton, always said. "Those who win are the ones who can hold on for the entire length of the ride." Lyndon was holding on all right—his grip had never been stronger—but the dizzying ascents and plummets were threatening to throw him off balance.

He had plans to stop by Skip Morley's house on the way home. Skip was his main man in Homeland Security. A former CIA agent, he'd cut his teeth in Colombia where he earned a reputation for unconventional but highly effective intelligence techniques. In the end he proved too edgy for the agency and had to leave. Lyndon had dug him out of premature retirement, creating the position of executive liaison. Lyndon didn't like him, but maybe it was better that way.

Skip had a townhouse in Georgetown, a bachelor pad where the nutcracker next to the bowl of walnuts was in the shape of a naked woman's legs. He had other erotic paraphernalia too—hard-core porn in the bathroom, a busty Marilyn Monroe statuette, sexy lingerie on the towel rack—but never a sign of a real woman. The rumor about town was that it was all a charade and Skip was a gay cross-dresser. Lyndon didn't want to know, didn't need to know, or at least he hoped he didn't.

Skip was doing the dishes when Lyndon arrived. "I saved some food for you if you want," he offered. "Nothing fancy—linguine with low-fat Alfredo sauce. Might seem like a contradiction in terms, but I make it with just a little margarine and no-fat half and half. Have you tried it?"

"The half and half?" Lyndon guessed, and Skip nodded. "No, I haven't."

"The doctor told me to cut back on fats—I've got high cholesterol."

"Too bad."

"Yeah, it's a drag. No more ice cream either."

Lyndon was hungry so he accepted a plate of pasta. Skip hovered over him, watching him take the first bite. "What do you think?"

"It's great," Lyndon lied. The sauce had the consistency of Elmer's glue. He picked under it for some plain noodles. "So you got some news for me?"

Skip hung the dish towel on the refrigerator door and sat down across from him, their knees almost touching under the kitchen table. In the glare of the overhead light, Lyndon noticed an oily sheen to Skip's face. His craggy features, protruding forehead and long bumpy nose reminded Lyndon of a rough bust abandoned by a frustrated sculptor. Except for perfectly straight teeth, there was nothing refined about him. Skip sighed. "Barrett's meddling," he told Lyndon.

"She's always meddling. What's it now?"

"Her aides are nosing around the Mohammed case. Young woman named Lisa Derby was spotted with his lawyer in New York. Another aide named James Madison—catch that—has been to North Carolina to see Mohammed's mother and sniff around the Muslim community in Raleigh."

"I'm not surprised. She'd love nothing better than to call for a thorough investigation."

"Does that concern you?"

"Of course it concerns me, but not too much. We just need to keep a handle on it."

"How?"

"Keep doing what you're doing. At this point information is the key. If we know her moves in advance, we can beat her at the game. It's as simple as that."

Skip raised an eyebrow. "Think so?"

Their knees touched, and Lyndon pushed back his chair a few inches. "It's all about endurance, Skip. You know that."

"There are different kinds of endurance."

"What do you mean?" Lyndon noticed Skip's arms looked oily too—maybe he'd just had a massage.

"Most of my time these days is spent enduring the bureaucrats at Homeland Security. I used to think the CIA was bad, but compared to this outfit it was a piece of cake. Getting permission to do anything operational is like pulling teeth."

"That's why you get Daybreak directives straight from me."

"And you get them straight from the President?"

"You don't need to know."

"To protect him?"

"You do your job, I'll do mine."

"Look, Lyndon, all I'm saying is I need some protection too. I'm in deep now and I don't want to find out I'm alone in a shit pile."

Lyndon pushed his plate away. At most he'd eaten half of the wretched stuff. "I've never seen you nervous, Skip. What's happening?"

"What if something goes wrong? What if we don't win the election?"

"We're going to win—that's what this is all about."

"Got contingency plans?"

"We don't need them."

"You'd better have them, Lyndon. I've been screwed before and I don't intend to get screwed again. I want a good retirement package ready and waiting."

"I'll see what I can do."

Lyndon left shortly after that, declining the offer of a dessert of canned peaches with Cool Whip. Back in his car, he switched from the radio to the CD deck, playing Aretha's greatest hits. He turned it up loud. Why was Skip so anxious? Was someone on to him? Was there some closet liberal in Homeland Security who was using Skip's cross-dressing sex life—if he really had one—to try to force information out of him? Lyndon hoped that Skip knew how to keep his fly zipped.

Chain, chain, chain, chain of fools...

Why were men so weak? Lyndon had been weak once too, but he had overcome it. His first epiphany came the night he drank so much booze and snorted so much cocaine that he found himself huddled in the corner of his bedroom, in a pool of his own vomit, shaking and quaking with fear like a hunted animal. Only he was the hunter too, he was the one pointing the gun. When anyone came near him, he screamed for them to go away, and so they all left, even the girl he'd just had sex with—no one even bothered to call a doctor. There was nothing to prove he almost died, but he knew it was a close call. He knew next time the hunter would bag his prey.

After that, he joined an AA group in Washington full of men like him, lobbyists and legislators on the make but not making it through the day without a couple of drinks at lunch and more at dinner. He dried up and followed the twelve steps and found religion or rather religion found him by way of the President, who was just a rookie congressman back then. The congressman wanted to show him the way to Christ, but Lyndon resisted until epiphany number two. It happened in the shower room after a game of squash. He dropped a bar of soap and as he picked it up, he noticed with surreal clarity the stunning whiteness of the congressman's feet. He had the whiteness Lyndon needed to make it to the top, and Lyndon had the brains he lacked. Their two halves made a powerful whole. And so he struck a deal with himself. Believe what the congressman believes, follow him until he has to follow you. Embrace Christ. Embrace eternal power for the sake of the temporal. Find God within yourself.

The plan had worked well until now, but he could see that in the weeks and months ahead he was going to have to work hard to keep the President and his little army of loyalists in line. Professor Maxwell had never talked about that in political science class: how the true leader needs to keep a lid on the cravings of weak mortal men. He would be tempted to tell the professor that when they met at Lyndon's twentieth Princeton reunion in June. The Lewinsky factor, Lyndon would call it, even though it wasn't just about sex. It was about longing and self-destruction. It was about getting caught with your proverbial pants down.

What the hell was he doing? Nick asked himself on Saturday morning on his way to the roller rink. Going to Sam's birthday party set a bad precedent. Now all the kids in the after-school program would want him to come to their parties too, and even if he could afford the time, he couldn't afford the presents. Lisa had told him not to get one for Sam, but he had anyway—a Wizards basketball.

Face it, he told himself, you're going to the party because you want to see her. Had she invited him for the same reason? On the phone she couched the invitation in terms of Sam: how much he'd appreciate having Nick there. "Don't worry, I'm not expecting you to manage the kids," she assured him. "I'm sure you do enough of that during the week."

It crossed his mind that she wanted him to fill in as the father figure, but he hoped that wasn't the case. "I'll bring my roller blades," he replied, "but I refuse to play Laser Storm."

She laughed. "I don't blame you."

She was already out on the rink when he arrived, skating a few feet behind Sam who remained outside the pack even at his own party. Dressed in jeans and a T-shirt, she looked more like Sam's big sister than his mother. Her hair was tied in a ponytail, but one side had already come loose. As she skated over, she pushed it behind her ear. "Thanks for coming," she told him.

"Everything going OK?"

She nodded. "I think so." Behind her Sam stopped himself by plowing into the wall. "He needs to learn how to brake," she said with an air of irritation.

"Hey, Sam, let me get my skates on and I'll teach you how to stop," Nick offered.

His attention to Sam paid off, not in terms of improving the boy's skating abilities—he was as awkward in the rink as on the basketball court—but in raising Sam's status among the other boys. Mr. Connor was cool and if he chose to be with Sam, well, then, Sam must have something going for him. Nick played the pied piper, leading the boys around and around and around the rink until centripetal force drew Sam into their circle and Nick was free to skate away in search of Lisa.

She was watching from a bench. "Your turn to skate with me," he said, extending a hand to help her up. It was such a time warp, asking a girl to skate, so innocently adolescent as if the demands of boy meets girl extended no further than a brief touch of fingers. For the first few minutes he sustained the illusion, timing his stroke to hers, but then the hip hop music blaring from the loud-speakers returned him to the present, mocking his reverie with its sexual crudity.

On their second turn around the rink, the boys surrounded them. "We want our pizza now," Sam demanded with new-found authority.

"All right, all right," she said, "I'll tell them to get the table ready."

As Nick helped her cut the pizza and serve the birthday cake, she kept thanking him until he finally told her not to. Their eyes locked in that moment and he felt let in, but let in to what? She suddenly seemed frightened, vulnerable. A moment later she was the harried mother again, telling Sam to slow down as he tore open the wrapping paper on his presents. She picked up the discarded rib-bons from the floor, wrapping them around her fingers. When Sam opened the package with the basketball, she looked at Nick again. "Thanks," she said.

He left before the other parents came to pick up their kids, not wanting to engage with them. On the way home he convinced himself there was nothing between Lisa and him. She needed him to help and who could blame her? Single motherhood is rough. But at 5:00 that evening, just as he was deciding what to have for dinner, the phone rang. "Nick, it's Lisa," she began. "I just wanted to thank you again for coming."

"I think you've thanked me enough."

"You wouldn't believe what happened."

"What?"

"Jake asked Sam to sleep over tonight—it's the first invitation he's got since we moved here."

"That's great."

"It means I'm free. Free at last." She paused, and he wondered what she wanted from him. "If you don't have plans, I'd like to treat you to dinner."

"I'd like to come, but you don't have to treat me."

"Oh, yes, I do. How about I pick you up in an hour?"

"OK," he said, "as you like."

When he got off the phone, he walked over to the window, looking out at the neighbor's dogwood tree which was about to bloom. He liked dogwoods. There was something elegant and spare about the blossoms even when they were in profusion. He should plant one himself, pay more attention to his poor excuse for a garden. It mirrored the neglect of his own life: a few flowers and shrubs placed haphazardly, watered and weeded only sporadically, just enough to keep them alive. Just enough. No more.

Lisa Derby wanted more of him, but more of what? At the health club, career women asked him out because they wanted sex with a he-man and nothing else. Making love to them left him empty and diminished because they didn't want to see beyond his muscles and his prick. That wasn't Lisa, but what was? Who was she? And why had she looked so scared?

6

At 12:45 on Thursday, Lisa hailed a taxi outside the Dirksen Building and told the driver to take her to the Osaka Restaurant in Dupont Circle. She watched out the window to see if she was being followed, but how would she know? Did she want to know? She had caught Richard Brown's paranoia like a virus and it was infecting every dimension of her life. It ruined her night out with Nick. At the restaurant where they ate dinner, she kept nervously scanning the room for the man in the blue parka. He wasn't there, but maybe someone else had taken his place. She wanted to confide in Nick, but she couldn't so instead she made stupid small talk. First date, last date. How long had it been since she slept with a man?

Trying to buy some luck, she gave the taxi driver a big tip when he dropped her off. It was starting to rain so she hurried into the restaurant. Richard Brown was waiting for her by the hostess post. "All the regular tables are taken so we have to go native and sit on the floor," he told her. "I hope my knees can take it."

The Japanese hostess, dressed like a geisha but with the walk of someone accustomed to jeans, showed them to a section of low tables set off from one another by painted screens. "At least we have the illusion of privacy," Richard said, lowering his body onto the seat cushion. His stomach brushed the edge of the table. "There," he sighed. "The real challenge will be getting back up."

She tried to read his face, but the light was dim, the bulb encased in a paper lantern. "How have you been?" she asked.

"All the 'D' words," he replied, "Demoralized, Depressed, Despairing, Defeated, but not yet Dead. How about you?"

"About the same."

"Oh, but you don't look it." His smile was flirtatious. "The advantage of youth."

"I'm quickly aging."

"Washington does that to you."

A waitress came and set two menus in front of them, then asked if they wanted anything to drink. Richard ordered a bottle of sake. "And two cups," he added.

"I don't drink at lunch," Lisa told him.

"Just have a sip. It's good for you on a rainy day." After the waitress left, he inspected the menu, then closed it and frowned. "How are you really, Lisa?"

She closed her menu too. "Scared, I guess. I was followed."

"Followed here?"

"No, I don't think so. It was after I left you in New York—I saw that man in the blue parka the next day. He followed me from the Metro to Dirksen."

"Oh, I wondered where he went. Have you seen him lately?"

"No, and I've been looking."

"There's probably someone else on you now. There's someone else on me— a blond kid, can't be older than twenty-five, he still has pimples. They want to make us nervous."

"But why? It just means we take more precautions."

"They figure most people screw up when they're nervous, because guess what, most people do. Or they get scared and back down, even if they won't admit it to themselves and fabricate some other reason. Do you want to back down, Lisa? Because if you do, I'll understand. We'll just have a nice lunch and shake hands and say good-by."

"That's not why I came here."

He stared hard at her. With her eyes adjusted to the light, she could see the dark circles under his, a spot of red in the corner of his left one. His face had the puffy but haggard look of a mourner. She leaned back—maybe his fatigue was contagious too. He was about to say something when the waitress came with the sake and poured two cups before taking their orders. As she left, Richard lifted his cup in a toast. "To Senator Barrett," he said, "and a successful investigation."

Lisa took a sip. "So you found something."

"Let's say someone found me."

"Who?"

He glanced around the room and then leaned forward, whispering. "It's between you, me and Senator Barrett, OK?" Lisa nodded. "Because this guy's sticking his neck out, taking a huge risk." She nodded again. "It's a guy in the CIA, counter-terrorism expert. He helped oversee Mohammed's interrogation in the Nevada prison. He didn't like how the military was handling it. He told me the power outage was intentional."

"Do you trust him?"

Richard shook his head. "I don't know. Maybe he's just playing games—some of the older types don't like how the Pentagon is taking over their turf. But he's all we've got so far, and if he's telling the truth, it's dynamite. It could bring the whole rotten house of cards tumbling down."

"And he's willing to speak?"

"Not to the press, at least not yet. He wants to go the official route—probably figures it will give him more protection. He wants a private meeting with Senator Barrett at the end of next week. He wants to see if he can get more information before he blows his cover. I told him sooner would be better, but he wouldn't have it. Do you know the senator's schedule?"

"She's going to Minnesota to campaign on Monday, coming back Friday morning."

"Are you going with her?"

"Yes. My son has spring break and I'm taking him out to stay with his grandparents while I travel with her."

"We'll shoot for Friday afternoon then. Just tell the senator to keep her schedule flexible. She's about to land a big one." He drained his cup of sake and then poured himself another. "You're not making much progress on yours, I see."

"I told you I don't drink at lunch."

"When this is all over, I'll get you drunk at dinner then." She nodded noncommittally. "I'll take you to the best restaurant in town."

When the sushi came, he ate with relish, popping chunks of raw tuna into his mouth like bonbons. Despite herself, she drank a full cup of sake, needing something to blunt her anxiety. She hoped this CIA guy was for real and wasn't leading Richard on, feeding him false information that would make Senator

Barrett look bad in the end. Richard was a brilliant lawyer—that's what everyone said—but it took a different kind of intelligence to manage something like this, a street-smart deviousness they didn't teach in law school.

By the time they finished lunch, he was tipsy enough to reach across the table and place his hand on top of hers. It was warm and sweaty and covered her hand completely. "Lisa, Lisa, I sense this is just the beginning," he said. Whether it was a come-on or political comment, she couldn't tell, but in either case she didn't want his touch. She wanted Nick's and so she drew her hand away.

———

Lyndon didn't like horses. He overcame his fear of them at summer camp, but there was something about them—their smell or snout or snort, he never knew—that repelled him. He rode reluctantly with the President and Trudy on their periodic retreats to the family horse farm near Lexington. Lonesome Hollow it was called, like the name of an Appalachian fiddle tune. The President, by contrast, loved horses. Sometimes when he was particularly stressed out, he escaped to the barn and talked to the horses as if they were his advisors, with the advantage that they never talked back.

Air Force One had flown them to Kentucky late Thursday night. The worst unemployment figures in a decade, coupled with uncharacteristically clever Democratic ads featuring closed public libraries, roads full of potholes, and a laid-off construction worker eating in a soup kitchen, had bumped Hartley's rating in the polls up to 52 percent and the President was flipping out. Lyndon had urged him to stay in Washington and take the heat, but Trudy insisted her husband needed a rest at Lonesome Hollow. "You can talk strategy there as well as here," she assured Lyndon.

The plan was to talk strategy on an early morning ride, just Lyndon and the President, but when Lyndon got to the barn, it was Trudy who was waiting for him. "He woke up with a bad headache and I told him to sleep it off," she explained.

Lyndon looked her in the eye. "He's not drinking, is he, Trudy?"

"Of course not," she said a little too defensively. "Don't be paranoid. The President's entitled to a headache every once in awhile, isn't he? He said to wake him up when we get back and we can do a Bible reading together."

"When we get back?"

She tossed her head so that her perfect hair swirled around like something out of a shampoo commercial. "I thought you and I could go riding instead. The horses are already saddled up and the Secret Service guys got up early to follow in a jeep. I wouldn't want to disappoint them."

"All right," Lyndon agreed, though it was the last thing he wanted to do.

"I'm riding Moonbeam, you've got Sparkler."

"But I usually ride Moonbeam," Lyndon protested. If he was going to suffer the discomfort of riding, the horse had better be one he knew how to handle. "He knows me."

"I got Sparkler for my birthday—I thought you'd like the chance to try him out." Her smile had a devious turn to it. "He's a bit wild, but I'm sure you can hold him in check."

So that was it, he thought. She wanted him to play the fool in her personal little rodeo, cut him down to size by giving him a bruised butt and saddle sores. If Lonesome Hollow was a plantation, Miz Trudy would have pulled down his pants and whipped him for being an uppity nigger houseboy. He considered refusing to ride Sparkler, but he wasn't one to walk away from a challenge. "Bring on the wild horse, you bitch," he muttered under his breath.

Sparkler was the tallest horse Lyndon had ever mounted, pure black except for a hint of brown in the mane. With one hand he gripped the saddle, with the other the reins, aware that if he fell, he'd fall hard. They set off down the road at an even trot, the Secret Service jeep a couple of hundred feet behind them. The sun was just rising and in the morning mist the bluegrass looked like sea water and the hills in the distance like waves. It was beautiful country, Lyndon had to admit, though he still preferred the dry scrub and gnarled cottonwoods of the Texas hills where he spread his parents' ashes.

His parents died early, one after another, his father from a heart attack, his mother from heartbreak. Although their intimacy often excluded him, he viewed it as heroically romantic, something he would never attain with a woman. His only real romance happened the summer he turned eighteen when he fell in love with a counselor from the girls' camp across the river. They met at a dance and then he swam the river the next night and they made love on a blanket under a willow tree. She thought it was amusing that he was a virgin. He could still remember the promise of sexual pleasure in her deep, guttural laugh. "I like the color of your skin," she said, holding her creamy arm up to his. And then she touched him down there. "But this is what I like the best."

"Sparkler's all right, isn't he?" Trudy broke his reverie, drawing her horse closer to his. "I was just kidding when I said he was wild. He's just fast, really fast.

Comes from a line of racehorses, but he doesn't have quite enough speed to be competitive. I'm going to take you to a meadow where we can gallop."

"I don't think that's a good idea."

"Oh, c'mon, Lyndon. I've seen you gallop before. You're good—you're going to like him. Just let him go—he's smooth, really smooth." The smile she gave him was almost friendly, just like the morning sun was almost warm.

"You've galloped with him before?"

"Lots of times."

He wondered if she was luring him into a trap, planning for the horse to throw him so he would die or wind up paralyzed. But without him, her husband was nothing. She must know that. And without her husband, she was just a has-been Southern belle, a former First Lady.

She was right. Sparkler was very fast, but very smooth. Lyndon leaned forward into the motion, pressing his legs into the horse's sides and loosening the reins, relinquishing his fear. Trudy hadn't tricked him after all. The gallop was perfect, and by the end he wished the meadow stretched all the way to creek that bounded the property. "How'd you like him?" she asked when she caught up.

"Fantastic," he said breathlessly.

"Tomorrow before you leave you can ride him again."

Her newfound generosity perplexed him. When she suggested they dismount to give the horses a rest, he wondered what was next. She pulled a tangerine from her pocket, peeled the skin and gave him half, and then leaned against a poplar tree. "Lyndon, I know you don't like me," she began.

With the back of his hand he wiped the tangerine juice dribbling down his chin. "That's not true, Trudy."

"Oh yes, it is. I don't blame you. I'm not very nice." She said it without apology. "But I need your help."

"The President's drinking, isn't he?"

"No, I didn't lie about that."

"Then what is it?"

"Well, he wants to drink."

Sparkler swished his tail, brushing off a fly. "That's nothing new," Lyndon replied, wishing he could brush off this problem just as easily.

Trudy ground the tangerine peel into the ground with her boot. "It's getting worse. The temptation is so strong I can see it in his eyes. He can't look at me straight any more. He can't look at Brendon either. It's like a whole big part of himself is about to break loose and roll down the hillside like a runaway boulder."

She put her hand on her forehead as if to block the sun, but he could tell the real reason was to hide the desperation in her eyes. In the tall grass he noticed a spider web glistening with dew and pointed it out to her. "See that, Trudy. See how finely spun that is. Sometimes God's way is simple and beautiful, like the spider web, sometimes it's difficult and even ugly. But it's God's way and He has a pattern—a reason for everything. Maybe he's teaching you how to help your husband."

"I don't believe in God, Lyndon."

"What?"

"Neither do you. I know you're faking it, but you have to and so do I. So let's get that clear. No more parables, please. I need more than a lousy spider web."

Her frankness took him aback. For a moment he thought of insisting on his faith, but she wouldn't believe it. She was smarter than he thought. "So what do you need?"

"Support, I guess. It's going to be hard work keeping him from drinking."

"Do you have someone you can talk to?"

She shook her head. "You lose all your real friends when you're First Lady. The only people who seek you out want something from you. I can't trust anyone, Lyndon—except for you, and we don't even like each other."

"You can talk to me anyway."

"All right, I will."

They barely spoke on the way back, however. She sat stiffly in the saddle as if trying to regain her dignity. He almost felt sorry for her, but he felt sorrier for himself. The President was closer than he'd thought to self-destruction. The falling boulder could flatten them all.

Matt stood at the living room window of his brother Luke's vacation house in North Carolina, gazing out at the sea. The house sat high above the beach on stilts, an old cottage among newer condos, primitive but comfortable. The afternoon was warm and a little humid, with big white clouds that periodically blotted out the sun, but when they moved away, the light seemed all the more intense. The waves were perfect for body-surfing, but he was long past that now. A Federal Appeals Court judge he knew broke his neck at the Jersey shore, trying to act twenty on his sixtieth birthday. He survived, but it was a miracle he wasn't paralyzed.

What should he do with what was left of the day? Dr. Levinson's instructions were simply to get away on his own and relax. Matt ran his finger over a dry crab shell, one of many crustacean specimens lining the window sill. His brother was a high school biology teacher who preferred the natural world to the social one. Sometimes Matt envied him.

What should he do? What did "relax" mean exactly? The word had long ago disappeared from his vocabulary. He could sit in the rocking chair and doze like the old man he was becoming, but he didn't want to become that old man, not yet. There was too much to do, too much at stake. If there was a way to re-open the Mohammed case, he was going to have to find it. He was Reynolds's main challenger now, holding the center, but could the center hold?

The rocking chair beckoned. Relax, give in, it seemed to say. But he had an urge to get out, to go for a ride even though he didn't like to drive. The tree he hit in high school was always around the next bend, waiting to crack his windshield and shatter his bones. But what if he could will it to disappear and just get in the rental car and drive because it was a beautiful day? It was a worth a try.

He drove down the coastal road, passing the turn-off to Maidenhead Beach where Salim Mohammed's mother lived. How strange that it was so close, but of course it was—he knew that. He shouldn't go there, it might prejudice him, but how? It was a town with a beach like any other town with a beach, a place he might take a walk. No, he wouldn't go. Yes, he would. No, yes, no, and then a mile down the road there was another turn-off. Yes. He turned right.

He found a place to park on a side street, a hundred yards away from the beach. A sign said "private access," but no one seemed to care that an old white man was parking there. How insignificant he was without his judicial robes. He walked to the beach, rolled up his pant legs and took off his shoes. The sand was cool but not cold, soft and firm at the same time. He went down to the water and tested it with a toe. He guessed it was in the lower sixties, swimmable if you were tough enough.

As he walked along the water's edge, he could feel his anxiety drain away like sour milk poured down the sink, yet there was a residue left, a bad taste in his mouth that he couldn't shake despite the ocean's allure. It came from a chance encounter with Justice Fox in the corridor a couple of days ago. Fox liked to gossip; he was always pulling you aside to tell you some faux pas of Reynolds's or a malicious tidbit about Merritt's dominatrix marriage to a law professor six inches shorter and ten years her junior. Usually, Matt didn't take him seriously, but this time the subject was himself. "Is your health OK, Matt?" Fox asked him.

"Fine," Matt lied. He hadn't told anyone at the Court about his high blood pressure.

"Well, your head clerk doesn't think so."

"What do you mean?"

"One of my clerks mentioned that Scott told him your heart's acting up."

"Scott doesn't know what he's talking about."

"I shouldn't tell you this, but he also told my clerk that your obsession with the Mohammed case is clouding your judgment—you won't put your mind to any other decisions."

"Scott said that?"

Fox shrugged. "My clerk said he said it, but who knows. They're vicious basketball competitors—they play one-on-one every evening before they go home. Could be my clerk wants to get Scott in trouble."

"Sounds possible."

"Watching how the nine of us operate is not exactly a model for good behavior."

They left it at that, but it worried Matt then and it worried him now. How did Scott know about his heart condition? He hadn't told him anything. Was Scott secretly looking through his appointment book? And claiming Matt was losing his judgment—who did Scott think he was? What game was he playing? Had he struck some kind of deal with Reynolds to undermine Matt? Next week he would have to confront him, but he knew Scott would weasel out of it, tell him he never said such a thing. There were no solid grounds to fire him. But Matt would hide his appointment book from now on.

It took almost a mile of walking before he rid his mind of Scott. Before turning back, he stopped to rest in an empty lifeguard's chair. He had been a lifeguard one summer in college, tanned so brown he could almost pass as black. "Nigger," some of his friends jokingly called him, and he wondered if they still used that word or had mastered the language of the New South. He had saved three people that summer, one a kid pulled out by the undertow, the second a drunk student who swam out too far, the third an old man who had a minor stroke in the water. That could be me now, he thought. I could need saving.

He gazed south down the beach where a long-legged black boy was dashing in and out of the waves, watched by an elderly woman in a dark dress. He was too far away to see their faces, but somehow he felt it was Faith Jones with her grandson, the boy who said on TV that he wanted his daddy back. That had touched Matt more deeply than anything else about Mohammed's death. A boy saying he wanted his daddy back.

It would be right that they would be there, to remind him of the justice still undone, the payments he still had to make. He had to tame his wild heart so he could keep going, keep the Court on course.

———

By the time 5:30 rolled around, the after-school kids were literally bouncing off the gym walls. Maybe it was the anticipation of spring break that made them so hyper. Nick wished he could look forward to the vacation, but it meant he wouldn't get paid for the week, and there were no extra hours to pick up at the fitness club.

He surveyed the room to make sure no one was doing anything dangerous to themselves or someone else. There was such a fine line between fun and danger at this age. Maybe that was the case all through life; it's just that the risks took different forms, like sex and AIDS for his generation. Already he could tell which kids were going to push their bodies to the limit. Josh Tyson was fearless; he climbed ropes to the ceiling, hung like a monkey from the rings, led the charge no matter what the sport. Sam was a different matter. You could see his mind working, weighing consequences, holding back. Too much restraint. Maybe it was because Sam didn't really have a father in his life, someone to hang him upside down and roughhouse with him. But no, there were other kids raised by single mothers who didn't hesitate to take physical risks. Sam was just Sam, that's all. At least he was part of the gang now. The other boys had taken him in as a kind of mascot, someone who would cheer on their own daring.

He wished Lisa was picking Sam up today, not Mrs. Cummings. He hadn't seen her since their date last weekend, if you could call it a date. Better to call it a disaster. He had wanted to ask her why she was so anxious, but he held back. The holding back was tearing at him now. What had there been to lose? A little pride if she rebuffed his concern, but he was past pride. He was a little scared, to tell the truth. Scared of the longing she induced, longing for sex that was something more than sex, more than the fine line between fun and danger.

He looked around the room again. Two boys were wrestling on the tumbling mat and it was threatening to turn ugly. As he walked toward them, contemplating whether to blow his whistle, he noticed Lisa in the doorway. She waved at him and he waved back. "No wrestling unless I'm there to supervise," he told the boys, but one kept pinning down the other. "Get up, both of you. I don't want to have to tell you again." He waited until they were disentangled, then walked over to Lisa.

"The senator let me out early," she explained, "so I thought I'd pick up Sam so he can come home for a little while before he goes over to Josh's. Another sleep-over invitation—can you believe it?"

"I can. The other guys really like him now."

"It's a huge relief." She paused, fiddling with her purse strap. "I wanted to apologize for Saturday night," she said, her face flushing. "I wasn't feeling well."

"That's all right."

"No, it isn't. You must think I'm rude."

"That's not the word I'd use."

"I'd like you to give me another chance. How about coming over tonight? We could watch a DVD."

"I have to work until nine."

"Come over after, then. I can't do tomorrow. Sam and I are leaving for Minneapolis in the afternoon."

"OK." He noticed another parent coming down the hall. "Can I bring anything?"

"Just yourself," she said and then called to Sam.

When Nick reached her apartment around 9:30, it looked as if she had done nothing to prepare for his arrival. A bag of potato chips lay open on the couch, a few greasy crumbs on the pillows. A partially packed suitcase sat on one chair, a laundry basket on the other. Lisa herself looked disheveled in an old pair of baggy jeans and a faded University of Minnesota sweatshirt. Nick didn't know what to think. She didn't apologize, just swept the crumbs off the couch so he could sit.

The DVD was a Gene Hackman thriller he'd seen at least three times before. He didn't tell her, since watching it was a good excuse to sit close and say nothing. In the middle of yet another car chase, he ventured an arm around her shoulder. When she didn't pull back, he put his hand behind her head, playing with her hair as he drew her close to kiss her. There was no hesitation in her, no recoiling, as he lifted her sweatshirt and found her breasts. "Nick, let's go to the bedroom," she whispered.

The bedroom was neater than the living room, the bedspread and sheets folded down as if by a night maid in a hotel. He undressed her slowly, and then told her to roll over so he could give her a massage. He worked her neck and her shoulders, listening for her breathing to become easier before he slid his hands along the sides of her breasts. He drew her legs apart and massaged her thighs. "Nick," she said in a familiar way, as if she'd known him for a long time. "That feels so good, Nick."

Even though he was aroused, he felt infinitely patient. Giving her pleasure was a kind of meditation that shifted something inside him, something that had been lodged in the wrong place for too long, like a tree fallen across the road. Gently, he turned her over and lifted her legs so he could explore her with his tongue. Her coming was the sweet end to his meditation, the beginning of a journey he hadn't risked for so long. A journey toward wanting, needing, needing to be inside her, a sex of hope.

And it was all he hoped for. She danced on top of him with a wicked lustiness, taunting and tantalizing. After he came, she gazed down on him, pleased with herself, smiling in a way that made her more beautiful than any woman he had ever seen.

7

Reluctantly, Faith Jones unlocked the front door of the fish store on Monday morning. Every day it was getting harder for her to cut and clean the fish she bought at the wholesale market. Blue fish, swordfish, halibut or tuna, it didn't matter. She wanted to take a break, but this was her living, and she had Samira and Ali to support. Maybe someday Samira would help her, but for now she was incapable of doing anything except watching TV. Faith worried about the look in her eye, as if she were staring off into the distance, only the distance was a vast dry desert inside her. If Samira was Christian, Faith could at least take her to church, where there was one young widow mourning her husband's death and another coping with her husband's life sentence. These days there were too many young women without a man, too many boys without a father.

Ali's father was dead and his mother's soul was dying. Faith knew it was up to her to keep the spirit alive in him, but she wondered if she had the strength. Her physical strength wasn't in doubt. She might be over sixty, but she could still lift heavy bags of ice and stay on her feet all day long with only a few varicose veins to show for it. Inside she was tough too. She was a fighter, always had been, and she wouldn't stop fighting until she cleared Jackson's name. That was a given, a God-given.

But it takes a different kind of strength to raise a child. A child is not a bag of ice you can lift off the floor. Your heart has to be strong to raise a child. You have to have so much love inside you that there's always some left over when the child takes all he can take, because he'll demand even more another day. She had given that kind of love to Jackson, but now she felt drained by his death, hollow where the love used to be, so hollow she was scared the Devil might come to fill the empty space.

She said a little prayer to ward off the Devil, and then went into the back room to clean some shrimp. She could get a better price if she shelled it—ten dollars a pound instead of eight. Halfway through the task the phone rang. She was reluctant to answer it, afraid it was another hate caller saying her nigger traitor of a son deserved to hang. Instead, it was the young man from Senator Barrett's office who had visited her last week.

"Nice to hear from you again, Mr. Madison," she said.

"I wanted to confirm that you're still willing to come to testify."

"Of course. I told you I would. Nothing would change my mind on that."

"It could be as early as next week. I just wanted you to be prepared."

"You've found something out, haven't you?"

"No, not exactly, but we're optimistic."

Optimistic was a word Faith hadn't heard in a long time. "You just tell me when," she said, "and I'll be there."

After she hung up, she stood for awhile by the sink, unable to get back to cleaning the shrimp. The idea of testifying made her less nervous than the prospect of traveling. The farthest she'd been since her husband Paul's death was to Raleigh. She wished he could take her to Washington. He knew how to handle things—how much to tip the taxi driver, where to eat, how to read a map.

She picked up a shrimp and pulled off its shell, then removed the black vein from its translucent body. "I need your help, Paul," she said, throwing the shrimp in with the others.

So they were getting the old lady ready to come to Washington, Lyndon thought as he read over Skip's latest phone transcripts in the privacy of his office. The wiretap on Faith Jones's phone had yielded little until now, but this tidbit was worth it. He knew the mother was only backdrop though, providing a little atmosphere for the main act of the play that Barrett and Brown were planning to stage. But try as Skip might, he still hadn't identified the star actor, the source of the information they were all excited about. Lyndon had to hand it to Richard

Brown. He'd made plenty of security errors along the way, but he hadn't yet blown the identity of his mystery source. He probably would in due course, but would it be soon enough?

It was frustrating, sitting and waiting for Skip to deliver the goods. Too much waiting these days for a man like Lyndon, "a classic man of action," a profile in the *Wall Street Journal* once described him. Its sketch of him made him look like a gnarled version of Denzel Washington. The *Journal* got its portraits of white people right, quirky and individualized, but it hadn't mastered the art for African Americans.

He stood and paced the room, following the design of the oriental carpet as if it were a map that might lead somewhere. He only had a few minutes left before he met with the President in the Rose Garden for a heart-to-heart about drinking. Trudy had come to his office yesterday and begged him to do it. "Please don't tell him I came to see you," she said.

"But how am I supposed to approach him then?" Lyndon asked.

"Pretend you're the one suffering from temptation. He'll respond to that."

Lyndon reached the Rose Garden before the President and studied him as he approached. He looked awful. Instead of his usual jaunty stride, his legs shuffled, and the bags under his eyes made his expression droop like a basset hound's. Lyndon knew he was just coming off a long meeting with his campaign staff. Usually that left him fired up, not dragged down. "Sorry I'm late," the President apologized. "They started fighting with each other and I couldn't afford to leave."

"Let them fight—they'll sort it out."

"This re-election business is so much harder than the first time around."

"These are hard times. You've got to play that up, remember. Hard times and hard choices require a President hardened by experience."

"I don't feel hard, Lyndon, I feel soft, real soft."

Lyndon nodded sympathetically. "I know what you mean. I'm feeling that way too. That's why I wanted to talk to you."

"What is it, Lyndon?"

They strayed off the path onto the grass. The afternoon sun was warm on Lyndon's neck. Another time, another place, he might sit on a bench and give himself five minutes to bask in it. Instead he knew this spring would just pass him by like all the other seasons. "I'm feeling the thirst again," he began. "It's all I can think about sometimes."

"Have you drunk anything?"

Lyndon shook his head. "I've come close, too close for comfort, but then I think of our mission and the Lord stays my hand."

"You're lucky."

"What do you mean?"

"That He comes to your aid like that. I pray for Him to do that, but nothing happens and I feel more alone than ever."

"You're feeling the thirst too?"

The President looked down, lowering his voice. "The desire is consuming me, Lyndon. I'm hanging on, but my will power's running out. I've lost interest in, well, just about everything, even my wife. I'm damned if I drink and damned if I don't, because either way I'm useless. They squabbled at the meeting today because they sensed my weakness. I'm not mentally present, Lyndon, and people are starting to notice. Does it ever happen to you—your mind just goes blank and you stare off into space? I can't afford to do that. What if it happens at a press conference?"

"It won't," Lyndon asserted.

"How can you be sure?"

"Look," Lyndon took the President's arm and guided him back toward the rose bushes, "see those thorns on the branches." The President nodded dutifully. "Well, when I was out here waiting for you, I realized something really important. Remember when Jesus was crucified, they put a crown of thorns on his head?"

"Yes, but what does that have to do with me?"

"He wore those thorns and he suffered to save us all, didn't he?"

"Of course he did."

"Well, there's a crown of thorns on your head too."

"What, Lyndon, are you nuts, comparing me to Jesus?"

"All true leaders have to wear a crown of thorns. You see, if they don't suffer, they won't understand suffering, they won't know how to put it right. You're suffering now because God is preparing you for the next big challenge, the next four years of putting this country right. You need to bear it nobly. You need to say to yourself, yes, I'm suffering, but that's what makes me stronger."

"It makes me weaker, Lyndon. You've got it all wrong."

"That's what you think now, but in a week or two the weakness will pass and you'll wake up a new man, like after a bad flu when the fever burns you clean."

"And you?"

"The Lord is staying my hand so I can help you."

"I hope you're right, but I'm not cured yet. I've still got a bad case of flu."

An idea suddenly struck Lyndon. "Exactly," he said, snapping his fingers, "brilliant."

"What are you talking about?"

"It's time you called in sick—with the flu."

"But I'm not sick."

"When things are going really badly, you know what most people do? They call in sick even if they aren't. Why don't you give yourself the rest of the week off and spend it in bed in Lonesome Hollow with the ministrations of your lovely wife. Let her love you—love heals, you know. We'll have a bedside photo shoot when you're getting better. She'll be sitting next to you with a bowl of chicken soup."

"But people don't like the president to get sick."

"Not real sick, but a little sick—it proves you're human. And when you're down like that, Hartley can't kick you, can he? It would make him look too mean. It's a break all of us can use."

"You'll run things in my absence?"

I run them in your presence too, Lyndon wanted to say, but refrained. "Of course. I'll be in constant touch."

"It's a good plan, Lyndon. I'm feeling better already."

"But you need to start acting like you're feeling worse."

The President bent down to examine a rosebud. "How long do you think it will be until they start blooming?" he asked.

From a corner of her eye Lisa glimpsed a waitress carrying a bread basket and hoped it was time to eat. She was in the Minneapolis Sheraton at the Democratic Business and Professional Women's luncheon in honor of Senator Barrett. Working the crowd had given her an appetite. She knew she needed to fortify herself for the trip to Thief River Falls. The town was in the northwest corner of the state and they were chartering a small plane to get them there on time. The senator had family there and was making a folksy visit to a church dinner to dispel concerns that she was just a big city politician.

Ever since she dropped off Sam with her parents Saturday night, Lisa had been on the go, accompanying the senator from one fundraising event or speech to another. In between, in taxis and limos and planes, the senator tutored her on who to greet and what to say; she was teaching Lisa how to campaign like a political insider. Late at night they had also spent time strategizing about the upcoming meeting with Richard Brown's CIA source.

Senator Barrett's unspoken message was that if Lisa performed well, she could be next in line. "When I finally give up the ghost, I want another woman to replace me," the senator told her, "but not just any woman. That's not the point. It has to be someone who's not afraid to tell it like it is. There aren't many people like that in Washington, men or women. I want someone with mettle—that's an old-fashioned word, but it says it all, doesn't it? People raised here in the northern Midwest have more mettle, I think. Must be something in the soil or maybe it's the cold winters that freeze the bullshit out of you."

Lisa was gratified to be trusted and singled out this way, but there was another part of her, the part that looked hungrily at the bread basket, that wanted to turn and walk away. She studied the senator wondering if that could be her in twenty years, high on adulation but low on love. Was it so wrong to want to be loved? To want a normal family life? Was that what Nick represented, the possibility of a normal life? Did that account for her attraction to him?

A tap her on her shoulder broke her reverie. "Lisa, I hoped you'd be here." She recognized the voice of Melissa Patterson, a former colleague at the law firm. She was a smart and imposing woman, tall and wide-hipped, but she didn't dress to her advantage. Today she was clad in something polyester and frightfully lime-green.

"Oh, hi, Melissa. Great to see you," Lisa said.

"Great to see you too. I see you've gone on to bigger and better things."

"You think so?"

Melissa laughed. "Well, I'm jealous."

"Don't be."

She gave Lisa a shrewd look. "Well, I have heard the senator's not the easiest person to work for, but then again the firm isn't exactly a joy ride either. I guess we so-called business and professional women just have to pick our pain."

"Maybe all women do."

Melissa drew in her breath in mock surprise. "Lisa, what's happened to you? You always used to be so upbeat."

"I like the senator, really. It's great work—I'm just tired."

"Ditto. Thoroughly exhausted. Did you hear I made partner?"

"Congratulations." Lisa meant it. Melissa surely deserved partner more than a lot of the dumber guys in the firm who sucked up and sailed to the top.

"I'm the token female, but I'm grooming others. If the senator loses, I'll make sure you're welcomed back."

"Thanks, but she's not planning to lose."

"The Republicans are pouring in money from all over the country."

"I think that's going to backfire. People in Minnesota like to think they choose their own senators."

Melissa shook her head. "Don't be so sure. Things are changing here, just like they're changing everywhere. This town's getting mean, losing its charm."

Lisa heard her cell phone ringing and reached into her purse. "Excuse me for a second, OK?"

"Sure. I'm at your table—we can talk more later."

Lisa flicked open the phone and starting making her way to a quieter corner of the room. The connection was bad, but she could make out her mother's voice through the static. "Sam had a bad fall," her mother said.

Lisa's heart raced. "Is he OK?"

"He was jumping off the hay bales in the barn."

"But is he OK, Mom?"

"He's getting X-rayed right now. They think his left arm's broken."

"Oh God."

"I think you'd better come home. We can't get him to stop crying."

Soothing pain was not her mother's strength. She thought everyone, even little kids, should be stoics like herself. "Can I talk to him?"

"When he gets out of X-ray."

"I'm supposed to be going to Thief River Falls this afternoon." She paused, hoping her mother would say to go ahead, but of course she wouldn't. Her silence meant only one thing: you have to come home. "I'll talk to the senator and see if I can skip the trip—especially if his arm's broken."

"Oh, it's broken all right—you can see the bone sticking out."

"Why didn't you tell me that?"

"I didn't want you to worry."

"Call me back when he gets out of X-ray, will you. I want to talk to him." Lisa hung up, but kept clutching the phone, her concern for Sam tinged with anger. She had jumped off hay bales all during her childhood and never hurt herself. Why was he so clumsy? Why couldn't her mother deal? And then she was angry at herself for having these thoughts. Sam's arm was broken and she was his mother. End of story—and perhaps the end of her political career. Senator Barrett wouldn't be pleased she was leaving.

With trepidation she made her way toward the senator who was in deep conversation with Virginia Morgan, a female VP of General Foods and a particularly generous supporter. Lisa knew the senator wouldn't take well to being interrupted, but she had no choice. Luckily, as she approached, an announcer told people to find their tables and Virginia took leave. "I need to have a word with you," Lisa told Senator Barrett.

"What's up?"

"My son broke his arm and my mother wants me to come back. It means I won't be able to go to Thief River Falls. I'm really sorry, I…"

"Lisa, aren't you getting tired of spending your whole life apologizing to me? Go to your parents' place if you have to—the trip to Thief River Falls is no big deal and I can do without you tomorrow. Just make sure you're on that plane to Washington Friday morning. I need you with me for that meeting."

"Thank you."

"You can quit thanking me too." She paused, waving to someone who was coming her way. "You forget I have a son. It's always a question of priorities, even now. You're lucky he broke his arm today. Just be ready to work on Friday."

A cold rain was falling when Lisa set out for her parents' farm. Sixty miles down the highway it began to freeze. Spring in Minnesota, she thought as she struggled to keep the rental car from skidding off the road. The cell phone lay on the seat next to her, awaiting Sam's call. The battery was getting low and she was afraid the phone would die before she heard from him. At exit 30 she turned off and stopped at a roadside diner for a cup of coffee and some food to keep her going. The old man behind the counter told her they were supposed to have freezing rain all night.

Back in the parking lot, she turned on the defroster to melt the ice on the windshield. She closed her eyes for a minute, imagining what it would be like to have someone like Nick along with her, someone to share the worry and the driving, to lie in bed with her at her parents' house and remind her that she was a grown woman now, not the little girl who filled her days with fantasies of escape. But wasn't Nick a fantasy too? An impossible fantasy of love and care and the white picket fence?

She picked up the cell phone, wondering if she could remember Nick's number. She shouldn't call him—it would run down the battery—but she needed to hear his voice. The number came to her and she dialed it, though she hesitated a few seconds before pressing the send button. His phone rang six times before she got the answering machine. "Nick," she said, "it's Lisa. I just wanted you to know that Sam broke his arm, but he's going to be OK. I'll try to call you later."

The freezing rain forced her to drive slowly, and she didn't get to her parents' farm until dinner time. Sam greeted her at the door, proudly displaying his cast. "You can be the first one to sign it," he said.

Matt didn't really like watching basketball on TV, but the game was an excuse to stay up later than Dora, to take some time for himself. Ever since his trip to the beach, he had become needier in that respect, wanting peace and quiet so he could think more clearly. He was like the Wizards player now standing at the foul line, needing a little extra time to center himself, bend just so, calculate the arc to the basket. Swish, in the ball goes, so he gets another shot. This one dances on the rim, but goes in again. Not as dramatic as a breakaway dunk, but two points all the same. The Wizards were up by eight.

Was Matt ahead or behind at the Court? It was too early to tell. At least he had started to reassert control over his own office. On Tuesday he dusted off his old prosecutorial skills and called Scott in for a grilling. "I hear there are rumors circulating about my physical and mental competence," he told him.

Scott played dumb, of course. He certainly hadn't heard anything, he claimed. On the contrary, people were remarking on Matt's strength in standing up to the Chief Justice.

"Oh, they are, are they? That's not what I hear." Matt zoomed in on him then, searching Scott's face with the full force of his fierce eyes.

Scott blinked nervously and his leg jerked as if someone had tapped his knee to test his reflexes. "You know this place is full of rumors."

Matt nodded slowly. "Oh yes. In fact, I heard a rumor that it was my head clerk spreading rumors about me."

Scott blinked again. "That's not true"

"What's not true—that such rumors are circulating or that you're the source of them?"

"They could be circulating. I don't know, I don't hear everything, but I'm certainly not the source. Who told you I was?"

"I don't think you need to know. My purpose is not to launch a vendetta against anyone. But I warn you that if I find sufficient evidence that you're spreading these stories, your clerkship will be terminated immediately." Matt paused and clasped his hands together on the desk. "And I can assure you I will do everything in my power to make sure you don't have a future in the federal judiciary. Do I make myself clear?"

"Yes, but…"

"You're excused. We'll meet at 2:00 to go through those cert petitions."

Matt smiled to himself. How good it had felt to watch Scott quiver. He turned his attention back to the game where the Celtics had cut the Wizards' lead to five with a perfect three-pointer. A few more of those and the Wizards would be in trouble. They had a habit of losing the lead at the end of the first half, ceding the locker room advantage. Basketball was such a psychological game, almost as bad as tennis. Sometimes it was painful to watch.

Just as the Wizards missed a lay-up, a ticker tape news alert ran across the bottom of the TV screen: Commuter plane carrying Senator Pamela Barrett and her aides reported missing in northern Minnesota. Stay tuned to this channel for more information. Immediately, Matt began channel surfing, looking for a longer report. On one news channel a local Minnesota reporter described how the plane had taken off at 8:30 PM from the airport at Thief River Falls during an ice storm. When the pilot made his last radio contact at 8:50, there was nothing to suggest the plane was experiencing difficulties. Authorities were still hopeful.

Half an hour later, they were no longer so hopeful. There were a number of reports from the White Earth Indian Reservation of a flaming object in the sky south of Route 113. Rescue vehicles and helicopters were on their way to the area, but it could be a long while until they found the exact location of the crash.

A chill settled over Matt as he stayed glued to the television, watching the drama unfold in small increments: sound bites from political figures, interviews with aviation experts, touches of local color from Native Americans who witnessed the fire in the sky. He draped a throw blanket around his shoulders, but it did little to ward off the cold. He had no love for Senator Barrett—who did?—but it wasn't the right time for her to die. She said things that needed to be said.

They found the wreckage after midnight, plane and body parts scattered over a field. There were no survivors. At 12:30 AM the White House issued a statement from the President who was recuperating from flu at his home in Lonesome Hollow. Throughout her political career, Senator Barrett had done great service to her country, it read. The President deeply regretted her untimely and tragic death and offered his deepest condolences to her husband and son.

Frantically, Nick tried Lisa's cell phone number, but the call wouldn't go through. The message she left on his answering machine said Sam had broken his arm. Did that mean she had gone back to her parents' house to be with him, or was she on the plane? It was 2:00 AM and they hadn't yet released the names of the other passengers because they were still trying to contact family members. Why didn't she call to tell him she was all right? Maybe she hadn't even heard about the crash. Maybe she was safely asleep in a farmhouse somewhere in Minnesota. He tried to believe that. Her survival would be a sign that his own life meant something.

part two

8

The late May weather was perfect, clear and a bit on the cool side, as the oldest living Princeton alumnus, centenarian Douglas Wright, led the annual parade down Nassau Street and through the iron gates of the university. The spry old man walked with only the aid of a cane which he periodically lifted to greet the crowd. Behind him, the twenty-fifth reunion class bore the gleeful look of kids finally let out for recess. They all wore identical T-shirts and straw hats festooned with the orange and black Princeton colors.

On the insistence of the Secret Service, Lyndon marched inconspicuously in the middle of the throng of successful middle-aged professionals. It had been a long while since he'd last visited Princeton. He'd never attended a reunion before, but Professor Maxwell had invited him to be on an expert panel in the afternoon on "Princeton in Washington." Lyndon owed him that. In fact, he owed him much more.

Maxwell had been his mentor in college. His lectures were what got Lyndon out of bed in the morning, for the bookish, diminutive Maxwell was a brilliant orator, with the diction of a Shakespearean actor and the fire of an FDR. He also had a knack for spotting political talent. The rookie students he recruited to his team of favorites almost all rose to high places. Seeing beyond Lyndon's bad habits, Maxwell convinced him he was headed for power. "Once you believe it's your destiny, that's half the battle won," he instructed Lyndon in his senior year.

"A political life is like the priesthood. It's a calling, a vocation."

The band struck up "Old Nassau" and Lyndon mouthed the words. A little boy let go of a helium balloon and Lyndon watched it drift into the bright blue sky. The campus lawns were a dazzling green, the stone buildings as old as they can be in the New World. Despite the bad patch in the stock market, the university's endowment was clearly doing well. A perfect little world, Lyndon thought, like a theme park. That's why these people all come back, even ancient alums like Wright, to re-experience the security of a theme park world. There was a political lesson in there somewhere.

He felt a hand on his arm. "Hi, Lyndon. Remember me?"

Her face was familiar, but her name escaped him. "Sure I do," he said.

"Jeanine Turner."

"Right, so good to see you, Jeanine." He remembered her now, the shy black girl from Alabama who became a raging black nationalist her sophomore year. Her Afro was more modest now, graying in places, and she was rounder, softer, maternal looking. "What are you up to these days? Still making trouble?"

"No, I gave that up. Now I just try to help people, you know, one by one. I work for Legal Aid in Chicago—or rather what's left of it since the cuts."

"That's noble."

"I'm surprised you think that."

There was an edge to her voice that reminded him of the old Jeanine. "You think I'm opposed to helping people?"

"Yes, if they're poor."

"You still think I'm a race traitor too?"

"I'm beyond that kind of thinking now, Lyndon, way beyond."

"Well, at least that's something we have in common." Abruptly, he turned away and started walking faster, relieved when she didn't follow. Later, when the march came to a halt, he noticed she was with a balding Jewish guy who had an arm around her shoulder. She was pointing at Lyndon as if he were some kind of freak.

He enjoyed a warmer reception during lunch in the reunion tent where old Cottage Club buddies slapped him on the back and kids asked for his autograph. The photographer from the alumni magazine shot away. By the end of lunch, he longed for a rest, wishing for a moment that he was a man without consequence who could lie down unnoticed in the shade of the old trees. Instead, with his

Secret Service handlers trailing behind him, he headed for the Woodrow Wilson School of Public and International Affairs, where his panel began in half an hour.

The school was housed in a secular temple of white marble and stylized columns, endowed by its Japanese architect with a transcendent lightness of being. As a student, Lyndon had often cooled his feet or splashed his face in the fountain in front, cleansing himself when his life was far from holy. He walked up the steps and into the foyer, where he paused by the spiny metal globe in the center. He strummed it so that it made a tinny tinkling sound and then made his way to the auditorium.

Maxwell was already sitting at the table on stage, looking over his notes. Ten years had passed since Lyndon had last seen him, and Maxwell's shock of white hair was now reduced to a few fine strands. As he stood to greet Lyndon, he laid a hand on the table to balance himself. He was almost sixty-nine, Lyndon remembered, due to retire next year. A fellow classmate had been in touch about endowing a chair in his name. "Glad you could make it," Maxwell said, but there was little warmth in his smile. "Affairs of state often lead to last-minute cancellations. A little calm before the storm, is there?"

"Which storm are you referring to?"

"The election, of course."

"As you know, there are lots of storms in my line of business."

"Ah yes," Maxwell sighed, then gave Lyndon a penetrating look. "And some are more convenient than others. Like that ice storm in Minnesota."

"I wouldn't call that convenient—it was a tragedy."

Maxwell raised an eyebrow. "Really? Well, I'd enjoy discussing the ramifications with you. If you're not too busy, I wonder if you'd like to stop by the house after dinner for a little coffee in the den, for old time's sake?"

"I'd like that."

"Oh, here comes one of your fellow panelists. Scott Hanson—do you know him? Also a former student and very up-and-coming, people tell me. Head clerk for Supreme Court Justice Matthew Pomeroy."

"I haven't met him," Lyndon quickly replied.

"Well, you will now. Between you and me, Lyndon, he lacks a little je ne sais quoi—call it charm, maybe, or just open-mindedness. The younger ones all do, at least from my own observation. These days it's so competitive to get into Princeton that the freshmen arrive prematurely hardened, smug or so well-rounded you long for some rough edges. There's no such thing as an ingénue any more. They're too driven for my taste. Starts in preschool, I hear. I don't like them as much as your batch. Frankly, they're not as interesting. Time to retire, I guess."

Besides Lyndon and Scott, the panel included Brenda Axelrod, a Congresswoman from Pennsylvania, and Lydia Fuller, the CEO of a pro-labor lobbying firm. Maxwell kept Lyndon for last. Scott and Brenda's remarks were dull and predictable, but Lydia was a dynamic speaker, and her humorous anatomy of influence was a hard act to follow. While she spoke, Lyndon tried to think of a few funny stories he could add to his prepared speech, like the time he talked in his sleep on Air Force One and a nosy reporter on board recorded his gibberish as gospel truth.

In the end, he didn't deviate from the vacuous phrases his speechwriter had thrown together like soup made from leftovers. In fact, it was all he could do to make it through to the end. A few lines in, he noticed Jeanine and her balding partner sitting in the back row, fumbling with something. Jeanine raised a hand and in unison about twenty people in the back row stood up, silently unfurling a banner. THERE'S BLOOD ON YOUR HANDS, LYNDON TOTTMAN. On the white background were red handprints and sketches of a noose and a plane bursting into flames.

———————

Lisa pushed the shopping cart down the cereal aisle, searching for a new brand of cereal Sam had seen on TV, Monsterpuffs, featuring little green Frankensteins and cocoa Draculas. She shouldn't buy it—sugar was probably the main ingredient—but these days she had to pick her battles. Since Nick's entrance into her life, Sam had become less whiny but more combative. Nick said all the boys Sam's age were starting to feel their oats. Feeling their oats but eating Monsterpuffs. Go figure.

On Saturday afternoon the grocery store was crowded and she made slow progress down the aisle. Nick was back at the apartment, watching another playoff game with Sam. She didn't mind that they weren't helping with the shopping—or did she? Lately, she felt herself sinking into a dull domesticity both at home and at work. Since Senator Barrett's death, her job seemed more like office housekeeping than legislative analysis. The Governor of Minnesota had appointed a milquetoast retired Congressman, Harold Lundberg, to fill out Barrett's term. He was only interested in hobnobbing with his former buddies and securing a few government contracts for local firms back home. He had no interest in pursuing the investigation of Salim Mohammed's death.

What did it matter anyway? Richard Brown's source was no longer willing to talk. The senator's death had scared him off. The aviation authorities still maintained the plane crash was an accident, but she didn't believe it. The only real accident was Sam's fall, an act of fate that had saved her life. She had to finish the senator's unfinished business, but how? Come the new election, she would be out of a job. She had her feelers out, but prospects weren't bright for a congressional aide branded as Barrett's protégée. She was too controversial.

Her eyes scanned the shelf. There they were, Monsterpuffs. She grabbed a box and stuck it in the cart, then headed toward the meat aisle. As she reached for a family pack of chicken legs, she felt a hand on her arm and looked up in surprise. "Good lord, Richard, what are you doing here?"

He put a finger to his lips. "Shh, let's just shop together for awhile, OK."

"All right." She glanced at him curiously. She hadn't seen him since the day of Senator Barrett's memorial service, when he told her everything was off and he was going into hibernation and she should too.

"You shouldn't get that chicken," he advised. "It's shot full of hormones."

"What isn't?" she replied as she put it in the cart. "How'd you find me anyway?"

"I followed you from your apartment."

"You followed me?"

"You're not being so careful any more, are you?"

"I'm in hibernation, like you're supposed to be."

"It doesn't matter. You should have noticed I was following you."

She studied his face, trying to gauge if he had finally gone over the edge from paranoia to lunacy, but he appeared much the same except perhaps a little fatter and grubbier. His beard needed a trim and his shirt had a yellow stain on the pocket. He guided her to an empty section of the housewares aisle and picked up an egg beater, pretending to inspect it. "Our source has been in touch again," he whispered. "I guess his conscience is pricking him and he needs to talk."

"But I can't do anything, Richard. I have no authority to call for an investigation and the last thing Lundberg wants is to rock the boat."

"Do you want out?" He turned the handle on the beater and watched it spin. "That's why I came to see you—to find out whether you want in or out."

"What good is it if I'm in?"

He shrugged. "Think of it this way. It makes a good story. Senator Barrett's aide, the Midwest farm girl who narrowly escaped death, bravely pursues the truth and takes on the administration almost single-handedly. The press will love it like they never love the ACLU. Good for your political career too."

"My political career is about to end."

"Only if you let it. Look, Lisa," he said, watching the progress of a woman with a baby as they turned down the aisle, "I'm not saying you have to be involved or that you're indispensable. For you, maybe it's not worth the risk and I understand that. You've got a young kid. Mine are all grown up. Just think about it. I'm meeting our friend Tuesday evening. Show up if you want in."

"Where are you meeting?"

As he waited for the mother to pass, Richard put the egg beater back on the hook. "Don't make them like they used to," he commented. "That piece of crap will break in a couple of months." And then under his breath, "Our friend will be jogging around the high school track in Reston. We'll meet by the water fountain at 7:45 when it's starting to get dark. If you come, wear jogging gear and take a few spins around the track so you look thirsty. This time make sure you're not followed." He didn't wait for her reply. "Whatever you do, don't buy the egg beater," he said, and walked away.

———

In the Supreme Court building, Matt sat alone at his desk, bending a paperclip with his fingers as he skimmed a long, boring legal brief. Usually, at least one of his clerks was in on Saturday, but Scott was at his Princeton reunion and the others had been seduced by the fine summer weather. He was grateful for the solitude—in fact, that's why he'd come. At home Dora was driving him to distraction. The wedding was two months away, but you'd think it was tomorrow. She couldn't stop talking about it. And when she wasn't talking to him, she was trying to phone Jessie, who had become more and more unreachable. "She's never home," Dora complained, though he suspected Jessie had just stopped answering the phone. "I have to check with her about what kind of hors d'oeuvres she wants."

"Jessie will go along with any decision you make," he told her, which was true. His daughter could care less about such details, especially when they had to do with food. But precisely because they had to do with food, Dora was insistent, a throwback to the anorexia days when mother and daughter were locked in bitter battle. He could see it coming—there was going to be a blow-up and he would be forced to intervene. As if there wasn't enough on his plate already. He tossed the mutilated paperclip into the garbage and started on another.

Well, at least the wedding was an event with closure, unlike the drama unfolding at the Court. The term might be over in a month, but the break would bring little reprieve from his nagging malaise about the Mohammed case. Chief Justice Reynolds was still doing his best to bury it, drowning them all in trivia by making a big deal of little cases, like the one Matt was reading about now. A dispute about a tax-free smoke shop on tribal land in Rhode Island. Maybe it would be interesting in different circumstances, but now he couldn't care less about the cost of a pack of cigarettes. No one should be selling them anyway. He felt a pain in his chest. Heart or heartburn? He went through the checklist Dr. Levinson gave him and decided on the latter. He was tired of worrying about his heart. To hell with it. To hell with Reynolds. He shoved the brief away and tossed paperclip number two.

There was a knock on the door. "Come in," Matt said more gruffly than usual.

Justice Fox poked his head in. "Am I disturbing you?"

"No, no, Eric. By all means, come in."

Fox remained in the doorway, his battered leather briefcase in hand. He had inherited it from his father whose monogrammed initials were still visible amidst the scrapes and scuffs. "I was just going for a drink at the University Club before I head home. Want to join me?"

Matt debated with himself. Fox always had an ulterior motive, but what did it matter? The conversation would at least be interesting. "All right."

"Meet you in a couple of minutes in the lobby?"

"Sounds good."

At the club they sat in the grill room at a table too close to the TV for Matt's liking. Fox ordered a Manhattan, Matt a Diet Coke. The television was tuned to a local sports news broadcast. Two announcers, one black, one white, laughed at each other's jokes, slightly off cue. Both bemoaned the fact that the Wizards had lost by fifteen points. If they lost again on Monday, the party was over. "I hope they make it," Fox said. "I sprang for tickets for the opener with the Lakers. I know it's like fiddling while Rome burns, but I need some diversion. Want to come?"

"Me?"

"Yes, you, my friend. You look glum, like you need some cheering up."

"I am glum."

"And the reason?"

"The same as yours, no doubt."

"Your health's all right?"

Matt's shoulders tightened. "I don't know why Scott spread that rumor."

Fox peered over his spectacles to give him one of his penetrating looks. "I'm only asking because it's going to come down on you the hardest and you need to be prepared. None of us other justices can play the role you're going to be forced to play."

"And that is?"

"I keep my ear to the ground—you know that, Matt. And I hear a lot of nonsense. Most of it I just shrug off. If all the conspiracy theories one hears were true, you wouldn't trust anyone, even your wife. Of course I don't have a wife, but you know what I mean." He paused and stirred his drink. "But I heard one recently from a very credible source. Don't ask me who it is because I can't tell you. But this person has a perfect record. One hundred percent accuracy over the ten years that I've known him. What he told me last week has been weighing heavily on my mind."

"And what was that?"

Fox took a sip and leaned forward. "He told me the administration is developing a contingency plan for the election. If it looks like they might lose, they're going to find some grounds to postpone it. They'll use the provision in the second Citizen Defense Act that Senator Barrett made all that fuss about. In the event of a terrorist attack, or credible evidence of an imminent one, they can declare a state of emergency and suspend the normal operations of government."

"I find that hard to believe."

"Harder to believe than that they killed Salim Mohammed? Or arranged Senator Barrett's plane crash."

"No, but…"

"But what?"

"They'll find a way to win the election anyway, so why should they bother?"

"Did you see today's poll? Hartley's up by eight points, his strongest lead yet. If the Chinese make good on their threat to convert their reserves to euros, the stock market could crash. Hartley will leap ahead."

Matt looked away toward the window where he caught a glimpse of sky. It was still bright out. The days were getting so much longer. Fox could be right; God knows, they would stop at nothing. Evil. He wished he could say that to Fox: they're evil. But it was his role and responsibility to submit each of his judgments, private or public, to long and intensive scrutiny. He wasn't prepared to use the word "evil" yet, and even if he was, he wasn't sure he would say it to Fox. You couldn't trust the man to keep a secret.

"I'm only telling you this, Matt, because if it happens, you're going to be the one in the hot seat. If we're asked to rule this fall on the constitutionality of postponing the election, the Court will split the same way we did in the Mohammed case, and you'll be the swing vote again."

"I'll vote my conscience, you know that."

"Yes, and the administration knows that too."

"What are you suggesting?"

Fox stirred his drink again, swirling what was left of the ice cubes around the glass. "I'm not sure. But I know they'd like nothing better than the opportunity to replace you. So, please, do your best to stay healthy."

Sunset brought a chill to the air, and Lyndon wished he had a warmer jacket as he walked down Prospect Street to Maxwell's house. He passed his old eating club, but gave it only a fleeting glance. Its Georgian elegance had seduced and betrayed him; he had collapsed drunk into its plush couches like a drowning man. The walkway to Maxwell's house was framed by an old trellis, strangled by vines and missing slats here and there. The fieldstone was cracked and uneven, and in the overgrown garden only a few lilies competed successfully with the weeds. By contrast, the red door was freshly painted. Lyndon lifted the brass knocker, but before he could let it fall, Maxwell opened the door. "I saw you coming," he said.

The professor had changed his suit for a pair of baggy corduroys and a fraying sweater. As they passed through the living room to the den, he explained that since his wife's death, he hardly used the large room any more. "It's remarkable how one's personal geography shrinks with age. Here I have this huge house, and I confine myself mainly to the den. There's probably some Freudian angle to it—a retreat back to the womb." Lyndon nodded, unsure of what to say. He remembered Maxwell's wife as a dumpy little lady who brought refreshments, though later he learned she was a highly acclaimed classical flutist.

In the den they sat in twin leather arm chairs patched with duct tape. "I forgot to offer you something to drink," Maxwell said. "I can make some coffee—regular or decaf."

"Don't bother," Lyndon replied.

Maxwell leaned back and closed his eyes, and for a moment Lyndon thought the old man might be nodding off to sleep. But when he opened them, he looked alert and sly as a fox. "Did the protest upset you?" he asked.

"I've been through worse," Lyndon replied, though the truth was it had unnerved him. He hadn't expected it at Princeton.

"They were quiet, anyway. Not much I could do about it."

"I didn't expect you to do anything."

"You didn't want me to call in the campus police?"

"Of course not."

"Why? Because it would have been embarrassing, or do you still believe in freedom of speech?"

"Of course I believe in freedom of speech."

The professor smiled, but not kindly. "I invited you here because I have several questions for you," he continued. "A little tutorial for old time's sake. Only this time you don't have to answer them, but I, on the other hand, have to ask them. It's one of my last duties before I retire, and before my mind goes."

"I doubt your mind will ever go."

"My short-term memory is already going, Lyndon. I'm heading down the road toward senile dementia. But maybe these days it's a blessing in disguise to remember the distant past but not the present." He paused, turning and leaning on his armrest so his face was closer to Lyndon's. "That brings me to my first question."

Despite himself, Lyndon felt a stab of student anxiety. "Yes?"

"How did a smart boy like you end up working for an idiot like the President?"

Lyndon squirmed. "He's not as dumb as he seems."

"Or is it that you're not as smart as you seem? Perhaps I overrated you. What did you learn from me, Lyndon? Didn't I teach you the value of democracy?"

"Yes."

"Well, then, why have you forgotten it? You can't claim dementia, not at your age."

"I haven't forgotten it."

"You just don't believe in it any more?"

"I didn't say that."

"No, but your actions speak louder than words."

"This is insulting, Professor Maxwell…"

"I told you that you don't have to answer, but I have to ask. Here's my next question: Who killed Senator Barrett?"

"It was an accident. I had nothing to do with it."

"But maybe someone else did?"

"You mean the pilot?"

"No. I mean someone in the administration."

"It was an accident. The weather was terrible."

"Convenient, wasn't it? Just like the electricity going out precisely when Salim Mohammed decided to hang himself. Come now, Lyndon, how do you expect me to believe these things?"

"You also taught me about contingency, Professor Maxwell. Never underestimate the role of contingency in politics, that's what you said."

"Contingency might explain one death, maybe, but not two."

"The world doesn't run according to probability tables."

"Then how does it run, Lyndon?" Maxwell raised his voice. It had echoes of its old robustness, and his expression was fierce. "Is it God's hand we're talking about? Divine providence? That's what your President would have us believe. Do you believe that too, Lyndon, or are you just putting it on? Tell me, it's my last question, and your answer is off the record. I won't repeat it to anyone. Exactly what do you believe in, Lyndon?"

"Why do you want to know?"

"If your behavior is rooted in religious conviction, I might feel easier about it. But if what motivates you is raw power, well, you know that spoils like meat. Goes rotten, like I taught you. I'm starting to catch that whiff about you."

"It's time to end this conversation," Lyndon said abruptly. "Don't get up— I'll let myself out."

The professor sighed, making no move to discourage him. "As you wish, Lyndon, as you wish."

Agitated and angry, Lyndon left the house and walked fast to the boathouse even though he had plenty of time before his last meeting of the day. Maxwell still had the power to shake him up and he didn't like it. He should have never come back for the reunion. THERE'S BLOOD ON YOUR HANDS, LYNDON TOTTMAN. The red hand prints on the banner looked like a child's finger painting and the sketches were amateurish too. Maybe Jeanine had put her kids up to it. Her mixed-race kids. I'm way beyond that now, Lyndon.

After he reached the boathouse he stood on the edge of the dock, looking out at Lake Carnegie. The moon was not quite half full, but the night was clear enough that it cast a strong reflection on the water. He wished he still had a key to the boathouse and could take out one of the sculls. It would feel so good to row, to lose himself in that simple, rhythmic motion. Exactly what do you believe in, Lyndon? No one had ever asked him that before, probably because people assumed they knew the answer.

He sensed footsteps by the play of the boards beneath his feet and turned around. Scott walked toward him with his arm extended, anticipating a handshake, but Lyndon kept his hands in his pockets. "Hope I'm not late," Scott said.

"No, we're both early."

"I got a little lost—I never came here the whole time I was at Princeton."

"I did crew my freshman year," Lyndon said, "and then I gave it up."

"Had to get up too early in the morning?"

"Something like that."

"So what's up?" Scott asked. "Why did you want to see me?"

"To get your sense of things."

"Pomeroy is digging in his heels, if that's what you mean."

"Any possibility of bringing him over to our side?"

Scott shook his head. "Doubtful." He paused, as if unsure whether to reveal more information or not. "I don't think he trusts me any more."

"You think he suspects something?"

"I didn't say that," Scott replied defensively. "He just doesn't like me. It's a good thing there are only a few weeks left in the term."

"And his health?"

"I told you what I know. You'll have to find out the rest. He's anxious about his daughter's wedding, by the way. Very anxious." Scott took a step closer. "How's my appointment coming?"

"Fine. Ninth Circuit Court of Appeals—what you asked for."

"What if he tries to sabotage it?"

"He dislikes you that much?"

"I'm nervous, that's all."

"There's no problem unless you make a problem. You need to lie low, stop antagonizing him. Can you do that?"

"Yes, of course."

Scott sounded offended, but Lyndon pushed harder. "I mean it, Scott. If you want that appointment, lie low, lie very low. I may need you one last time."

Nick lay wide awake in bed, worrying about Lisa. The swath of moonlight that filtered through the curtains seemed brighter than it actually was, too bright, as if someone were shining a flashlight in his eyes. When he got up to pull the shade, Lisa asked what was wrong. "Nothing's wrong with me," he said, "but something's clearly bothering you. You've been acting strange ever since you got back from the grocery store. Want to talk about it?"

"I can't."

"Why not?"

She rolled over to lie on her back. "I have to make an important decision, let's just leave it at that. It has nothing to do with you."

"Sure it does," he said as he got back in bed. "I'm practically living with you."

"I don't want to involve you, I can't involve you." She took his hand. "Trust me, this is about work, not us. I'll be all right once I figure out what I'm going to do."

"And you can figure that out alone?"

"I have to."

"No, you don't. Have you ever considered that I can help you? And I don't mean just with Sam. I have a brain, you know."

"Of course I know that, Nick."

"Sometimes I'm not so sure." He regretted saying it, regretted revealing his insecurity. Smart women never liked that. They needed to pretend the male was fearless, invincible, up to any challenge they posed. Ultimately, they were always disappointed though. Was it better to disappoint her now or later? He was like the scarecrow in the Wizard of Oz: If I only had a brain...

"Don't be ridiculous, Nick."

"Then let me help you."

"All right," she said. "Tell me what you would do. Would you risk everything, maybe even your life, to get at the truth, or would you just shut the book and play it safe? That's my dilemma."

"I'd share the risk."

"What if it can't be shared?"

He wove his fingers through hers. "In the war I risked everything for a lie. To risk it for the truth would be a nice change."

"It's not so easy, Nick. There's Sam too."

"That's why you need to share the risk."

"Maybe," she said. "Let me sleep on it."

She fell asleep before him, and he lay awake for another hour, keeping vigil without knowing why.

9

Above the horizon, the setting sun was the ugly orange of a duck egg's yolk. The heat was intense, the air thick with smog and so still it made you beg for wind. Lisa ran the first lap of the Reston high school track at a brisk pace, but by the second her sides hurt and she fought for breath. Two more laps and it would be time to go to the water fountain. Was the man passing her Richard Brown's source? In the fading light she could make out a tall and gangly figure, his legs so long they looked like stilts. He ran fast but without elegance, stooped forward as if moving through a tunnel with a low ceiling.

Her sweat mixed with the chill of fear. She didn't want to be here. Raw courage wasn't her strong suit. Her first mistake had been to unburden herself on Nick. She was sure he would persuade her not to come, but like an actuary, he had weighed the potential risks and come to the opposite conclusion. Only later did she realize his calculations might be skewed by a desire to prove himself. If she put herself in danger, he would save her and prove his manhood. It was a game she had no interest in playing.

But then came the wild card—the unscheduled visit of Faith Jones to her office two days ago. She arrived fresh off a Greyhound bus from North Carolina, with a return ticket scheduled for the evening. "You have to let me see Ms. Derby," the old woman had pleaded with Marla. "I came all this way."

"But she has an appointment with someone else in ten minutes."

"I don't care. I need to see her—right now."

"But Mrs. Jones…"

Overhearing the conversation from her office, Lisa had opened the door. "Please come in Mrs. Jones," she said, and then turned to Marla. "See if you can reschedule that appointment for later in the afternoon."

Lisa offered her a seat and she sat down on the edge, her hands folded around her big black pocketbook as if someone might whisk it away. "I need your help," the old woman said after they shook hands. "You're the only one left who can do something. I want to testify. Mr. Madison called me. He told me to come to Washington."

"Mr. Madison's dead, Mrs. Jones," Lisa responded, "and so is Senator Barrett."

"I know that. My son's dead too. But that's not stopping me. Grief is hard, Miz Derby, but you can't let it get in the way. You can't let them scare you either. There was a reason you weren't on that plane, a divine reason. God is expecting something from you. I'll be waiting for your call."

"Mrs. Jones, I'm really sorry, but I can't promise anything…"

"I'll be waiting." And with that the old woman got up, straightened her skirt, and left.

Was that why Lisa was running around the track now—to appease an old woman mourning the loss of her son? I have a son, Lisa thought, and he's playing safely at a friend's house, thank God. She shot a glance at the road. Nick was circling the perimeter of the school in the getaway car, only there was no getting away if the tall jogger had hostile intentions. She heard his footfall behind her. He'd already lapped her. It would be easy for him to pull a gun and shoot her in the back, and then knock off Richard Brown who was doing stretching exercises near the water fountain. Almost 7:45, time to meet. Well, she could use a drink; her thirst was real enough.

After passing her, the jogger left the track and headed toward the fountain. Lisa slowed her pace to a walk and pretended to be relaxed as she followed him. "Hot, isn't it?" the jogger remarked when they reached the fountain. He gestured for her to go first.

"Sure is." She took a few gulps of water and then splashed her face.

"I'm impressed you both could run," Richard said as he joined them. "I just took a walk and I thought I was going to faint."

"Not many people out," the jogger replied.

"No, I didn't see anyone," Richard answered.

"Good," the jogger said. "Wait a minute and meet me under the stands."

It was dim and fetid under the bleachers, the last dredges of light leaking through the slats overhead. The high school hide-out was littered with cigarette butts, empty liquor bottles, and a spent condom that Lisa took pains to avoid. Richard stood close to her, but it didn't make her feel any more secure. He looked ridiculous in a tight baby blue track suit, like an overgrown kid in Dr. Denton pajamas. He was bulky but not strong, and she doubted he could throw a punch. "Tom Dougherty," the jogger said, extending his hand to Lisa as if they were meeting at an official function. "I want you to know how sorry I am about the senator's death. You'd be surprised, but a lot of people in my line of work respected her. She was right—we don't need all of these new laws. I've been in counter-terrorism for thirty years and what works now is what's always worked— a little intuition and a lot of attention to detail. And superiors who take information seriously. That's getting rare these days."

"Richard said you were involved in Salim Mohammed's interrogation."

"I was in charge of it, or at least that's what I thought at first. I flew in from Washington once or twice a week. In between, the other interrogators were supposed to follow my orders. It didn't take me long to realize something else was going on. You see, I encouraged Mohammed to unburden himself on me. Not because I'm a nice guy, don't get me wrong, but because I find that's the most effective way to get information. He told me they were torturing him—nothing that showed, no beatings or burns, just making him stand in the sun for hours and refusing him water. I gave him all the water he wanted and he drank like a horse.

"I confronted the prison authorities, but they denied it and at first I didn't know who to believe. But I could tell Mohammed was losing his grip and not in a way that would be useful to us. In interrogation there's a fine line between vulnerability and insanity. You want them vulnerable, but crazy is useless. If they go crazy, you can't trust the information they give you. They'll say what they think you want to hear, or spout nonsense, or they won't speak at all. The last time I saw Mohammed, they had just about driven him over the edge. I put my foot down, threatened disciplinary action. Only I began to realize I had no real power—someone else was running the show."

"The Pentagon?" Richard asked.

"That's the easy answer," Dougherty replied. "It's a military prison, after all.

But even so, there was such an air of impunity that I started to think there was protection at even higher levels."

"How high? The Commander-in-Chief?"

"Maybe not the President personally, but someone close."

"You told me you have evidence they hung Mohammed."

"I do," Dougherty said and then looked around again. He took a few steps further under the bleachers until he reached the point where he could no longer stand straight. He pulled a handkerchief from his pocket and wiped sweat from his face. Lisa noticed his forehead looked prematurely wrinkled, a smoker's brow though she doubted that he smoked. More likely he was a chronic worrier, like herself.

"Do you think they know you have this evidence?" she asked.

"I'm being watched, if that's what you mean. They're watching everyone associated with the Mohammed case. But that makes them inefficient—they're spreading themselves too thin. And the boys who watch, well, some of them are my friends. I've been in this business a long time."

"So there's room for maneuver," Richard said.

"Yes." Something eased in Dougherty's face when he said that, and the lines on his forehead faded like invisible ink. "I did some digging around after Mohammed's death," he continued. "I knew I was being lied to and I don't like that. I went through the records of the other prisoners and discovered one had been released two days after the hanging. His name's Toby Edwards, court-martialed for consorting with the enemy in Syria. I'd interrogated him a couple times. His only crime was falling in love with a woman whose brother happened to be a suicide bomber. I decided to pay a visit to his home in Denver, but his mother said he was off on a camping trip. She claimed she didn't know where he was, that he was traveling from park to park. I got the license plate number of his pickup and tracked him down at a campground near Durango.

"I scared the wits out of him when I showed up. He was fishing in a creek when I came up behind him, and he jumped a foot high. At first he wouldn't talk but out there in the wilds, a man's conscience has the need to come clear. He told me he was offered an early release if he killed Mohammed. His cell door would be unlocked during a blackout and all he had to do was slip down the hall and strangle him in his sleep. Mohammed would be deep asleep, out on sleeping pills. And then Edwards was supposed to string him up and return to his cell. Edwards said he refused at first, but then they threw the stick in with the carrot. They threatened to torture his Syrian girlfriend and make him watch it on video. He broke down on me, and I told him there was a way to redeem himself—to come clean. He was worried about what they'd do to his girlfriend, so I told him she was already dead. She was rendered to a prison in Egypt, mauled by dogs—pretty awful. There was nothing he could do to save her."

"Is that true?" Lisa said.

"Of course it's true," he raised his voice slightly. "I told you I don't like lies."

"So where is he?" Richard asked.

"Hidden away, under my own personal witness protection program."

"And he's willing to talk?"

"Yes, if I tell him to. He's fragile though, shaken by the death of his girlfriend, his fiancée really. They were planning to get married."

"We should move fast then."

"Hold on." Dougherty put out a hand as if to restrain him. "I need a little more time."

"But that gives them time too," Richard insisted.

"That's a risk, of course. But there's one other thing I need to find out. You see, Edwards didn't recognize the man who cut the deal with him. He wasn't a prison official as far as he could tell. I want to find out who he was."

"Do you think you can?" Lisa asked.

"I have an idea, but I'm not a hundred percent certain. As soon as I am, we move forward. You have everything in place, ready to go."

He spoke with them a while longer, making arrangements for how to be in touch. Then he left, running into the dusk, where a lone pink streak across the sky marked the divide between day and nightfall. Lisa followed a few minutes later, jogging in the opposite direction toward the parking lot where Nick would meet her. The adrenaline from the encounter lifted her, making her feel strangely lighter, as if she had shed a burden rather than taken one on.

The visiting Chinese foreign minister sitting next to Lyndon picked at his pecan pie as if the nuts were an exotic North American species of beetle that politeness dictated he eat. He didn't like the coffee either, grimacing as he took his first sip and then adding several teaspoons of sugar. All in all, the meal hadn't been a great success, or at least the Chinese were playing it that way. They were still threatening to convert to the euro, holding out for more concessions. A state dinner in honor of the foreign minister obviously didn't impress them enough.

No one looked happy on either side of the cultural divide, except perhaps Phil Douglas of the Federal Reserve who would use the Chinese recalcitrance in his continued push for higher interest rates. He had that I-told-you-so look on his face that Lyndon despised.

Lyndon made eye contact with the President, signaling that it would be better to end the dinner sooner rather than later. Trudy, meanwhile, was trying to sell seconds on the pie. "It's my mother's own recipe," she announced, "a Southern favorite." The Chinese ambassador's wife, as wide as she was tall, nodded but refused another piece. Trudy made one more offer, but the silence was deafening, the sound of no hands clapping. A look of defeat crossed her face, but then she rallied, smiling her widest smile as if posing for a picture. She leant forward provocatively, attracting whatever male libidinous energy was floating around the room. "I really want to go to China some day," she said in her most languorous Southern drawl. "I told the President he has to take me there. I've got to see the Great Wall."

Lyndon felt a little stab of admiration. She was a good actress, better than her husband whose struggles, both internal and external, were starting to paint dark circles under his eyes. His skin was turning sallow and flaccid. His posture was going downhill too. He slumped in his chair like an old man who has eaten too much and needs a nap. By contrast, Trudy was fresh, pert, perfect. She had remade herself recently, getting a new layered haircut which put her on the front pages of the fashion magazines. A change in eye make-up made her look less matronly and more intense, like a New York model inhabited by intriguing demons. She could be a real asset to the campaign, he thought, a newer, sharper image for the White House.

After they rose from the table, she made her way to the mantel where Lyndon was standing with the foreign minister, showing him the famous portrait of Abe Lincoln. "These words carved into the mantel, they're famous too," she told the minister. "John Adams, one of our first presidents, wrote them on his second night in the White House. Why don't you read them out loud to us, Lyndon."

"I pray Heaven to Bestow the Best of Blessings on THIS HOUSE and on All that shall hereafter inhabit it," Lyndon read. "May none but honest and Wise Men ever rule under this roof."

"A noble aspiration," the minister said, lifting an eyebrow, and then with a slight bow, turned away.

"I need to talk to you, Lyndon," Trudy whispered.

"Not now."

"Of course not now. Tomorrow morning, after the Bible reading."

"The President cancelled tomorrow's reading—he's got a meeting."

"You come anyway," she said, and touched his arm. "Please."

"All right," he agreed reluctantly.

What was she going to tell him that he didn't know already? he wondered as he made his way to the diplomatic reception room to bid good-by to their ungrateful guests. That the President was edging closer to drink and despair? He knew that, and he knew it was his job to keep him from going there. Like artificial respiration, Lyndon breathed willpower into him every morning. So what else did Trudy want? For him to breathe willpower into her too? He had an image of bending over her, hands on her chest, lips meeting. Perish the thought.

But it stayed with him as he drove to Skip's house in Georgetown. His fantasies of overpowering her were changing into something worse—saving her, making love to her. He tried to convince himself it was all in his head; he was simply projecting his desire to save the President onto her attractive body. But then why was he clenching his jaw and holding the steering wheel so tightly it hurt his hands? As a shield against feeling the feelings he shouldn't feel but did? How dangerous was it to imagine unbuttoning her cashmere sweater to find the purple lacy thing underneath?

He had more important things to think about, that was the real problem. No time for diversions, even of the imaginary sexual kind. Focus your mind, Lyndon, he chided himself.

Skip met him at the door, dressed in sandals, shorts and a striped golf shirt that had lost its shape. He ushered Lyndon into the living room where there was a plate of brownies on the table and the TV was turned up loud. Skip pressed the mute button, but his eyes kept straying to the screen. The comedy routine he was watching seemed pointless without words. "Do you mind turning it off?" Lyndon asked.

Skip picked up the remote and pointed it at the set. "It was pretty funny," he said, chuckling nervously. "Want a brownie? I made them with egg substitute— they don't taste half bad."

"No, thanks."

"Are you sure? I'm getting to be a pretty good cook."

"No, thanks," Lyndon repeated, more forcefully this time. He noticed Skip's toenails were long and yellow, hideous. He wished the man had the decency to wear shoes, but then decency wasn't the reason he hired him. "So why did you want to meet?"

Skip put down the remote and looked up at Lyndon. "I'm afraid Toby Edwards has disappeared."

"What?"

"My guys lost track of him a couple of weeks ago."

"A couple of weeks ago?" Lyndon responded incredulously. "He was supposed to be dead a couple of weeks ago. I thought you had that all worked out."

"He disappeared from Durango before we could get to him."

Lyndon was furious. He felt like standing up and hurling something, anything, the brownies, the lewd nutcracker, the TV itself if he was strong enough. But he contained his rage as he always did, releasing it slowly through a sluice in the dam, in the flow of his words, his voice. "Where the fuck is he?" he demanded.

"I don't know, Lyndon. We're looking."

"Why didn't you tell me before?"

"Because I thought we'd find him."

"Well, that was wishful thinking, wasn't it?"

It was Skip who stood up. He walked over to the kitchen doorway, looming there as if to remind Lyndon of his superior size. "Don't forget you were the one who told me not to touch Edwards until he was out of prison for awhile," he said angrily. "I held back against my better judgment, so don't blame me."

Lyndon turned to face him. "It was too risky, you know that. One death in the prison was enough."

"Riskier than the present situation?"

"He wasn't supposed to get away."

"I'm stretched thin, Lyndon. I don't have enough men to keep tabs on everyone."

"Then hire more."

"The ones I've got are the only ones I trust. I sent two of my DC guys to help look for Edwards, but that leaves me shorthanded here."

"How big a problem is that?"

"It wasn't until a few days ago. That's the other thing I need to talk to you about."

"Would you sit down, Skip. It's hard talking with you standing up like that."

Reluctantly, Skip sat down on the couch, but he didn't lean back. "Richard Brown's prowling around Washington again."

"What's he up to?"

"We're not sure. He's gotten better at evading us and like I said, I don't have enough men. We know he contacted Lisa Derby—we saw them come out of the same grocery store. I wonder if he's on to Edwards."

"How could he be?"

"A leak somewhere. It would only take one person looking at the prison records to see Edwards was released shortly after Mohammed's death."

"I thought those records were supposed to disappear."

"They did, but not until a week later."

"Fucking hell." Lyndon could feel his temper rising again. "You mean to tell me it took a week to press a delete button on a computer?"

"The military's incompetent, Lyndon. They don't know how to run a prison. Sometimes it's a plus, sometimes a minus. We had a free hand, after all." Skip paused. "And we still do."

"What's that supposed to mean?"

"You want my advice?"

"Sure," Lyndon said, trying to keep the sarcasm from his voice.

"It means we don't make the same mistake twice. We act now, not later."

———

The phone rang on Sunday morning just as Matt settled into a chair on the deck with a cup of coffee and the Sunday papers. Dora was at church and he debated whether to answer, deciding against it until he heard Jessie's voice on the answering machine. He hurried back to the kitchen and picked up the phone. "Jessie," he said, "are you still there, Jessie?"

"Hi, Dad."

He carried the phone outside, taking care not to spill his coffee as he sat back down. "Have you looked at the front page of the Post yet?" she asked. "Hartley's ahead in the polls ten points now.

"Well, that should make life interesting," Matt replied.

"Do you think he can win?"

"Do you?"

"I'm going to vote for him. And you?"

"I have to keep my vote a secret."

"You can tell me."

"I think you can guess." He took a sip of coffee, wishing he could reveal Fox's fears that the administration might do something to put off the election. But even though he trusted her with most everything, she might tell David and then David might tell someone else. His future son-in-law didn't exactly have a big mouth, but he liked to impress people a little too much. It was the one thing about him Matt didn't like, but he'd been much the same in his early thirties. Age had worn his ego down, got rid of the rough edges, like the weathered arm of his Adirondack chair where he set his mug. "Your mother's not here," he said. "She's at church."

"I know. That's why I called now."

"Uh-oh. More conflict with your mother about the wedding? I may be a judge, Jessie, but it's hard to remain impartial at home. I'm not a very good mediator."

"It's something else." When she paused, he found himself wondering if there was something wrong between David and her, but her next words dispelled his fears. "I'm pregnant."

He let out a loud gasp of surprise. "That's wonderful, honey."

"Twins, Dad. Can you believe it? I know there are some twins on Mom's side of the family, but I never thought it would happen to me."

"Do you know if they're girls or boys?"

"I told them not to tell me."

"How many months?"

"Four. I didn't want to tell you until I was over the worst risk of miscarriage. I miscarried before—I didn't tell you and Mom." He wanted to ask why, but was afraid of the answer. And why was she telling him and not Dora about the twins? Shouldn't a mother be the first to know? Jessie must have read his mind, for she continued, "You don't think Mom will be upset?"

"Upset? Are you kidding? She'll be thrilled."

"She won't be upset that I'll be almost six months pregnant at our wedding? I'll be showing by then. She's pretty traditional about these things."

"She's less rigid than you think, Jessie. She accepted you and David living together the past four years."

"But she's exacting the price now—we have to have a perfect wedding. Being six months pregnant spoils that."

"I don't think so. Having grandchildren is much more important to her than a perfect wedding. Give her credit. She may get caught up in details, but it's your happiness she wants. Believe me."

"I want to, Dad, but sometimes it's hard."

"Why is it easier to believe the worst?" Once he said it, he realized that was the crux of the matter. Mother and daughter found it easier to mistrust each other than to trust. It was an old bad habit, a sort of emotional laziness. Maybe two bawling babies would force them out of it. David's mother was dead and his well-heeled stepmother was not the nurturing kind. Jessie would need Dora's help.

There was also something he could tell her now that might make a difference, something Dora had sworn him to secrecy about many years ago. But old secrets have a way of becoming bad habits too. "You know your mother was pregnant when we decided to get married," he said.

"She was?"

"She had a miscarriage at about ten weeks and you know what she told me?"

"What?"

"That I was free now, that I didn't have to marry her. As if I was marrying her just because of that. We didn't have a perfect wedding—she was still grieving. Maybe that's one reason she's so set on yours going well."

"I wish you'd told me that sooner."

"She never wanted anyone to know. She miscarried twice after that, and once more after she had you. You don't think she'll be happy you're pregnant?"

"God, Dad…"

"Why don't you pretend you didn't call me? She'll be home at noon. Call us both with the good news."

"OK," Jessie agreed with uncharacteristic humility.

His coffee was cold by the time he returned to it, but he didn't care. He didn't even care that half the morning paper had blown onto the grass. Let it blow all the way to end of the yard. He was going to be a grandfather—a grandfather of twins. That was the only news that mattered.

———

For the past few weeks Faith Jones had noticed a subtle change in Samira. It was as though the sap had started running again in a tree you took for dead, the kind of tree that looks like one more gust of wind will blow it over. Samira's hands were more agitated when she watched TV; a hint of a smile crossed her face when her son, longer and lankier by the day, nestled up to her for some affection. Yesterday on a whim Faith asked if she wanted to get her hair done, and to her amazement, Samira agreed.

The three of them went to the beauty parlor together, Ali playing in the lobby with his Game Boy. When Samira traded her veil for a cape to keep her shoulders dry, Faith was struck by how young and pretty she still was. Samira stared at herself in the mirror as though she was greeting herself after a long absence. Her hand touched her cheek to make sure it was real. After the haircut, Faith paid for her to have a manicure and she chose a pink pearly color for her nails. Such was the power of vanity that Samira didn't put her veil back on for the walk to the car. It was only a few steps, but Faith took it as a good sign. Back home while making lunch, she probed Samira about her faith. Unlike Jackson, Samira had grown up as a devout Muslim and she still said her prayers five times a day. "It's what keeps me going," she told Faith. "Praying is the only time I feel any hope." Faith could relate to that; she was the same way herself. If she didn't pray at night, she was in a dark mood the next day. It was the veil she didn't like. Maybe she was prejudiced, but she sensed Samira hid behind it and not just for religious reasons. It was a way to prolong her mourning and keep from making decisions. It wasn't doing her or anyone else any good.

Finally, she summoned up her courage to ask Samira why she wore the veil. "Not all Muslim women do," Faith said. "I know a Muslim lady who teaches in the high school and she only wears a head scarf and sometimes not even that."

"Salim liked me to," Samira replied.

"Well, I'm his mother and I think you should take it off. It's too hot to wear it in the summer." She paused, cutting a peanut butter sandwich she'd made for Ali. "Besides it's keeping you from getting back into the world. You need to fit in here. And I need your help."

"In the store?"

"Yes, but I need your help in other ways too." She wiped her sticky fingers on a paper towel. "I'm waiting for a call from that woman in Washington, the one I went to see on Tuesday. If she calls, you'll be in the news again and I want people to see your face."

"Why, mama?"

Samira had never called her mama before, but Faith tried not to look surprised. "Because you've got a pretty face and they'll look at you and see you're not a devil. You'll help Jackson that way."

"How can I help Salim when he's dead?"

"He's got a soul, doesn't he?"

Faith thought about Jackson's soul the next morning as she sat in church. Was it Christian because he was baptized, or Muslim because he had died a Muslim—died, in fact, for being a Muslim? Or did it really matter? Reverend Lee would say it did. He was delivering a sermon now that Faith had heard before. He was getting old, repeating himself, the fire in his voice flickering like a candle burned down to the end. Since his wife died last year, he wasn't taking care to trim the tufts of gray hair that sprouted from his ears, making him look like a cross between a man and a bear. Oh, Reverend Lee was no expert on the soul.

She closed her eyes, trying to find her way to Jackson's soul, to send him her message: I'm doing everything I can, but I need your help to bring Samira back to life. Maybe he heard her, because when she returned home from church, she found Samira out in the front yard with Ali, a scarf wrapped around her head, pulling weeds from the flower garden.

10

Instead of taking his usual straight-backed chair for the Bible reading, Lyndon sat in the President's place on the couch. Brendon poked his head in the door. "My mom says to tell you she'll be a few minutes late," he said. "Last day of school," he added, smiling widely. His mouth was so full of braces it would probably set off a metal detector. He was thirteen and remarkably well-adjusted for a political brat.

"See you at the game tomorrow," Lyndon told him as the boy turned to go. Trudy followed five minutes later. Lyndon was shocked when he saw her. It was the first time she had appeared before him without make-up or blow-dried hair or clothes carefully chosen to set off whatever it was she wanted to show off that day: her eyes, her mouth, her breasts, her hips. She looked like she had just rolled out of bed and traded her nightgown for a T-shirt and sweatpants. She sat down beside him on the couch and took his hand in hers. She had never initiated physical contact with him before and he felt wary and flustered like an awkward boy asked to dance by the prettiest girl in the room. "I need you to see me, Lyndon," she said, gazing directly into his eyes, "really see me."

"I always see you, Trudy," he responded, "or at least I try."

"No," she shook her head, "no one sees me. Do you know the last time I let someone outside my immediate family see me like this? In college, in my sorority. Sometimes late at night I'd sit around talking with the girls. We'd bare our hearts, you know, the way girls do. But the next morning before class we'd compete over the mirror in the bathroom and start fighting over the boys again. But I lived for those times when I was just plain me, you know. Plain me." As she spoke those words, the pressure of her hand increased. He couldn't tell if it was a come-on or not. God, he hoped not, but God, he hoped so. God, Jesus, weren't they supposed to be reading the Bible? Thou shall not commit adultery. Thou shall not covet thy President's wife. She laced her fingers through his. "Help me," she said.

"How?"

"See me."

"Believe me, Trudy, I do."

"How do you see me?"

"You're a strong woman."

"Plain me is strong?" she asked with a touch of the old coyness in her voice.

"Yes."

"Like plain you? I haven't seen plain you yet, Lyndon. You cover up everything, don't you? You never let down your guard, even to yourself."

"I can't afford to."

"Because of my husband?"

"Is he drinking, Trudy?"

She didn't answer the question. "The weaker he gets, the stronger he forces us to be, doesn't he, Lyndon? But it's not fair to either of us. We can't be ourselves."

"I don't want to be myself, Trudy."

"Why not?"

"Because at my core I'm weak, a drunk, just like him. Maybe he's doing me a favor. Maybe he's doing you a favor too. Forcing us to rise above ourselves."

"That sounds trite, Lyndon."

"Sometimes life is trite."

She shook her head. "No, it's too full of longing ever to be trite."

"Even longing can be trite."

"In the mind, maybe, but never in the body. Kiss me, Lyndon."

"Trudy, you know I can't…"

"Just once, I'll never ask again. To keep me going so I can keep him going. Or would you rather I kiss you?" She reached up and drew his face toward hers. "Plain me kisses plain you," she whispered.

He let her kiss him because he had to, but then he wanted to and he did what he wanted, passed his hands over her breasts to feel the hardening of her nipples through the thin cotton of her shirt. He pulled it up and kissed her there until she sighed and drew away. "Thank you," she said. "I'd better go now." She stood up and walked toward the door, but turned around before she left. "The longing will keep us both going," she told him. "Trust me."

He stayed behind in the den for a few minutes, trying to recover the trust he used to have in himself. She promised she would only ask him once for a kiss. He'd have to make sure she never had the chance to ask again. Why hadn't he been able to refuse? He rationalized that it was all part of propping up the President, just like she said, but he knew he was lying to himself.

The plain truth was that plain Trudy was the closest he'd come to the girl he met that summer at camp, the girl he swam the river for, the girl who disappeared, like all girls disappear, into the faces of disappointed and dissembling women.

He straightened his shirt and got up, hoping he wouldn't see her on his way out. She had disappeared, but left music playing in the living room, a female vocalist he hadn't heard before, a cross between country and jazz, Dolly Parton meets Billy Holliday. She was singing about love, about longing. He wished he could stay there and listen, but Skip was waiting for another decision.

After his shift was over at the fitness club, Nick did his own workout. He got on the rowing machine and worked hard to do five kilometers in twenty minutes. There was a guy at the club in his early seventies, Dan Ellison, who was faster than that. Last year he won the indoor rowing competition in his age group. Tonight they rowed side by side in a companionship of sweat and sheer endurance. Through the glass window in front of them, Nick looked out at the pool at the even strokes of the lap swimmers. Yesterday he had brought Lisa and Sam along to swim, and his new-found status of family man was now duly noted. "Got your hands full now," Dan remarked when they finished rowing and headed to the locker room. "Happened to me too. A kid came along with the package."

"How did you get along?"

"Better than with my own son. That was the problem." He sighed. "Still is."

Nick thought of asking more, but Dan was the kind of guy who didn't like too many questions. Except for a small towel wrapped around his waist, he stood before Nick now in full naked splendor. There was something awe-inspiring but also slightly unnerving about his muscularity, as if a younger man was trapped inside the skin of an older one, struggling valiantly but futilely to get out. "You like the kid?" Dan asked, stooping to pick up his soap dish.

"A lot."

"That's good."

Nick nodded, not knowing what else to say, still a stranger to family talk.

"Does he like basketball?"

"Oh, yeah."

"Taking him to the game tomorrow night?"

"I wish."

"I've been holding on to two tickets, hoping they'd lure my son to come see me, but he claims he's too busy. He's a lawyer in Philly—never has any time. And my stepson's off in Africa, working for the UN. What's your kid's name?"

"Sam."

"I'll give you the tickets half-price. Then you can take Sam to the game."

"Are you sure?"

"Sure I'm sure. I don't like crowds. You'll enjoy the game much more than me." And then, as if to offset his generosity, he added, "They'll still cost you a hundred bucks."

"I don't have my checkbook on me," Nick said.

"Not to worry. Give me the money next week." He fumbled in the pocket of his pants hanging in his locker and pulled out his wallet. "They're pretty good tickets," he said as he handed them to Nick. "High up, but smack in the center."

They showered in silence and spoke only a few words while getting dressed, as if the ticket exchange had used up their quota for intimacy. "Have fun," Dan told him as they parted in the parking lot. There was a wistful quality in the way he said it, and Nick could tell he missed his sons.

———

Until the very last minute it was kept secret that the First Lady would sing the national anthem on the opening night of the Wizards-Lakers NBA championship series. Dressed in a blue suit with red trim and a white blouse, she stood in the middle of the floor of the vast Verizon Center, facing the flag above the scoreboard. Fox, who was an opera buff, nudged Matt as they rose to their feet. "It's bad enough listening to her husband speak, but now we have to suffer through her singing. Gilbert and Sullivan couldn't have dreamed this one up if they tried. Are we living in a farce or a tragedy, Matt?"

"Both," he answered. To his untrained ear, her voice wasn't bad. At least she could hit the high notes. He looked up at the VIP box where the President stood at attention with his hand over his heart. So high up he seemed smaller than life, vulnerable perhaps. Was he hoping that his wife's performance would help him in the polls? Hartley was here too, and no doubt the TV cameras would zoom in and out on him all night long as he played the role of regular guy in the crowd. The cameras might search out Fox and himself as well. He would have to be mindful of that, avoid the little things that could make you the object of ridicule, like scratching your nose or dribbling mustard from your hot dog.

And the rockets' red glare, the bombs bursting in air...

"Oh, how I wish I could put my hands over my ears," Fox whispered to Matt. "It's execrable."

Gave proof thro' the night that our flag was still there...

"Who allowed her to sing?" he continued. "The owner of the Wizards is a Democrat, for God's sake."

"This is a non-partisan sports event."

"Oh right, with the Führer up there in his bullet-proof box. On second thought, do you suppose it is bullet-proof?"

"Don't know," Matt replied.

Oh say, does that star-spangled banner yet wave,
O'er the land of the free and the home of the brave!

A loud hooray went up from the crowd as Trudy turned and waved at each section of the arena, in the end blowing a kiss toward her husband who blew one back. "How sweet," Fox muttered as they sat back down. "You know some people say he's drinking again."

"Really?"

"Friends of mine who have the same problem say you can see it in his face."

"I don't suppose we'll ever know, so there's no sense speculating."

"Trusty Lyndon will prop him up. Look, he's standing behind him right now—the man's a human crutch."

"An intelligent one."

"A cunning one. There's a difference between intelligence and cunning."

"There used to be," Matt said, "but you forget, we're old school."

Fox smiled. "Speak for yourself."

The Wizards team came out on the floor to great applause. But ten minutes into the game the mood had turned despondent. The Lakers scored twenty points in a streak of easy rebounds and turnovers that made the Wizards look like a high school team. The Wizards finally broke the spell with a free throw, but at half time the Lakers were still up by fifteen and heads hung low on the way to the locker room. Matt felt tired, ready to go home, sorry he'd accepted Fox's invitation. "Bad show," Fox said, "but who knows, they've performed miracles in the second half before." He swiveled his knees to let a boy get past on his way to the aisle. "Why don't we go out too," he suggested.

"No, I'll stay put. It's always so crowded by the concession stands."

"No, come with me. I have a friend who wants to talk to you."

"Out there?"

"Yes, out there."

Matt followed Fox down the stairs and out into the hallway, wondering what he had up his sleeve now. Of course, Fox had an ulterior motive for inviting him to the game—Matt was naïve to have expected differently. As Fox navigated deftly through the press of bodies, Matt had a hard time keeping up. He thought about his heart, but then tried not to. On the faces of passers-by he saw a few stunned looks of recognition. Yes, I am Supreme Court Justice Matthew Pomeroy, he expressed with the faintest of smiles. But don't stop me, don't talk to me, don't have your child ask for my autograph. He trampled on a pile of spilled popcorn and just avoided getting Coke splattered on his shirt. Finally, near the entrance, Fox drew him into a corner by a row of phone booths. A man stepped forward from one of them. "Meet my friend Lenny Schurman," Fox told Matt. "He works in the Attorney General's office."

"I'm a long-time admirer," Lenny said, shaking Matt's hand vigorously. He was a short, squat man with the flattest head Matt had ever seen. It looked like someone had sat on top of it while his skull was forming. He was completely bald, but his dark brown eyebrows and goatee suggested he was still in his forties. His pants were too long, the cuffs bunched up around his shoes.

"Never thought I'd see you wearing a Wizards sweatshirt, Lenny," Fox remarked.

"For protection," he replied. "Look." He lifted the sweatshirt to reveal a Lakers T-shirt underneath.

"Lenny's from L.A.," Fox remarked.

"Riverside," Lenny corrected him.

"Close enough. Lenny has something he wants to tell you, Matt. I'm just going to duck into the men's room while you two have a chat."

Lenny checked to see there was no one near enough to overhear him, and then spoke in a low voice. "I thought you ought to know something about your head clerk," he began. "Were you surprised by his appointment to the Ninth Circuit?"

"It would be impolitic of me to say," Matt replied.

"Lots of people I know were surprised."

"Oh?"

"There was another guy in line for the appointment—someone much better qualified. An old law school acquaintance of mine. He thought he had it in the bag, but then there was an intervention and Scott Hanson was nominated."

Matt frowned. "Who intervened?"

Lenny smiled. "Evidently, he has friends in high places. It was Lyndon Tottman."

"How do you know?"

"You'd be surprised how many people know. They're just keeping their mouths shut, for obvious reasons. Besides, this kind of stuff happens all the time now. After a while, people just get used to it, lower their expectations and adjust to the new merit system."

"You sure your friend doesn't just have sour grapes?"

"Oh, he's got sour grapes all right, but for good reason."

"Why would Tottman intervene on behalf of Scott?"

"Ah, that's the question, isn't it? I've heard two different rumors. The first is that they're both Princeton grads, old school and all that, but I don't put much stock in it. They were there at different times. The second is that Scott rendered services."

"What kind of services?"

"Fed information about you to Tottman." A trace of a blush passed over his face. "Not impossible, is it? I hear he's a little weasel. I just wanted you to know. Fox insisted I tell you myself. So there it is. I don't know what you want to do about it, or can do about it. As far as I know there's no paper trail or smoking gun. But these days suspicion is the better part of valor."

"Well, thank you for your candor."

"My pleasure." Lenny extended his hand again. "Like I said, I'm a long-time admirer." He waved at Fox who was coming out of the men's room. "Well, enjoy the game," he added. "I'm glad I'm rooting for the Lakers."

Only a handful of people were left on the Metro by the time the train pulled into the station at Silver Spring. It was 10:45 and most of the DC area was watching the dismal end of the Wizards game. They were losing by thirty points, a fellow passenger told Lisa. Taking advantage of the fact that Sam and Nick were at the game, she had stayed late at work to sort through the last file drawer of Senator Barrett's papers. She had hoped it would give her a sense of closure, but instead it gave her a sense of things left undone, a life ended prematurely, and she grieved anew.

The station parking lot was deserted so she took out her keys, sliding them through her fingers so she could jab a mugger in the eye. Fat chance she'd emerge the victor, but the illusion of self-defense at least allowed her to proceed. Much of her life seemed propelled by illusion now, like the illusion that Nick could protect her. There was no such thing as real safety any more. Had Senator Barrett felt that too, the afternoon she boarded the plane? The keys felt cold in Lisa's hand.

She put on the radio as she drove home. The game was over and the Wizards coach was on, so she switched to a jazz station. Nick had told her that if the game was a blowout, they'd leave early to avoid the crush. She hoped so—Sam needed his sleep. She yawned and a wave of exhaustion passed over her. Who was she kidding? She was the one who needed sleep.

She parked in the apartment lot, noticing that Nick's car wasn't back yet. As she opened the door to step out, a voice startled her from behind. "Lisa, wait a second." She turned to face Richard Brown.

"What are you doing here?"

"I've been waiting for you. I heard from our friend. We need to talk."

"Here?"

"In the car. I've been followed all day—finally shook them off in the crowds near the Verizon Center." He walked around to the passenger side of the car and got in, easing his bulky body into the seat.

"So what did he say?"

"He knows who gave Edwards his orders. He wants..."

By the time she saw the man with the ski mask, it was too late to lock the car doors. He swung open the door on Richard's side and pointed a gun at them. "Give me your wallet and your purse," he ordered. "Fast."

Lisa picked up her purse from the floor. "Here," she said, handing it to him. Richard reached into his pocket and pulled out his wallet. The man grabbed it from him and stuffed it in his jacket. For a moment she thought he might leave, but then his hand took aim and there was a muffled pop and Richard's body slumped against hers. She tried to hide behind it, but the shots kept coming. One hit her shoulder, another grazed her face. And then there were headlights, the sound of screeching tires, and maybe Nick's voice—she couldn't tell. The shots stopped. Richard's body pinned her to the door. She felt his blood, or was it hers, trickling down her arm as she sank into darkness.

Lyndon woke in Lonesome Hollow with the first boom of thunder. From his bed he saw a bolt of lightning strike the crest of a distant hill and a curtain of rain approaching swiftly over the bluegrass. He checked the clock—5:20 AM. Was it a dream, his nighttime ride with Trudy? No, no, her smell was still on his fingers, her whispers still in the air. Come in, Lyndon, come in now.

She had arrived at his door around midnight, suited up for riding, complete with red leather cowboy boots. "Want to go for a night ride?" she asked as she stepped inside. "The moon's out and there's plenty of light. I had Bob saddle up the horses."

"Who's going?"

"Just you and me. Your friend the President got whopping drunk and is now sound asleep."

"You mean your husband the President."

"It's the same man, I believe."

"Drunk?"

She nodded. "Or you could describe him as pissed, intoxicated, inebriated, soused… Take your pick."

"This is disastrous, Trudy."

"Don't you think I know that?" Her eyes were sad and her mouth angry, a tension that enlivened her face, making her more appealing. "Come for a ride with me, please, Lyndon. My favorite Secret Service guys are on duty tonight and they're very discreet. I need some relief."

He agreed, telling himself it was a chance to talk more with her, figure out what to do with the President. Twenty minutes later they met in the barn where they mounted two of the quieter horses. They set off down the drive at a slow trot, turning on a dirt road that led through the fields to a pond where there was a barbecue pit and a screened gazebo. The moon was almost full, dimmed by haze like a light in a smoky room. The horse's rhythmic movement relaxed him even though he knew he should be on guard, ready to refuse her if she wanted more than just longing.

In the gazebo she lured him into stripping off his clothes to go skinny-dipping in the pond. "I do it all the time," she said, "just wrap yourself in this towel." She had two towels and a blanket—too prepared, he thought, but he followed her instructions. It was a hot night, a swim would feel good.

"What about the Secret Service guys?" he asked.

"They're trained to look the other way."

Entering the pond, she took his hand as if he were a child who needed encouragement. When it was deep enough to swim, she released him, diving underwater and emerging ten feet away. "Keep away from the sides," she told him. "It's mucky over there." He followed her as they swam the length of the pond and back. He was glad he couldn't see the water. It smelled brackish and there were warm spots where he suspected gases from decomposing leaves were bubbling up. He tried not to think of snapping turtles and snakes. He'd always imagined her as a swimming pool kind of girl, happy only in chlorine, but here she was, more fearless than him. He was treading water while trying to keep his feet from touching the soft, muddy bottom when she dove under again and came up right behind him, her breasts brushing his back. She wrapped her arms around his waist, and then a hand slipped down between his legs. "Do you feel the longing, Lyndon?" she whispered.

"Of course."

"Will you make love to me in the gazebo? No one can see inside."

"I thought it was only longing you wanted."

"You think that will go away if we make love?"

"What if the President finds out?"

"He won't because he doesn't want to. He only does what he wants to do, you know, sees what he wants to see. Sometimes I think he never grew up. You take so many chances on his account, Lyndon. Why not take this one for yourself?"

He knew all he had was a few seconds to make the choice. He could break free and swim away to the other end of the pond. She wouldn't follow, she was too proud for that. They would put on their clothes and ride back, and tomorrow they both would pretend nothing happened. But he let the seconds pass. He gave in because he was desperate to give in to something, and she was safer than his other temptations.

She was right. The longing didn't go away. Back in the gazebo she put on her boots and danced for him and then slid down his front, seeking him with her mouth, her warm lovely mouth. The sweat ran down his face, his chest, his legs, conducting a current that made him tingle everywhere. He came fast, he couldn't help himself and then he couldn't help himself from crying out. "Hush," she warned. "We don't want them to think we're having too much fun." She spread the blanket on the floor and lay down. "Now pull off my boots, plain Lyndon."

The feel of expensive leather in his hands gave way to the smooth underside of her thighs. He licked her like a cat licks milk, but she was the one who purred. He tasted her sweetness and her bitterness and he liked them both. After she came, he licked the tears from her face, suckled her breasts until she asked him to come in. He needed to be asked, he realized. He still wanted to be the one giving in. He rolled on top of her, bracing his hands on the hard wood floor. His arms felt strong enough to hold himself up for an eternity of pleasure, the same way he felt that first time at summer camp with the girl he crossed the river for.

Now, in the dawn's light, he realized that he had crossed another more treacherous river for Trudy, and there might be no turning back. He had shifted his allegiance from husband to wife.

He got up and walked to the window. Another flash of lightning. He counted the seconds until the thunder arrived. The center of the storm was only two miles away. The rain was coming down in sheets now. He should close the window, but instead he opened it, sticking out his head for anointment. Holy water. His parents baptized him late, when he was six, hedging their agnostic bets. He remembered the dunking—how scared he was in advance, but how fast and easy it had all seemed in the moment. Maybe there was a lesson there.

And a banana split afterwards, a reward for good behavior.

Trudy, Trudy, Trudy...

He pulled back from the window and grabbed a towel to wipe his hair. He noticed the morning papers were already slipped under his door. Maybe they would help take his mind off her. He sat down in a rocker and opened the Post. First, he looked for the good news, or rather the absence of news. No more stories on Richard Brown's murder. The mugging story had taken hold and the reporters had moved on. They were like a herd of cattle always looking for greener pastures, never staying on a topic long enough to get to the bottom of things. It was a contemptible feature of American journalism, another symptom of the culture's attention deficit disorder. The trick was using it to your own advantage.

Moving, moving, moving, keep them dogies moving...

So what had they moved onto today? Bad economic news was the lead. The dollar was plummeting on all major foreign exchanges after the Chinese converted to euros. Those bastards had played the game to the very end, squeezing all the concessions they could from the Americans, and then doing what they had set out to do all along—screwing the U.S. Hartley had already issued a strong statement promising "to restore faith in the American economy," and he was planning a major speech on the steps of the New York Stock Exchange next Monday. The latest polls put him up by fifteen points. The pundits couldn't decide whether the surge in his popularity was thanks to the bad economic news or the buzz around next month's Democratic convention in Minneapolis. On the op-ed page, that irksome female columnist wrote about the President and his men fleeing to Lonesome Hollow under the cover of darkness. Was the President having problems walking not only a fine line but a straight one?

Smart bitch. Keep her moving too. Keep her entertained.

With the next flash of lightning, the lamp flickered and thunder shook the house. Lyndon closed the paper and looked out at the torrent of rain flooding over the gutters. Steal Hartley's thunder—that was the task at hand. The time had come to get the President's agreement, to initiate the next phase of Operation Daybreak. He hoped he could do it.

Fortunately, Trudy didn't show up at breakfast and he ate alone with the President. Sitting across from him at the table, Lyndon could spot the telltale signs of drinking on his face. His nose was red and his cheeks were puffy; he was inflated on the outside, deflated in. They only had an hour before the President's campaign staff arrived by plane, an hour in which Lyndon needed to secure his agreement. Hopefully, the drinking bout had made him more malleable, not less.

"We need to think outside the box today," Lyndon began.

"Well, sure, I'm willing to consider anything at this point, Lyndon."

"We've done some work on scenarios." Lyndon reached into his briefcase and pulled out a report. "Those focus groups I told you about. I know you're worried that if there's another terrorist attack, people will blame you for not protecting the country, but there's another side. The majority said they'd accept postponing the election if there was another attack on the scale of 9/11. They think elections should take place in a climate of stability."

"I don't get what you're driving at," the President said, pouring himself another cup of coffee. Good, Lyndon thought, the more caffeine, the better. "I thought we already had a media strategy in place if there's an attack—we're prepared…"

"We're not prepared to postpone the election."

"Should we be?"

"That's the question I'm raising. If we were prepared to do that, it might give us a cushion…"

"A cushion against what?"

"The downward trend. The Democrats coming out of their convention with a bounce that doesn't go away."

"But this presupposes there'll be an attack."

Lyndon shrugged. "Or the credible threat of one. The nation on high alert. The new CDA gives you the authority to declare a state of emergency when you deem it necessary."

"The Democrats would take it to the Supreme Court."

"We could make that difficult."

"I don't know, Lyndon," the President said, shaking his head. "This sounds awful risky."

"I'm not saying we do it. All I'm saying is, we keep it in mind. Might take a little pressure off you to know there's a fallback plan. You could use that, couldn't you?"

"I got drunk last night, Lyndon. Really drunk."

Lyndon nodded sympathetically. "There's too much pressure on you— reduce the pressure and I bet you won't feel the thirst. Think it over, but don't tell anyone else, not even Trudy. It's just between us, OK?"

Now that school was out, the three of them worked together in the store. Samira, neatly headscarved but still shy, worked the back room, filling takeout orders, while Ali worked up front with Faith. He had a knack for weighing fish. He took after her dead husband Paul who always knew how much a piece of fish weighed before putting it on the scale. Oh, what a precise man he had been. Wouldn't wear a pair of unmatched socks even if they were the same color and you couldn't tell the difference. It drove her crazy sometimes.

With the two of them working with her, Faith could take a break now and then and sit on the chair outside the back door to get some fresh air. This afternoon she put her feet up on an empty carton and leaned back and looked up at the sky. It was hazy with dark clouds to the west that might bring a storm later on. She wouldn't mind that. Truth was she was feeling down, and rain would suit her mood just fine.

Why was everyone so blind? she wondered. The TV claimed it was a mugger who shot Richard Brown dead and almost killed Lisa Derby. A mugger! As big a lie as Jackson taking his own life. She told that to one of the reporters who called her, but so far her words hadn't appeared anywhere. People were out of the habit of telling the truth. Truth is a habit, a good habit, like brushing your teeth. Stop doing it and your teeth start to decay, but you don't notice until it's too late. A mugger!

She clasped her hands together. What hope was there? What was she going to do? They had murdered Jackson's lawyer and they would murder Lisa Derby if they had another chance. Maybe it wasn't a reporter who called her, but someone from the government. Maybe they would even kill her if she kept speaking up. But what did it matter? She was an old lady with a clear conscience, ready to meet her Maker whenever her time was up.

She watched a tan pickup truck pull into the parking lot, one she hadn't seen before. She should probably go back in and help Ali with the customer. She rose slowly from the chair, feeling a familiar pain in her hip. At least she'd grabbed a few moments of rest, enough to see her through to the end of the day.

―――――――

From the couch in her parents' living room Lisa looked out the window at the gathering dusk, dreading nightfall and its challenge of sleep. She couldn't sleep, not really. The pain in her shoulder was still sharp enough to cut through the drugs, and the drugs gave her demented dreams that forced her to wake up to fight off the demons. But even when she was fully conscious, the demons lingered. She could feel their breath in the breeze that rattled the screens and hear them in the cries of hunted animals in the fields and the creaking floorboards as her parents visited the bathroom in the middle of the night. It was in those moments that she was relieved Sam was in California with his father. She didn't want him to inhabit this twilight land of fear, but she missed him and she missed Nick too.

She flicked through the channels on the TV, piecing together random fragments of shows like word magnets on a refrigerator, trying to make sense out of senselessness. She wished she could sit outside, but it was black fly season and her parents had never invested in the luxury of a screened porch. Her mother was in the kitchen making dinner, her father closing the barn for the night. Nick delivered her to Minnesota at the beginning of the week, stayed two nights and then flew back to DC. Her parents liked him better than they had ever liked Kevin. Nick knew how to talk to them. He asked questions about the farm, whereas Kevin had shown little interest, hiding out in the upstairs bedroom where he made phone calls and racked up billable hours, counting minutes like a miser counts his gold.

She hadn't wanted to come here, but Nick had persuaded her she needed to recuperate in a safe place. No place is safe, she told him. Well, then, safer, he said. Was it safer? Would they leave her alone now? Her father had taken his hunting rifle out of its case, cleaned and loaded it, and now he carried it wherever he went, even to bed. She tried to convince him the official story was true—it was a mugger who shot them—but he was nobody's fool, least of all his daughter's. When her shoulder was better, he told her, he was going to teach her how to use a gun.

She turned her gaze from the TV to the ceiling fan, watching the blades spin in a lazy circle. The wind had died down and the room was hot and stuffy, but she didn't have the energy to get up from the couch to turn up the fan. She closed her eyes, but the sensation returned of Richard Brown's body slumped against hers. In death he had saved her, a human shield. She took one bullet in the shoulder; another, grazing her cheek, left a red mark like a branding. According to the autopsy, Richard died almost instantly with a bullet to his head.

They should stop, she told Nick before he left. It wasn't worth risking their lives. But he was bent on finding Dougherty, carrying on her mission as if she had bequeathed it to him. There was a stubborn resilience in him, a blind intent that surprised her. Who was this man she shared her bed with? And who was she who wanted him? Did she want him? How could she possibly judge?

Trapped creatures lose their judgment. They struggle so hard to break free that they exhaust themselves, exhaust the possibility of freedom. She was trapped by her body's need to heal, by her parents' concern, by the momentum of circumstances that propelled Nick forward and left her behind. Was that why she told him to stop, because she didn't want him to outpace her?

The drugs wouldn't let her think clearly. She wanted her mind back even more than the use of her shoulder. Maybe she would cut back on the painkillers, a little less each time. Maybe it would be easier to live with the pain than with this stupor.

The front door swung open and she heard her father in the hall. "Building up for a scorcher tomorrow," he said as he came into the living room. "How are you feeling?"

"Better," she lied.

"You don't look it." He put his palm on her forehead. "No fever."

"No."

"Well, that's good." The back of his shirt was soaked with sweat and the layer of fine dirt that covered his arms made his skin appear darker than it was. Almost imperceptibly, his blond hair had turned to white so that he looked little different at sixty than he had a decade before. "I'm going up for a shower," he called to her mother in the kitchen.

"Make it quick," she replied. "Dinner will be ready in fifteen minutes."

The phone rang before he reached the stairs. "For you," he said to Lisa as he handed her the receiver. The voice on the other end introduced herself as Michelle Wang, assistant program coordinator for the Democratic convention.

"We're planning to have a short tribute to Senator Barrett on the opening day," she said, "seeing as she came from Minnesota and put so much effort into bringing the convention here. Your name kept coming up as the right person to speak. But I know about the," she paused, searching for words, "well, I know you're still recovering from the attack and we didn't know if your health would allow…"

"I'll do it," Lisa cut her off. "Tell them I'll do it."

———

For the third evening in a row Nick waited at the Reston high school track to see if Dougherty would show up for a run. So far, no one tall and lanky had made an appearance. "He runs funny," Lisa had told him, "he leans so far forward you think he'd lose his balance." Nick was walking around the track now, ten pound weights in each hand, but he didn't know how much longer he could take it. An hour had passed already and first the gnats and then the mosquitoes attacked him. The track brought back unhappy memories of high school football games where he warmed the bench because the coach didn't like his father. In fact, as far as he could tell, no one liked his father and he couldn't blame them. At the bank his father foreclosed on mortgages and at home on feelings. Nick's mother divorced him and he died a lonely man. Over time Nick had come to understand his father's loneliness because he suffered from it too, suffered from a kind of aggressive emptiness that allows nothing and no one to fill it. But then Lisa and Sam came into his life, and now the loneliness he felt came from real absence, real desire, real fear of losing them.

The weights were growing too heavy in his hands. As he walked to the edge of the track to drop them on the grass, he caught a glimpse of a man doing stretches near the goal post. Tall and lanky. He resumed walking, hoping the stranger was Dougherty. He let him run by once before attempting contact. Like Lisa said, the runner leaned far forward. Nick began to run too and when he came abreast of Dougherty, he said, "I'm a friend of Lisa Derby's and I need to talk to you."

Dougherty didn't even turn to look at him. "Under the bleachers in twenty minutes," he clipped. "I go first."

It was almost nightfall by the time Nick slipped under the bleachers. A few fireflies punctuated the dark like the first stars dotting the sky. A light breeze cooled him off, or was something else bringing on a chill? Suddenly, it seemed foolish to have searched out Dougherty. Maybe he was on the other side, maybe he gave the order to shoot Richard and Lisa. It wasn't too late to turn back and head for the car.

But he kept going, pulled by a momentum he'd come to recognize but couldn't name. He tried to remember the self-defense maneuvers he learned in the military, but he'd lost them in the long forgetting that he had needed to heal. Was he truly healed? How quick were his reflexes if they were put to the test?

"I know who you are," Dougherty said as they faced each other under the bleachers. "You saved your girlfriend's life. That's enough, Mr. Connor. You don't need to do anything more."

"There's unfinished business."

"Like what?"

"Just before he was shot, Richard Brown told Lisa you know who sent Edwards to kill Mohammed."

"Maybe, maybe not. Maybe I'm going to choose not to remember."

"Why?"

"You're asking me why?" Dougherty asked in disbelief. "Your girlfriend almost got herself killed, Mr. Connor. There comes a time when it's just not worth it any more. You do a cost-benefit analysis. They'll kill anyone who gets close to Edwards."

"They haven't killed you."

"That's only because I have friends who protected me, but they can't protect me any more. People are getting suspicious. I'm on my own now. I have a little time, but not much. And I've lost him—last week he took off from the safe house where I hid him and he hasn't returned. I need to find him before they do."

"I can help."

"By getting shot like your girlfriend?"

"You need us, Mr. Dougherty. You find Edwards, and Lisa makes it matter. On the news, in the Senate."

He took a while to answer, coolly inspecting Nick's face. "I'll think about it," he finally said. "In the meantime you lay low and wait for me to initiate contact."

Matt lay in bed, unable to sleep. He put a hand over his heart as if to protect it. Thank God the term was over at last. Scott was out of his life, unless he showed up at Jessie's wedding, and then he would be only one guest among hundreds, easy to avoid. Dora was sound asleep next to him, snoring lightly. He nudged her, but she kept snoring. Even though the wedding arrangements were running her ragged, she and Jessie were getting along better than before. Just as he'd expected, the pregnancy was bringing them closer together. Dora had already figured out how to let out the wedding gown to accommodate the bride's expanding waistline. When Jessie was home last weekend, she ate more than he'd ever seen her eat before. Maybe twins were the final cure for her eating disorder. For the first time since she was a toddler, his daughter's cheeks were rosy and plump.

That was one good thing about the world. He should try to think of more. He had to get Scott off his mind. What was it Fox's friend had said at the Wizards game? These days suspicion is the better part of valor. Maybe he was right and Scott had spied on him, maybe it was connected to the Mohammed case. Dr. Levinson had called this week to warn him that someone had hacked into the computerized patient records at the practice. "Perhaps they were just after social security and credit card numbers," he said, "but you're our most famous patient, Matt. No telling what journalists will do these days."

No telling what the administration will do, Matt had wanted to reply. The murder of Mohammed's lawyer—was that their dirty work too? How could it have been a mugging, especially with Senator Barrett's aide sitting next to him in the car? No, the two of them must have been on to something people high up didn't want them to know. Part of him wanted to contact Lisa Derby to ask her, but it would mean stepping out of professional bounds and he had never done that before. He was a judge, not a sleuth. But what if he dropped dead from a heart attack? His suspicions would die along with him. Or what if they killed him like they had killed Richard Brown?

Natural or unnatural, his would surely be a convenient death. With him gone, the administration could make an appointment to the Court that would ensure a majority for the President.

Suddenly, the sound of the crickets outside irritated him. He longed for the dead quiet of a winter's night, the kind of clear, cold weather that cuts through everything—your jacket, your hat, the muddle in your brain. Barring that, the only way to get clear was to write. He hadn't written in his journal since the morning he learned of Mohammed's death. In his journal he could voice his suspicions, and if they proved unfounded, he could tear the pages out. But at least there would be a record in case he died. Just in case.

He got out of bed, grabbed his robe from the chair and went downstairs to his study. He opened the side drawer of his desk and took out his journal. The triumphant note of his last entry—how he had outsmarted both Reynolds and Lovins to come up with the Mohammed ruling—now seemed naïve and self-congratulatory. He put down the date and began to write, not worrying as much as usual about his choice of words or his handwriting. *If suspicion is the better part of valor*, he began, *then I am compelled to record my fears.*

12

He came almost every day to the fish store, a thin but muscular young man with an untrimmed beard and dirty clothes. He always wore dark glasses and never took them off inside. At first Faith thought he was a beach bum, but he didn't have the oversalted look of a surfer. Then she thought he might be a day laborer who had migrated to the coast for summer construction work, but his hours were too random for that. One day he would show up at mid-morning, the next mid-afternoon. He bought the cheapest fish and stored it in a cooler in his truck. A camper maybe, but a loner. He always told Ali to keep the change.

One time she caught him looking at Samira working in back and worried he had lewd intentions. It also crossed her mind he might be a government spy, sent to keep an eye on them, but what was there to see? Two women and a young boy trying to make ends meet. What was suspicious about that?

Today she summoned up the nerve to ask him about himself. He wore the same orange t-shirt he had on yesterday, though his shorts were different, clean and pressed as if he just bought them off the rack. He pointed at the haddock. "I'll take a half pound of that, please."

"Ali, cut the man a piece," Faith instructed. The boy seemed sleepy this morning—must be growing, she thought. He had already grown out of the shoes they bought him in May. "Are you from around here?" she asked the stranger. He hesitated before saying "California" and she suspected it was a lie. "What brought you here?"

"I've been traveling across the country," he told her. "I never saw the east coast before."

"Do you like North Carolina?"

He nodded. "Beautiful beaches."

"How long are you going to stick around?"

"Until I feel the urge to move on," he replied, taking out his wallet to pay for the fish.

"Must be nice having that freedom. Where are you staying?" He mumbled something about camping, but nothing specific. "You cook the fish over a fire?"

"I have a little camp stove."

"Try grilling it over the fire sometime. Here, I'll throw in a piece of tuna for you—it's thick so it grills real good. I just got it this morning so it's fresh out of the sea." She reached in the case and pulled a chunk of tuna from the ice.

The man nervously checked his wallet. "Let me give you something for it."

"No, it's on the house. You're a regular customer."

"Well, thanks."

"Just let me know how it tastes."

She watched out the window as he walked to his truck. It was a different color from yesterday—it had gone from tan to red. She glanced at the license plate. She couldn't make out the name of the state or the number since it was covered with dried mud. No mud anywhere else though, not even on the bumper. There was something strange going on.

"Why'd you give him that tuna, Grandma?" Ali asked. "That was at least a pound—ten bucks worth."

"He looked hungry," she replied, keeping her suspicions to herself.

It was past midnight when Lyndon finally pulled into Skip's driveway, but he wasn't tired. On the contrary, he was pumped with adrenaline. Trudy had that effect on him. Their furtive sex was like a cocaine rush, a compressed explosion, higher than high. She took everything she could from him and more. Sometimes it was hard to stand up afterwards and they fell back down laughing. It was her laughing he liked best because it signaled their lust. Sometimes in the company of others, even her husband, she laughed like that to turn him on.

She was white powder in his nostrils, thrill without addiction, unless of course he was becoming addicted to her. He wanted her all the time, the same woman he'd despised only months before. "We hated each other because we wanted each other," she had told him tonight as they lay entwined on the couch in the First Lady's office.

"I thought you hated me because I was black."

She shook her head. "I hated you because you were so much smarter than my husband. I looked for ways to put you down—to make you smaller to make him bigger, but it didn't work. He just kept shrinking, you know, until I couldn't even feel sorry for him."

"Do you feel sorry for him now?"

"I feel happy for myself. How about you?"

Instead of an answer, he gave her a long kiss. "I have to go now, Sleeping Beauty" he murmured.

He sat in the car for a minute or two, forcing himself out of the fairy tale to the business at hand. Lately he found himself running on pure political instinct, and his instinct directed him to act tonight to set phase two in motion. No one but Skip, Scott, and he himself needed to know.

Skip was waiting for him at the door and ushered him through the living room and into the kitchen where Lyndon appeased him by eating one of his terrible desserts. This time it was a lemon bar made with artificial sweetener that left a metallic aftertaste.

"Let's talk outside," Lyndon said as he washed it down with a glass of equally metallic tap water.

The humidity was so intense that it was hard to tell whether it was dew or drizzle that dampened the skin. They walked to the bottom of the yard where Lyndon wiped his brow with a handkerchief. "Supposed to be hotter tomorrow," Skip remarked.

Lyndon nodded. "Typical Washington summer. Got the boat out?"

"Yup." Skip paused, breaking a dead flower off a stem and throwing it onto the grass. "Worried about the Democratic convention?"

"Yes and no."

"Meaning?"

"All indications are it'll be boring as hell. The press coverage will give Hartley's campaign a boost, but it won't last for long. And if it does, well, we'll have the ground prepared…"

"So you're telling me it's clean sailing?"

"Yes, clean sailing except for that fucker Edwards."

"We're closing in on him, like I told you."

"I hope so."

They stood quietly for a few moments, assuming the pose of people looking out at a vista except it was dark and the vista was only a neighbor's fence. "One other thing," Skip broke the silence.

"Yes?"

"I have pictures."

"Of what?"

Skip turned his face away from Lyndon and then with a sudden jerky movement, turned it back again. "You and the President's wife." He paused. "Naked in a pond. Fucking in a gazebo."

"Amazing what digital photography can do these days."

"Look, all I'm saying, Lyndon, is that we're even. You have your little secrets and I have mine. You play straight with me and I'll keep the photos safe and sound. But if you fuck me over, I'll fuck you over."

"Where'd you get the idea I was going to fuck you over? We're in this together, Skip."

"I just want to make sure we get out of it together, too."

"We will."

"Glad to hear it. Want another lemon bar before you go?"

"No thanks."

"No hard feelings, hey buddy," Skip said, slapping Lyndon on the back. "I'm glad you're having a little fun on the side—makes you seem more human."

Lyndon fought back an urge to punch him in the face. "Enough, Skip," he remarked coldly.

Skip smiled, extending his hand. "Let's shake on it, Lyndon. Happy days are here again."

That night Richard Brown appeared in Lisa's dreams. He wasn't dead or ghost-like—instead, he was walking down a street and looked pleased when he turned around and spotted her a short distance behind. He waved and she waved back, amazed that she could move her arm so freely. "Lisa, Lisa," he called with a familiar flirtatious air.

"Wait a minute," she called out. "Let me catch up and we'll walk together."

He shook his head, and then waved again and turned away, walking so fast that she soon lost sight of him.

The dream woke her and she got out of bed, tiptoeing down the hall to check on Sam who arrived a few days ago. The weeks in California had worn the father-son relationship thin. Kevin's affection flowed freely to his other boys, but trickled through a rusty faucet to his firstborn. Sam begged to leave and she agreed on the condition that he stay with her parents on the farm for the rest of the summer. Nick would pick her up tomorrow and escort her to the convention, and from there they'd fly back to D.C. She wanted Sam safe in Minnesota until she knew what was happening with Dougherty and Edwards. Dougherty still hadn't contacted Nick.

The night had cooled off enough that she pulled the covers over Sam. He was on his side, hugging his stuffed dog. She bent down to kiss him. She would miss him, but she was doing the right thing, or at least she hoped she was.

Back in her bedroom she turned on the light and again read through her tribute to Senator Barrett. They'd given her only five minutes—three hundred seconds—to keep the senator's legacy alive. It wasn't enough, but maybe that was the point. While the Democratic leadership had to acknowledge Barrett, they wanted to distance themselves from her more controversial stands. At least that was the position of Graham Olsen, the man who was running to fill her seat. Lisa didn't like him. Beneath his populist demeanor, he was arrogant and entitled, married to a Cargill heiress. She heard through the grapevine that he wasn't even considering her for his transition team. This five-minute speech was the last sop the pols would throw her. She had to make the most of it, but she wasn't satisfied with what she'd written. It was too canned, too sentimental, but that's what they wanted from her. The program committee had vetted the speech and she couldn't change it.

She read through it a few more times, working on where to pause, where to put emphasis. Her shoulder was hurting, but she didn't want to take a painkiller. She had to be sharp tomorrow, fully present. That meant she should go back to sleep, if she could. She put the speech on the bedside table, but before she turned off the light, she opened the drawer. Last week her father had bought her a pistol and taught her how to shoot it. It was in the drawer, its chamber empty now, but tomorrow she would load it. She ran her fingers over it as if it were an exotic art object, something that couldn't possibly belong to her.

Of course Nick was partial, but Lisa looked particularly striking up on the stage. Maybe because he knew her weaknesses and fears he saw more clearly her capacity to overcome them, her potential for power. At lunch she had pointed out the window at the sluggish, muddy flow of the Mississippi, diminished by a month of dry weather. "In grade school they took us on a field trip on an old riverboat," she reminisced. "I remember looking at the water and wanting to follow it all the way down to the Gulf of Mexico. Even then I knew I wanted to get out. But you can't get out, not really. Not if you want to be from here, get elected from here."

"Are you saying you want to move back?" Nick asked.

"Maybe. If I decide to give the good old boys a run for their money, if I try to take over where Senator Barrett left off."

"So you want to run for office?"

"Maybe, eventually." She looked out the window again. "I don't know, Nick. I'm pretending that's the case, trying it on. Would you come with me?"

He didn't hesitate. "Of course."

He watched her now as she walked to the microphone. Her injured shoulder threw her posture off, but she carried her head high, looking taller than she was, regal almost. A hush spread through the audience, a hush the speakers before her hadn't elicited. She played it smartly, putting her hands on either side of the podium and looking out over the vast expanse of the convention center like a ruler laying claim to a territory from a mountain top. Three hundred seconds. He could feel them starting to tick. Lisa began:

"I miss Senator Barrett. I miss her every day. Because of who she was and what she stood for. She spoke truth to power because she knew the power of truth."

She paused and picked up her speech, waving it at the crowd.

"The words I just spoke are written down here, and I have others too, others I've carefully rehearsed. But today as I sat here on the stage, I could feel her standing behind me. 'Don't talk about me, Lisa,' she said. 'They've already heard enough. Ask them questions. That's my real legacy—asking the hard questions.'"

Why was she taking such a risk? Nick wondered. She didn't have time to deviate from her prepared text.

"These are the hard questions I want to ask you today:

"One: Was the plane crash that killed Senator Barrett really an accident?

"Two: Was it really a mugger who murdered Salim Mohammed's lawyer Richard Brown and put a bullet in my shoulder?

"Three: Was Salim Mohammed's death really a suicide?

"Four: Why hasn't there been a serious investigation of any of these matters?

"Five: Why was Senator Barrett the only senator who spoke out forcefully against the Citizen Defense Acts, laws that under the pretense of protecting us, leave us defenseless against an imperial presidency that wants to strip us of the rights of citizenship and basic civil liberties?

"Six: Why do we allow the administration to act with such impunity?

"Seven: Is Bill Hartley going to win the presidency?

"I hope and trust that the answer to that last question is yes. Bill Hartley will win in the ballot boxes, I'm sure of it. He will win thanks to the hard work all of you have done to make that happen. But ask yourself this final question: Could that victory be stolen from us?

" 'Don't be afraid,' Senator Barrett often told her staff, 'but be vigilant every second of every day.' We have a hundred days left until the election. Ask hard questions and be vigilant every second of every one of them. Remember Senator Barrett. Remember her courage. Speak truth to power and trust in the power of truth. Thank you."

For a moment no one clapped. It was as if each one was waiting to see what the person sitting next to them would do. But then a gray-haired woman sitting near the front lifted her hands and clapped loudly and as others followed, the applause rose into a standing ovation. "Thank you," Lisa shouted. "Thank you!" She waited for a few seconds and then leaned into the microphone, leading the crowd in a chant for Hartley. As it gained momentum, people lifted signs and waved banners. Lisa picked up the pace.

Hartley for President! Hartley for President! Hartley for President!

The mood was electric and the cameras zoomed in on her.

Lisa's speech led the news that night. While liberal pundits cautiously debated the answers to her questions, Fox News labeled her "the Princess of Paranoia." Matt flipped through the channels, watching the coverage. Lisa Derby's fears were essentially the same as his. Did that make him the Prince of Paranoia?

13

"*He can't do it*," Trudy told Lyndon as they saddled Moonbeam and Sparkler on Sunday morning in the barn at Lonesome Hollow.

"What do you mean he can't do it?"

"He can't deliver the acceptance speech—it's hopeless. Have you heard him rehearsing? He's lost his powers of concentration."

"He'll pull it together at the convention."

"I wouldn't count on it."

Lyndon pulled down a stirrup. "But he's always managed to give speeches before—no matter what shape he's in."

"He's hitting rock bottom, Lyndon, and this time I don't think he's going to be able to get up again."

"So what are you suggesting?"

"Nothing. I'm just telling you." She flicked her hair to the back of her neck. "Now let's get out on the trail."

She rode Sparkler this time and he rode Moonbeam. He was grateful to have the mellower horse when he felt far from mellow. He had too many decisions to make and he couldn't see clearly. Was it sex or doubt, or both, that were clouding his vision?

Trudy broke into a slow trot and he followed, hoping the ride might shake some solutions out of his brain. He was up against it, that was for sure. Lisa

Derby's speech had thrown a monkey wrench into his plans, and he had to make his decision this morning. He looked at his watch. They were expecting his signal by noon. It came down to how he read the future. What if Trudy was right and the President really was incapable of functioning at the convention?

Trudy turned to look at him. "Catch up," she ordered. "The road's wide enough for us to ride side by side."

"Yes, ma'am," he muttered under his breath.

It was just before 9:00 and the sun was turning the corner from friend to foe. The last traces of the morning breeze were gone and the leaves hung from the trees like laundry that would take all day to dry. The bluegrass was no longer so blue, bleached instead to the gold of August. The same color as Trudy's hair. She pointed to a cluster of bushes on the left. "There's a pheasant in there," she said. He nodded, not caring whether he saw it or not. She knew her birds well—just like she knew her men. If she said her husband couldn't deliver his acceptance speech, she was probably right. "Have you ever hunted pheasants, Lyndon?" she asked.

"No, I don't like to shoot birds."

"Neither do I. My daddy took me duck hunting once and when I saw the first dead one in our dog's mouth, I almost passed out. Never ate duck after that." She paused, pulling the reins to slow Sparkler down. "Do you hunt anything else?"

"I don't hunt."

"I guess you don't need to."

"What do you mean by that?"

"You don't have to go out looking for things, they come to you. Like I did."

He wanted to tell her they were both hunted now by a hidden camera wielded by one of her favorite Secret Service guys, but he couldn't bring himself to do it. She wouldn't need to know, as long as he could keep Skip in line.

"Shall we gallop?" Trudy asked when they reached the meadow.

He thought back to their first ride alone together, her first confidences. "You gallop," he said. "I want to watch you."

"Watch me?"

"Yes, watch you." He pulled the reins tight, restraining any impulse of Moonbeam to bolt after his friend. "Go ahead."

She was an expert rider, at one with the horse, able to translate Sparkler's rhythm into the motion of her hips and thighs. That's what he wanted to see: perfect control. Maybe there was something he could learn from it, something he could apply to the decision at hand. Find that same rhythm of perfect control.

When he joined her at the other end of the meadow, she was looking at a group of large birds roosting in a tree. "Turkey vultures," she said. "You can tell by the red on their heads."

He loosened the reins to let Moonbeam graze on the grass. "What you told me about the President not being able to give the speech—you're sure?"

"Trust me, Lyndon," she said.

The sand was so hot underfoot that Faith made straight for the water's edge. In church this morning they sang "Wade in the Water" and it made her want to come to the beach. She sang it to Jackson when he was a little boy scared to get his feet wet. She dangled him above the surf, waiting for a wave to break and splash his toes. She could remember the magic moment when his cries of fear turned to squeals of glee. Then there was no keeping him from the water and she had to chase after him to make sure he didn't go too deep.

She walked further down the beach to get away from the Sunday crowds, stepping over the remains of sand castles collapsed by the incoming tide. She turned away from the sight of gulls competing over a fish carcass. She'd seen enough dead fish in her day not to bat an eye, but there was something about the way gulls picked and poked that repulsed her. "Damn," she said as a strong wave wet the hemline of her Sunday dress. At least Ali wasn't along to hear his grandmother curse.

A gust of wind caught her hat and sent it spinning toward the dunes. She chased after it, but a man got there before her, catching it in his hand. She recognized him at once as the strange camper in the repainted truck. She hadn't seen him since the day she gave him the free tuna. What was he doing here? She didn't know whether to be scared or not, but what could happen on an open beach in broad daylight? He handed her the hat. "Well, thank you," she said. "Did you enjoy the tuna?"

"I did," he replied. "I've been meaning to thank you."

"Haven't seen you for a spell."

"I traveled around a bit."

"And now you're back?"

"Yes," he said, "I wanted to talk to you."

"To me?" She wished he'd take off those damn dark glasses so she could see his eyes. There she was using "damn" again—at least she hadn't said it aloud. "What do you want to talk to me about?"

He hesitated, looking around to make sure there was no one near on the beach. "Your son Salim."

"You mean Jackson," she said. "That's his Christian name." She drew a little closer, scrutinizing his face. "Are you from the government?"

"No."

"Well, then where are you from?"

"Mrs. Jones, I..."

"Take off those glasses so I can see your eyes." Reluctantly, he removed them and put them in his pocket. She looked him in the eye. He was more scared than she was, that much she could tell. "What do you want to say to me?"

"I came to ask your forgiveness."

"Forgiveness? Why? I don't even know you."

"Mrs. Jones, I killed your son."

"What, boy? What are you saying?"

He said it more slowly this time: "I killed your son." As he repeated the words, the hat dropped from her hand, but she didn't care. She didn't care if it blew into the water and was carried out to sea. She felt heavy, short of breath. The stranger reached down to pick up the hat, but this time he kept it. "They made me do it, Mrs. Jones, I swear they did. I was a prisoner too and they told me they'd let me go if I killed him. When I refused, they said they were going to torture my fiancée to death and make me watch. So I agreed." He looked as if he was about to cry. "I knew it was wrong, but I was so weak and worn down that I did it. I strangled him in his sleep. He was drugged and never knew it was happening."

"My God."

"They let me go and I ran away. But another man came and found me, a man who interrogated me in prison. He told me my fiancée was already dead—she'd been dead for over a year. They lied to me. He wanted to find out who gave the orders to kill your son so he could expose them. He hid me away, claiming it was for my own safety. But I didn't know if I could trust him either. And so I fled and came here."

"To ask for my forgiveness?"

"Yes."

"For killing my son."

He looked down. "Yes."

She shook her head. "How do you expect me to forgive you, just like that?"

"I don't."

"I'm a mother. You killed my son, my only child. The Lord gave me one child and you took his life. With your own hands. You strangled him with your own hands and then you strung him up."

"I think about it every day, Mrs. Jones. I think about killing myself. I even tried to hang myself, but I couldn't do it. I needed to talk to you first, to tell you the truth…"

He was crying now, but she couldn't bring herself to comfort him—not this man who killed her son. Part of her wished him dead. Let him hang himself, what did she care? But another part of her saw in his despair a possibility, not of redemption—his soul was his own business—but of retribution. "Give me my hat," she demanded, and he handed it to her. "You want my forgiveness, you have to earn it, is that clear?"

"Yes, ma'am."

"Meet me at the fish store tonight around nine. Park your truck down the road and come in through the back door. I'll leave it open."

A beam of light pierced the stained glass window and pointed like an arrow straight at Scott Hanson in the back pew. Suppressing a surge of anger, Matt began walking his daughter down the aisle. Scott was a devil in the sanctuary, but he couldn't be allowed to ruin Jessie's day. Her arm was entwined around his and he felt, for one last fleeting moment, her protector. Was this what it meant to give your daughter away? To bid good-by to the illusion that you could protect her from all the ugliness in the world?

She looked lovely, her face radiant with the glow of mid-pregnancy, her belly well-hidden by Dora's artful tailoring. She was wearing flat shoes so as not to be taller than David. She was looking at David now, preparing to join him at the altar. Matt's role would soon be over, like an actor who only appears in the first few minutes of a play.

When he joined her in the pew, Dora was already starting to cry, dabbing her eyes with a crumpled tissue. He thought back to their own wedding day when they were all of eighteen. When he lifted Dora's veil to kiss her, she looked so terrified that he almost ran away. The bets were on that the marriage wouldn't last more than a year, especially since she'd lost the baby. His father had pulled him into his office the night before the wedding. "You don't have to go through with this, you know. Not for me. Not for your mother."

"I'm doing it for myself," Matt responded.

"All right then." And with that his father dismissed him as summarily as one of his staff.

David and Jessie were twice as old as Dora and he had been, but did that make them any more or less in love or likely to stay together? Did age really matter at all? Why was he thinking these thoughts? Why wasn't Dora taking his hand? He reached for hers. It felt cold, maybe because his was so hot. Sweat broke out on his brow. Scott was sitting in the back. Would he have the nerve to attend the reception too?

He focused on the words of the minister to break his negative train of thought. He was a compromise, a Congregationalist, neither Presbyterian like their family nor Roman Catholic like David's. He had a slow, pedantic delivery as if waiting to hear the echo of each word before starting the next. Self-important, Matt thought, but what did it matter? All that mattered was the happy look on his daughter's face as she repeated her vows. "I take this man to be my lawful wedded husband..."

Dora was crying in earnest now, fumbling in her purse for another tissue. It suddenly struck him that maybe she was crying for herself, for what she lost by marrying so young. He had always assumed the sacrifice was his, not hers. But it must be hard to live with a man who is always sitting in judgment, who can't even spare a tear for his daughter on her wedding day.

There was no veil to lift when David kissed Jessie, no look of terror on her face. Dora squeezed his hand, and then something shook loose and he gave himself over to whatever it was—envy, grief, joy, relief—and cried along with her.

At the reception, as the knife slid through the first piece of wedding cake, Matt worried he might cry again when it was time for him to toast the newlyweds. He was suffering considerably more performance anxiety than he ever had on the bench. What could he say that wouldn't sound trite, that hadn't been said already by millions of fathers? Or maybe that was the point: to feel connected to all those other fathers before him, to draw strength from custom. He reached into his jacket pocket for the notes he penned last night. Not that he would use them, but they gave him a sense of security.

He gazed out at the crowd. According to Dora, the wedding would be featured in tomorrow's paper. He couldn't care less, but you couldn't put this many

Washington luminaries in one room without some nosey columnist taking notice. He just hoped the tone wouldn't be snide. That would hurt Dora's feelings more than his own indifference. She was used to that.

She was sitting beside him, chatting happily to her younger sister Nancy who arrived in town at the last minute, always the drama queen. While Dora was dressed in a conservative beige silk suit, Nancy wore a tight red spaghetti strap dress with matching heels and hair color. She was now working on getting rid of her third husband to make way for a fourth. "You've got quite a sister-in-law," Fox had remarked to Matt in the buffet line. "Introduce me some time." And then he drew closer and whispered. "Can you believe Scott had the nerve to show up?"

"Unfortunately, I can."

"Some day I'm going to fix that little bastard."

Matt looked in the direction of the table where Scott was sitting, but his seat was empty. He wished he could forget him, but he felt compelled to monitor his whereabouts as if he were a naughty child prone to mischief. The waiters were distributing the cake now. He felt a slap on his shoulder and turned around. "Oh, Scott," he said, surprised.

"I just wanted to thank you for inviting me to the wedding. I wish I could stay until the end, but can you believe it, I have another one to go to this evening."

"It's wedding season," Matt replied coolly.

"Yes, I guess you're right."

"When do you start the new job?"

"At the end of the month, but I'm leaving DC this week."

"Well, good luck," Matt said, really wanting to say good riddance.

"Good luck with the new term. Should be interesting—no matter who wins the presidency." After Scott departed, Matt could still feel the place where he slapped him on the back.

The dizziness first hit him as he delivered his toast. He got through it all right—everyone at the table told him it was eloquent—but it took every ounce of his will power to stand up straight and he clutched the back of his chair like a cane. He hoped the feeling would pass when he sat back down, but one sip of champagne made his head spin. He drank a glass of water and loosened his tie. "Are you all right?" Dora asked. "You're awfully pale."

"I look pale?" he said with disbelief. "I feel hot."

"Well, it is getting warm in here with all these people. I'll tell them to turn up the air conditioning, especially as the dancing's starting soon."

"Good idea."

How could he possibly dance if he felt this way? He had promised Jessie the first dance as long as the band played a slow number. He had to pull himself together. He didn't want her to worry about him, not on her wedding day. One dance and he would be free to sit again. Maybe it was food poisoning. He did feel slightly nauseous. He'd wondered about the salmon, but would it hit him so fast? Please God, he prayed to himself, not my heart, not here at Jessie's wedding. He was cold now, starting to shiver. Surely the air conditioning wouldn't work so fast.

Somehow he managed to make it onto the dance floor and into his daughter's arms. The band struck up the old Sinatra tune, "Strangers in the Night," one of his favorites—she must have told them to play it. After a few steps, she sensed that he couldn't lead her, so she led him, but he couldn't keep up, his feet refused to move in time to the music. All his joints were stiffening. He felt like a man with wooden legs. "Are you OK, Dad?" she asked.

"I don't know, Jessie. Sometimes I get these dizzy spells."

"Why don't we sit down, Dad."

"What?"

"Sit down."

He leaned closer to her ear. "I've been meaning to tell you. My journal—it's in the bottom drawer of my desk. Read it if..."

"Dad, let's sit down, we'll get a doctor."

The last thing he remembered was resting his head on her shoulder.

Lisa's cell phone rang as she was sitting at her desk, preparing for yet another radio interview in the morning. In the space of a few weeks, she had given more than a hundred interviews to the press. While the conservative talk show hosts had crowned her the Princess of Paranoia, more liberal commentators saw her as a kind of modern-day Paul Revere, sounding the alert. She looked at the phone screen. It was Nick calling from the health club where he was working this evening. When they were apart, he called constantly to make sure she was safe. It was getting on her nerves. "What's up?" she asked curtly.

"The TV's on in the weight room and there was a news flash—Justice Pomeroy had a heart attack. It was at his daughter's wedding. He's in critical condition—it sounds like they don't think he's going to make it."

"Oh, Jesus. Why Pomeroy? Why couldn't it be Reynolds?"

"They're already eulogizing him—it's amazing how fast they've put the footage together."

"His poor daughter."

"He collapsed while he was dancing with her. Rumors are he's been having heart problems. Anyway, I thought I'd let you know. Sorry to be the bearer of more bad news."

She couldn't concentrate after she hung up, so she went into the bedroom and lay down. Her shoulder was still healing, the doctor said, that's why she didn't have her full strength back. She closed her eyes, but as usual she couldn't fall asleep. She remembered a conversation with Senator Barrett after the second Citizen Defense Act passed, another late afternoon confidence induced by a glass of Scotch. "Whether the Supreme Court holds the line—that's what matters now, Lisa," the senator told her. "After this last vote we can kiss the House and Senate good-by. I can count the number of principled legislators—from either side of the aisle, mind you—on my fingers. It didn't used to be like that. When I first came to Washington, there were a lot of us for whom politics was a higher calling, not the lowlife occupation it is today. The Court is our last defense against the imperial presidency. Who knows? The future of the country hangs on Pomeroy—which way he decides to go. What a burden that man carries on his shoulders. I can't say I envy him." She took another swig of her drink and smiled, more to herself than to Lisa. "On the other hand, maybe I do—envy him, I mean. That's real power."

Real power, Lisa thought. Real heart attack? Real plane crash? The only power she possessed came from being the Princess of Paranoia. She would use it tomorrow morning.

14

Matt felt as if someone was opening and closing a door to his brain. Sometimes light flowed in and then suddenly it would go dark again. When it was light he could hear them, but he didn't have the strength to make a sign. He'd been here before, after the accident in high school, so it had a familiar feel. And the same dream: a plantation of tall, straight pines with sunlight filtering through the needles in the shape of a star.

Someone was squeezing his hand. Probably Dora. What was she saying? Or was it Jessie's voice he heard? They were both talking.

Read this, Mom, you have to read these last pages from his journal. Here— I'll hold his hand.

Don't let go, the minute we let go...

I won't, don't worry. It's not so far-fetched what Lisa Derby said in that interview. He was afraid something was going to happen. And he was afraid of Scott. Scott knew about his heart condition.

What are you talking about?

Read it, I have his hand. His fingers are warmer than last night. He wants us to read it. He thinks Scott got hold of his medical records—some guy warned him that Scott was working for Lyndon Tottman. Scott was at the wedding, wasn't he?

What are you saying, Jessie?

I'm saying it might not be natural, the heart attack.

Your father has a heart problem.

Read it, Mom.

He would have told me if he was worried about Scott.

 Read it, please.

Silence, except for the blips and beeps of the machines which must be keeping him alive. If only he could will a muscle to move. Squeeze Jessie's hand. But if he tried, the door might close. It was taking all his strength to keep it open even a crack.

I need to get to a computer, access the database at the CDC. I'll find a computer in one of the offices...

I can't believe he didn't tell me this.

He didn't know for sure, Mom. We still don't know. There are tests they can run. Take his hand again. I'm going to find a computer. If the doctor comes, tell him.

Tell him what?

That it could be poison. That I'm checking. I'll be right back.

You can't leave. What if he... I can't believe he didn't tell me. Why didn't you tell me, Matt? What else haven't you told me? I always told you everything. Are you listening? Jessie's left for a few minutes. She'll be back. We're not going to leave you alone, not for one second. Can you hear me, Matt? We're not going to let you die.

The door was closing. Should he try to resist it, resist the dream, the path through the tall pines where the sunlight shone like a star? There was no choice, he was finally beyond choices, in God's hands, Dora's hands.

We're not going to let you die.

———

"What the fuck is going on, Lyndon? Please tell me what the fuck is going on," the President demanded as soon as Lyndon entered his private study in Lonesome Hollow. Lyndon had seen the wild look on his face only once before, the time he went after a copperhead in the woodpile, bashing its head in with a shovel.

"What do you mean?"

"You know what I mean."

Was this about his affair with Trudy, Lyndon wondered, and if so, what was he going to say? He looked up at the deer head mounted on the opposite wall. Cobwebs hung from the antlers like leftover Christmas tinsel. These days even the housekeeper wasn't doing her job.

"Do you want a drink?" the President asked. "I need a drink."

"You know I don't drink."

"And now you know that I do."

"Yes."

"Let's be honest with each other for a change." The President walked over to a cabinet in the wall where he took out a bottle of bourbon and poured a shot. "One shot after lunch—that's all I allow myself. It's called self-discipline." Lyndon nodded. "Bullshit, you're thinking, aren't you?'" Lyndon nodded again. "OK, let's play it straight then. I'm a drunk."

"So am I. I just don't drink any more."

"Well, I do."

Lyndon ignored the provocation. "What are we going to do about it?" he asked in a steady voice.

"We, Lyndon?"

"I am your friend, you know."

"You're my advisor."

"Yes, and your friend too."

The President scowled and shook his head. "Not any more. You lie too much, Lyndon, even to me. It's your lies that set me drinking again."

So it must be about Trudy, Lyndon thought as he adjusted his body language, relaxing his shoulders and chest so he could take the President's next punch like a pillow. Absorb it, then fluff out again, win him over with softness.

"Have you forgotten the Sixth Commandment, Lyndon?"

Here it comes, Lyndon thought: Thou shalt not commit adultery. But he was off by one.

"Thou shalt not kill," the President pronounced.

Lyndon didn't know whether to be relieved or not. "Of course I haven't forgotten that."

"But do you obey it?" The President's glass was empty, but he clutched it in his hand. "Too many people are dying on my watch."

"Excuse me, but there's a war going on."

"I don't mean the war. I mean Justice Pomeroy."

"The latest I heard is that he had a heart attack and he's still alive."

"Did you arrange that heart attack, Lyndon?"

"How on earth would I do that?"

The President's eyes narrowed and for a moment he seemed in command of himself. "You tell me. Tell me about Senator Barrett's plane crash too."

"That was an accident."

"Was it?"

"That's what the FAA concluded."

"But the FAA could be in your pocket too. Your pockets are so stuffed they won't hold any more—you've bought up half the town."

"Who's putting these ideas in your head?"

"Believe it or not, Lyndon, I can think for myself. I don't trust you any more. You're doing things behind my back. And now people don't trust me. It could cost me the election."

"Your drinking could cost you the election."

"It's not my drinking we're talking about, damn it."

"Well, we need to talk about it."

"Don't try to change the subject, Lyndon."

"Everything I've done, I've done to keep you in power. You know that."

"I don't want you killing people, breaking God's commandments to keep me in power."

"Killing people?" Lyndon guffawed. "The booze is making you paranoid, just like it did before. You were suspicious of everyone and everything when I first met you. What we went through—it was all about getting back to some level of trust, first in God, then in ourselves, then in others." He paused, letting the words sink in. "Believe me, I haven't killed anyone."

"Maybe not with your own hands."

"You're seeing things that just aren't there."

"Then why are other people seeing the same things as me?"

"You mean the Princess of Paranoia Lisa Derby mouthing off on TV? Stop drinking and the world's going to look a lot different."

"A lighter color of shit, you mean."

Lyndon took a few steps toward him and put a hand on his arm. "You need to go into treatment," he said more gently. "And I'm going to figure out a way that you can do that. Things are in place—we can put off your acceptance speech, even put off the election if we have to. You can get well."

"What if I can't?"

"You did it before, you can do it again."

"What if I don't want to? Have you ever thought about that?"

At the health club there were a handful of clients who drove Nick crazy and Sally Gleason was the worst of them. From one day to the next she couldn't remember how to operate the machines, and she was always calling Nick over in her whiny voice to adjust the settings. It didn't help that she was allergic to the words "thank you," or that she had the facial mannerisms of a squirrel. He had just finished putting her on the elliptical machine when he noticed a tall man standing in the entrance to the equipment room. It took a few seconds for the face to register. "Don't go too far, Nick," Sally Gleason said as he walked away. "You know I always have trouble with the treadmill."

"Maybe you can figure it out yourself this time," Nick replied, and then under his breath added, "There's always a first."

Dressed for work, Tom Dougherty looked different, his gangly legs hidden in gray flannel trousers. His sports jacket had a bulge in the side—probably a gun, Nick thought. "I'm thinking of joining the club," Dougherty told him. "Can you show me around?"

"Sure. Want to see the pool first?"

Except for a lone woman doing laps, the pool was empty. They walked around to the shallow end, standing near a box of kickboards and floats. "They traced Toby Edwards to a campsite in North Carolina last week," Dougherty began, "in the Smoky Mountains. He disappeared again, but they're on to him. They're scouring campgrounds and motels all over the southeast. The only hope he's got is that I find him before they do. I'm getting sent down there to help the search team."

"I thought they didn't trust you any more."

"They don't. Now they hope I'll lead them to him. It's going to be tough—I'll have to shake them off. I want you and Ms. Derby to stand by in case I find him. Tell her to get ready, but be quiet about it. And tell her to lay off the interviews for a while. Her profile's getting way too high."

"How will we hear from you?"

"Don't worry, you'll hear from me if I find him. But don't come looking for me under any circumstances." He paused, his eyes trained on the swimmer who was doing a nice even breaststroke. "They get wind of any connection between us and it's over, for all of us."

Sally Gleason opened the door and leaned into the pool room. "Nick, I need your help," she called. "Something's not right with the machine."

"Go ahead," Dougherty said. "I'll find my way out."

It was dark by the time Lisa pulled into the parking lot of the apartment house. She had changed her parking space to be closer to a lighted door, but even so it was always here that she felt most at danger, vulnerable to another attack. Ordinarily, she tried to reach home before sunset or phoned Nick to meet her downstairs. Today, she had stayed late in the office and Nick was working until nine. She reached in her purse for her gun.

It was no more than twenty steps from her car to the door, but she was hesitant to make them. Last night on the phone her mother had tried to persuade her that Sam should stay longer on the farm, enroll in the local elementary school for the fall. Lisa said no, but now she wondered. What if he was in the car with her now? He would sense her fear. And she would have to hide the gun.

She opened the car door and stepped out. "Miz Derby?" a woman's voice came from behind her. Lisa swiveled and pointed the gun toward the shadows. "Please, Miz Derby. I'm Samira Begum, Salim Mohammed's wife. I need to talk to you."

"Come closer where I can see you." Tentatively, Samira stepped forward into the light. Lisa recognized her face from the television. The young woman was wearing a simple cotton dress and headscarf. Her eyes were wide and frightened and she looked very young, almost girlish, and vulnerable. "Why are you here?" Lisa asked, lowering her gun.

"It's Toby Edwards. He's the man who killed Salim. He came to us and we're hiding him, but you have to come meet with him. He won't go public unless you convince him to. Please, please. We're so scared—"

Dad. The door opened a crack and let in some light. Dad, they took your blood, they're doing some tests. If it's what I think it is, there's an antidote. You just have to hang in there a little longer. Just hang in, Dad. Please. I want you to know the twins. I didn't tell you yet, but one's a boy and we're going to name him after you.

The pressure from Jessie's hand sent a slow wave of energy up his arm. If he could tap it, he might be able to move, make a sign. Enough to let her know.

We don't know what we're going to name the girl yet. Can you believe I'm going to have two kids all at once?

There were two kinds of light, he realized. One was the sunlight star in the pine forest, the other the light from the room. Maybe it was his choice after all. He would have to force himself to leave the forest, fight the part of himself that wanted to stay there forever. He opened his eyes, but the fluorescent light was too bright and he closed them again.

part three

15

Lisa woke with a jolt as the car swerved and the tires hit gravel on the side of the road. "Jesus, what's going on?"

"I think I fell asleep for a second," Nick told her. They had driven all night from Washington to North Carolina, turning off I-40 near Fayetteville onto deserted backcountry roads.

"Let's stop for a minute and finish the coffee. Want me to drive?"

"No, I'll be OK after some caffeine. I think we're almost there." He pulled over to the side and she poured the last dregs from the thermos, taking a sip of the lukewarm brew before handing it to him. It was bitter and full of grounds, but at least she had the foresight to bring it along. They were afraid to stop anywhere for food in case there was an alert out for the car. They had filled up with gas just once in an old Texaco station where the attendant was half asleep and there was no sign of surveillance cameras.

She looked out the car window. The road was still dark and empty, but she knew they should push on. She shone a flashlight on the map Samira had scribbled for her—it looked like the turnoff was in thirty miles or so. Nick handed her back the cup. "There's a chance they're already watching the house," she began, "in which case…"

"We could turn around. We don't have to do this, Lisa. We could have waited for a signal from Dougherty."

"Samira said there was no time."

"Whose judgment do you trust, hers or Dougherty's?"

"Do you trust mine?"

They reached the turnoff to the farm—Faith's cousin Henry's place—just before sunrise. There was no sign to mark the place except for a rusty old mailbox missing its door. They bumped along a rutted dirt road, bottoming out where it crossed a creek bed. The road then ascended, taking them through a wooded area where the trees were smothered in a dense mesh of kudzu vines. Lisa studied Samira's sketched map again. Henry's place was a quarter mile past the forest where the road came to an end. The sun was above the horizon now and the light on the windshield revealed all the minute imperfections of the glass.

Henry was standing on the front stoop of his house, pointing a shotgun in their direction. When Lisa called out her name, he nodded in acknowledgement and lowered the gun. He was a wiry little man, in his sixties or seventies, wearing baggy overalls and a baseball cap. He walked toward them with a slight hobble. "Came along for the drive, did he?" he pointed to Nick when he reached the car.

"This is my friend Nick Connor."

Henry squinted at Nick. "Before you get out, you better put your car in the barn. Give me a minute to get the door open. I don't move so fast any more."

The barn was part garage, part stained glass studio. In the window above the hayloft was one of Henry's creations: a stained glass depiction of the crucifixion, only this time Jesus was black. The style was naïf; the figures looked less out of the Bible than an African folktale. Lisa found it strangely unsettling. "You're an artist," she said as she got out of the car.

"Some days," he shrugged.

"Where's Mr. Edwards?"

"Sound asleep. He stood guard all night. I made him go to bed when I got up at five. That man needs to sleep. He's not in his right mind, I tell you. Mumbles to himself a lot and refuses to eat even though I can tell he's hungry. Prowls around like a cat with an empty stomach." Henry looked them over. "Looks like you could use some food and sleep too. I'll make you some breakfast and then you get some rest. Don't want you two going crazy on me too."

The old farmhouse, rundown on the outside, was impeccably clean inside, the wide wooden floorboards polished to a sheen. Henry was retired from his civilian job in the army; he'd managed the mess at Fort Bragg. "Didn't like it," he told them over a breakfast of sausage and eggs, "but it was a job and there aren't many jobs around here." He insisted on giving them his bedroom where family photos hung in neat rows along the wall. "That's Jackson," Henry pointed to a high school graduation photograph of a young man in a blue robe and mortarboard. "Salim Mohammed to you, I guess." Lisa recognized the face from mug shots in the news, though in this one he was smiling. His teeth looked touched up, unnaturally white. Henry pulled down the bedspread. "Clean sheets," he said.

After he left them, Lisa slipped her gun under the pillow. She was determined to remain alert, but stayed awake only a few minutes after Nick fell asleep. She didn't know if it was the heat that woke her in the late morning or the sound of footsteps pacing the hall. She reached for the gun and put it in her pocket. Leaving Nick to sleep, she got out of bed and opened the door, surprising the young man on the other side. "Toby Edwards?" she asked, but he didn't respond. "I'm Lisa Derby."

"I know who you are," he stated flatly.

His oily brown hair hung around his eyes, making it difficult for her to see into them. His beard was long too, masking his chin. He wore a thin green t-shirt and dirty jeans. The thought passed through her mind that they would have to clean him up before presenting him to the press. "We have a lot to talk about," she said. He mumbled something she couldn't understand and then walked down the hall to the bathroom where he closed and locked the door.

The choppy water of the Chesapeake Bay slapped violently against the boat as it accelerated beyond the slow zone near the yacht club. Lyndon grabbed the side of his seat and gritted his teeth. He had the rower's hatred for power boats, and today on top of it he could feel nausea coming on. The morning plane ride from Lonesome Hollow was bumpy the entire way and he drove straight from the airport to the dock.

"Feeling seasick?" Skip asked with the hint of a smirk. At the wheel he looked like a young kid out for kicks, gleefully taking each oncoming wave like a dirt biker making jumps. "I'll anchor a little further out and we can have our talk. Did you bring a lunch?" Lyndon shook his head. "It's OK—I brought enough for both of us."

Skip anchored and pulled up the canvas awning for shade. The sun was directly overhead and it was even hotter than yesterday, heading for the mid-nineties. Skip offered him a soggy tuna sandwich. "Low-fat mayonnaise."

"No thanks. I'm not that hungry."

"How about an apple?"

"Sure, I'll take an apple." It was a Granny Smith with a waxy skin, so sour it puckered Lyndon's lips. "Got some water?" he asked.

"You bet," Skip replied, tossing him a bottle. "Gotta keep hydrated on days like this."

They ate for a few minutes in silence, the water now sloshing more gently against the boat. It made Lyndon feel sleepy, but he couldn't afford to be, especially around Skip. They were in a chess match now, sometimes on the same team, sometimes opponents, and he had to be ready to block Skip's moves as well as to set them up. "OK, let's talk about Edwards first," he began.

"We're zeroing in on North Carolina. We've got a team down there based at Fort Bragg. We sent down Tom Dougherty too—the CIA guy who interrogated Mohammed."

"I thought you didn't trust him."

"That's the point. He might contact Edwards and lead us to him."

"In that case, you're going to have to get rid of him once he serves his purpose."

"I'm well aware of that."

"The agency won't like it."

"Screw the agency. We'll make it look like Edwards did it." Skip wiped his mouth with the back of his hand. "What else did you want to talk to me about? The President's drinking problem?"

"He needs to go into treatment," Lyndon said, tossing the rest of the sour apple overboard. "We have to put him out of commission for a little while, long enough to pull himself back together. First, we're sending him to Dallas this Thursday to campaign."

"Why Dallas?"

"A town with a history."

"So you want to relive the Kennedy moment, but with a happier ending?"

"No convertible this time."

"Of course not. The age of innocence has passed."

"A minor injury that we can make look like something worse."

"Oh, I can see it now—blood on Trudy's lovely pink dress. The sympathy will be enormous."

"Not only sympathy. We'll have grounds to postpone the convention—and the election."

"Very clever," Skip said, crumpling the brown lunch bag and sticking it under the seat.

"Can you manage it?"

"What haven't I managed?"

"Pomeroy's still alive."

"The odds are he won't make it."

"You screwed up, Skip."

"Scott screwed up. Using him was your idea, not mine. I told you I don't like amateurs." His smile had a touch of malice. "I just got some more photos, even juicier ones. You sure are having fun on the side, Lyndon. That another reason you want the President on ice? All the better to fuck his wife?"

Skip's cell phone rang before Lyndon could respond. Skip flipped it open, his face tightening as he listened to the caller. "You're shitting me!" he barked into the receiver. "Who the fuck let them get away? I thought we had GPS in both their cars." He paused. "They rented a car? You've got to be kidding. You have the plate? Put a search out for it." Snapping the phone shut with disgust, he turned to Lyndon. "Lisa Derby and her pal Nick Connor have gone missing. They left DC last night, heading south on 95 in a rental car. My guy lost them outside Fredericksburg."

"Maybe they're looking for Edwards too."

"Maybe they found him."

Matt opened his eyes. The room was dark. It must be night, he thought, relieved that he might have returned to a time measured in hours and minutes, days and nights. He moved his head to the right. Someone was asleep in the chair next to him. "Dora," he whispered. There was no response. To his amazement, he was able to repeat her name more loudly. "Dora!"

"Dad, it's Jessie." Her voice came closer and he could feel her breath on his face. "Jessie, your daughter."

"Where's your mother?"

"I made her go home to get some sleep."

"What happened?"

"You had a heart attack at my wedding—do you remember? Before you collapsed, you told me to read your journal. We think you were poisoned. They did tests, but they were inconclusive. In any case you had a heart attack, whether it was natural or not."

"Am I dying?"

"No," she said firmly, "but it's going to take you a while to recover."

"I'm so tired, Jessie."

"Yes, of course, you're tired.

"And you?"

"I'm all right—David's been spelling me."

"You have to take care of yourself. You're pregnant."

"Don't worry about me, Dad. I'm fine. I'm really fine."

"That's good." He closed his eyes. "I'm tired, Jessie, but keep talking to me."

"You should see all the cards and flowers, Dad. Not just from your friends, but from people you don't know, people from all over the country. The flowers could fill up the whole ward. We took some of them home, but gave the rest away, mainly to the children's ward. We thought you'd like that. Every day there's a story about you in the press. The fact that you're improving—well, it seems to give people hope. The hospital hasn't allowed any visitors besides the family, but your friend Justice Fox calls every day. You have no idea how admired you are."

"I ruined your wedding."

"No, you didn't. You're pulling through—that's all that counts. Look, I'm going to call the doctor. She wanted us to let her know as soon as you wake up."

"I'm tired."

"That's OK. Just rest while I go get her."

It was never night in the pine forest because the light that shone like a star never went away. Night returned his body to him, made him tired in a regular sort of way. He felt his own heaviness, the effort it took to move a muscle or take a breath. He felt pain in his chest, but it felt right to feel pain because it meant he was still alive.

"You try," Lisa told Nick in frustration as she came back in the house. "He's so scared he can't think straight. I keep telling him the longer we stay here, the more risk they'll find us, but I'm not getting through. Maybe you can."

"I doubt I'll do any better, but I'll try. Where is he?"

"He's pitched a tent in the meadow. He claims it's safer to sleep outside."

Nick grabbed a flashlight and headed out the door. The night air was dank and humid and the hum of crickets competed with the mosquitoes buzzing around his ears. The light from the barn where Henry was working cast a faint glow over the meadow. Nick trod through the tall wet grass toward the outline of a tent at the far corner. "Toby, it's Nick," he shouted as he approached, wanting to ensure he wasn't mistaken for an enemy. He knew Toby had a pistol and an assault rifle. "I want to talk to you." There was no reply.

By the time he reached the tent, his shoes and the bottom of his pants were soaked. "Toby, it's Nick," he shouted again.

"I heard you the first time. Come inside. They're too many bugs out there."

Nick unzipped the flap and climbed awkwardly inside. The tent was barely big enough for two grown men to sit upright. Even though it was hot, Toby was wrapped in his sleeping bag, his knees pulled up to his chin. "You OK?" Nick asked, and Toby shook his head.

"Turn off the flashlight, please."

There was something about sitting in the darkness that took Nick back in time, back to Kuwait, keeping watch with a buddy in that unspoken fraternity that only soldiers understand. "I'm scared too," Nick said after a few moments. "We'd be crazy if we weren't."

"Did you know they tortured my fiancée to death? They used dogs."

"Yes, I heard. I'm so sorry…"

"Every night I dream about it. I hear her screaming, but I don't know where she is. I can't get to her. I can't save her. And then I wake up and think about whether they raped her too. I want to remember her like she was before, how beautiful she was, but I can't. I don't even have her picture. They tore it up when they were questioning me."

Nick reached out and put his hand on Toby's arm. It was a risk, touching him, but he needed some comfort. "Are you afraid they're going to torture you too?"

"Yes." Toby hung his head. "It makes me feel weak, you know."

"That's what they want—for you to think you're weak. After the Gulf War, I felt weak for ten years, ten wasted years. I was diagnosed with everything from Gulf War Syndrome to depression, but the fact is the war just robbed me of my strength."

"How'd you get it back?"

"I finally quit thinking about it."

"It's not the same."

"I know. But all I'm saying is you have to get yourself to a place where you don't worry any more about being weak because you're not weak, Toby. What you've done is brave—incredibly brave, and now you just have to carry through."

"I don't know." He pulled his knees closer to his chest. "I'm not sure I can go through with it."

"You have to," Nick said more sternly. "You don't have a choice. They're searching all over for you. Sooner or later they're going to find you. The only way you're ever going to be safe is to go public. You can't keep hiding and you can't keep running."

"I'm just not ready."

"Do you think any of us are? Were you ready the first time they sent you into combat? I wasn't, but I went anyway. We should leave here tonight, after you get a few hours sleep."

"No, not tonight. I can't do it tonight. I won't talk—I can't. I'm not ready."

"Tomorrow night then."

"All right."

"You mean it?"

"Yeah, I promise."

"Get some sleep then. I'll stand guard by the house."

Nick unzipped the flap and crawled outside. He didn't know whether to trust Toby—he'd fled from Dougherty, after all—but it was a risk they had to take, along with all the other risks. He turned on the flashlight and made his way toward the barn to speak to Henry. There was no escape route from here. The one road in was the one road out, and the swampy terrain would make it difficult if not impossible to flee by foot.

As he entered the barn, the old man looked up from his work table where he was cutting a sheet of blue glass. "Toby refuses to go tonight," Nick said, "but he promises to go tomorrow. Is that all right with you?"

Henry finished cutting the piece and removed his protective glasses. "You can't force a man like that," he said. "You force him and he breaks. Shatters just like glass. You have to have patience to work with glass, and I have a lot of patience. You see my crucifixion up there?"

"It's really beautiful."

"You know how long that took me?" Nick shook his head. "Over a year. And then the church that commissioned it decided they didn't like it—they didn't want Jesus looking like a black man, looking like themselves. And so I put it up here in the barn."

"Some day it will hang in a museum."

Henry laughed. "You think so? Well, I'll be dead and gone by then, that's for ure." He picked up the piece of blue glass and held it to the light. "You know what Edwards does when he thinks no one's listening? He cries like a baby, just cries and cries. That's why he moved out to that tent—so he could cry and you and Lisa wouldn't hear him. He'll be all cried out by tomorrow. There are only so many tears a man can cry."

16

"*I thought they'd never let* me in to see you," Fox remarked as he took a seat at Matt's bedside. He was wearing a white linen suit and a festive red bowtie, more appropriate for a summer tea party than a hospital visit. He brought two presents, a bouquet of sunflowers and a book of political cartoons.

"Count yourself honored," Jessie told him. "You're the first person Dad wanted to see outside the family."

"Is that true, Matt?"

Matt nodded.

"But you're not to upset him," Jessie warned.

"Of course."

"Let us talk alone for a few minutes, Jessie," Matt said, pressing the button to raise the bed into sitting position.

"Just a few," she instructed as she exited. "I'll be back in five."

"She's worse than Dora," Matt told Fox. "Watches my every move."

"That's a good thing in your circumstances."

Matt sighed. "I suppose. So what are we supposed to talk about if you're not to upset me? You always upset me. I count on it. To tell you the truth I'm getting bored in here. They don't even let me watch the news. What is the news?"

"You really want to know?" Fox raised an eyebrow and held it there a second.

"Yes, as a matter of fact I do."

"Well, Hartley's maintaining his double-digit lead in the polls."

"That's good."

"The rumor is the President's back on the bottle."

"Much truth in it?"

"Could be. He looks terrible, like he's aged ten years in one month."

"So that's to Hartley's advantage."

Fox shook his head. "I'm not so sure."

"What do you mean?" Matt reached for the paper cup of water on the bedside table, willing his hand not to tremble as he brought it to his lips, but it did and Fox was watching.

"Here, let me hold the cup."

"No, no, I can manage," Matt insisted. "I'm trying to get my parts working again. Go on. I want to hear."

"It's just making them more desperate," Fox continued. "One of my sources says they're seriously thinking about postponing the election."

"Which source? Lenny Schurman?"

Fox shook his head, but it wasn't convincing. "Let's just say it's the one who usually gets it right. He's telling me to watch my back because it may go to the Court." He leaned closer. "He thinks you were poisoned. Were you, Matt?"

"I had a heart attack."

"But could it have been induced?"

"It's possible." Matt took another sip of water and put the cup back on the table, his hand steadier this time. Fox was still leaning close, too close. How much should Matt tell him? "They checked and didn't find anything, but that doesn't rule it out. Jessie says they didn't test in time. Some poisons leave the bloodstream fast without a trace. But there's a spot on my back where the skin's swollen, like an allergic reaction. Scott slapped me there before he left the reception. I remember it felt funny, or at least I think I do. My memory's hazy after that, I started feeling dizzy."

"So it could have been Scott."

"Yes, it could have been him." It felt good to say it even though he knew he shouldn't voice his suspicions, especially to Fox. He had no proof. Scott was innocent until proven guilty. "Maybe I just had a heart attack. I may never know— that's the hard thing. People like you and me are used to knowing. I'm afraid certainty's gone out the window, along with everything else."

"Along with morality, you mean."

"So it seems."

"Or is it that without morality, there can be no certainty?"

"You're going over my head there."

"Nothing's ever over your head, Matt."

"Thanks for the compliment, but I don't deserve it."

"False modesty."

"No, it's true."

Fox leaned back in his chair, putting his hands behind his head and rocking slightly, as he often did before making a pronouncement. "I'm pretty certain they poisoned you, Matt," he began. "And I wouldn't put it past them to try again. If not you, then me, or Lovins, or one of the others who would vote against postponing the election. None of us is safe. The time may call for some kind of preemptive sequestration."

"Like a jury in a murder trial."

"It seems that's what the Court's becoming, alas—a jury vulnerable to tampering." Fox stopped, studying Matt's face. "I'm sorry—I think I am upsetting you."

"No, I have worse fears than that. In a way, the heart attack put everything in perspective."

"Worse fears? Do you want to talk about it?"

Matt had never spoken with Fox about anything personal, but he needed a confessor, someone outside the family who wouldn't judge him unduly harshly for what he was about to say. "I've learned something about myself these past days," he said, "something that disturbs me."

Fox leaned close again. "What is it?"

"That death is seductive. I never told you this, but I was in a serious car accident when I was eighteen. I was drunk and hit a tree. I almost died. Part of me wanted to—to avoid the consequences, I guess. In the end there were no real consequences, legal or physical. I recovered fully. But I tasted death back then and it didn't taste so bad, and that's what frightened me. This time it was even more seductive—I kept having a vision of a beautiful forest where I could rest."

"Maybe that's a reward for leading such a good life."

"If I've had such a good life, wouldn't I want to resist my own death?"

"You did. You're still alive, aren't you?"

"Good point," Matt admitted just as Jessie opened the door and announced their five minutes were up.

From a window of Air Force One, Lyndon watched the skyline of Dallas emerge through a thick layer of smog. The city stretched endlessly in all directions, not a blot on the landscape but the landscape itself. It was nature that didn't belong here. He found Dallas an ugly, charmless city, but he was prejudiced. When he was fifteen, his parents shipped him off to an elite Dallas boys' school where he boarded with the sons of oilmen and ranchers. He became the butt of their tasteless pranks—cow shit under the pillow, a dead mouse in his shoe— until he finally pleaded racism and won the right to a single room. The bad boys then turned elsewhere, turned on each other, a process he observed with glee.

Those were hard years. To survive, he devoted himself to learning, studying the chemistry of cunning, the social physics of propulsion. He propelled himself to Princeton. Now there was no more time to learn, except perhaps about desire, the subject one never masters.

He had crossed an invisible border with Trudy. The infatuation was over, the daring sex, but he needed her more, not less. It was the way she settled into his body, lay her head on his shoulder, listened to him. He could see the top of her head a few seats in front of him. He wished she was closer so he could catch her eye, but then someone might notice, someone tuned into the force field of their desire.

"Tell me again, Lyndon," she said last night after their lovemaking. "Let's go over every detail one more time."

And so he ran through it again. "Just remember that sometimes you have to stray from the plan," he concluded. "No matter how much you rehearse the details, something happens and you have to improvise."

"You think I don't know that? I'm just nervous. I have to fix on something."

"I'm fixing on you," he said as his fingers traced her breast, "the details of you."

He broke out of his reverie when the plane landed and they taxied to the gate. As he disembarked behind the President, he noticed how his suit jacket fit a little too snugly around the shoulders. He was getting pudgy, compressing downwards, posture going to hell. He walked just straight enough to pass for sober, but Lyndon knew he'd been drinking last night.

In the limo Lyndon sat beside the speech coach, Jerry Fine, facing the President and Trudy. He noted with a certain satisfaction that she placed her leather purse between her and her husband, a small but tangible barrier. As they drove into town, Jerry reminded the President of what he was supposed to say in his first stop at the Dallas Public Library. Today's theme was domestic policy.

"Great to be back in Dallas, a city that invests in its people," Jerry said with his characteristic smiley-face intonation. "The best investments in a community are the ones the community makes itself. Little government works best for the little guy. Got it?" The President nodded, but Lyndon wasn't sure he was really taking it in.

As Lyndon watched the passing cars out the window, the dream he had last night came back to him. He was a little boy watching his father weed the garden, but when he moved closer he saw that instead of weeds, his father was pulling up flowers he had recently planted. "Don't watch me," his father said sternly. "Go help your mother." But Lyndon couldn't move. He felt paralyzed, as if his feet were growing into the ground and soon his father would have to uproot him too.

The dream unnerved him. When he shaved in the morning, his hand was unsteady and he nicked his chin. He pressed a Kleenex to the cut to stop the blood from running.

Blood on Trudy's pink suit. One of the details. She should stand close to the President, but not too close, and then rush to him.

"Hand me a Coke, will you, Lyndon," the President's voice cut through. "I'm thirsty as hell." Lyndon took a can from the limo's fridge. It was lukewarm, but the President wouldn't complain. On the campaign trail he had learned to drink Coke at any temperature.

The crowd at the Dallas Public Library was smaller than anticipated. Minus the press, there were maybe a hundred people milling around the reflection pool. The Secret Service shepherded the President and Trudy to the podium where the head librarian, a Chicana named Carmen Sanchez, was waiting to greet them. Lyndon waited by the limo, surveying the scene. Sanchez's handshake was less than enthusiastic, he noted, but her smile was good enough. Wooing the Hispanic vote was the purpose of the stop. Sanchez was well respected in the community, an up-by-the-bootstraps kind of girl, except now she was a middle-aged woman, graying and a bit dumpy in her plaid pant suit. It didn't matter; she made Trudy look good.

He watched Trudy edge away from her husband. A little further, he wanted to tell her, a few more inches just in case. But it was too late now. The play was in motion and he didn't even know the exact details of the script. Skip was in charge now. His eyes skimmed the library roof, taking in the usual contingent of sharpshooters. Could he trust Skip? Were his hands too full with the hunt for Edwards? And then there were the photographs. It turned his stomach to think of anyone looking at them. He started to break into a sweat and took off his jacket and hung it on his arm. His wallet and keys felt heavy in his pocket.

Look at her up there. She was the one with charisma now, not her husband. He prided himself on that. He was making her into something, providing her with an occasion she could rise to, like Jackie. His parents had loved Jackie more than Jack, loved her class. Trudy could learn that kind of class, he was sure of it. It wasn't so hard. Maxwell had taught him class, showed him how to tame his eagerness in favor of the subdued response. The good professor regretted it now, no doubt.

"I'm so happy to be back in this great city of Dallas," the President began "this city that knows how to invest in its people. Look at this beautiful library. The best investments for a community are the ones that a community makes itself. My good friend Carmen Sanchez here understands that." He gestured for Carmen to take his side on the podium and put an arm around her shoulder. It was a spontaneous gesture, a detail they hadn't planned for. "Just last year Carmen and her board raised more than three million dollars from the Dallas business community to update the library's computer system. Let's give Carmen and her board a hand. Let's give the great city of Dallas a hand..."

The President crumpled as the bullet hit his hip. Trudy rushed over from one side, bodyguards from another. All as it should be, Lyndon thought, until a second bullet narrowly missed the President and hit Carmen instead.

A gentle rain was starting to fall as Lisa kept watch from the porch in the late afternoon. The smell of fresh damp earth reminded her of the farm, and of Sam. If all went well, he would be able to come back to DC soon. And if it didn't? She understood herself well enough to know she was in denial about the effect her death would have on him. She couldn't go there, couldn't imagine him growing up with Kevin or her parents. The feelings of guilt would overwhelm her. For the last eight years of her life, she had waged an unremitting battle against maternal guilt and she couldn't afford to cede any of the territory she'd gained, especially today when so much hung in the balance. As soon as it got dark, they were taking Toby to a black-owned TV station in Wilmington where he would deliver his confession.

Rain. The beginning of a puddle where the gutter downspout was blocked. Heavier rain was predicted for later that night. The dirt road would be slippery, the creek high. Henry insisted they take his truck since no one would be looking or it. He was with Toby and Nick in the barn, checking over the truck one last time and putting a camper cover on the back.

Lisa leaned over the porch rail, catching a few drops of water in her hand. She wished she could call Sam and hear his voice. The night they left D.C. she left a message on her parents' voice mail, telling them she was going away for a few days' vacation. That's all they knew. All they might ever know.

At the edge of the woods she spotted a movement. Maybe a deer—a small herd of them had grazed in the meadow this morning. She took the gun from her pocket and pointed in that direction, but couldn't see much through the rain. Was that flash a white tail or white shirt? A few moments later a figure emerged from the trees, a tall man waving something white. As he drew closer, she recognized Tom Dougherty.

"Put down the gun, Lisa," he called as he approached the porch, but she kept it aimed at his chest. "Please," he said, waving the white handkerchief more forcefully. "Put down the gun. I've come to help you."

She let her arm drop. "How did you find us?" she asked as he mounted the steps. His clothes were soaked and splattered with mud, and he was breathing fast as if he'd been running.

"They're checking all of Mohammed's relations. They would have been here before me, if it wasn't for the chaos. I managed to slip away."

"What chaos?"

Dougherty looked incredulous. "You don't know? The President was shot this morning in Dallas. He's in the hospital and there's a national state of emergency. A woman standing with him on the podium took a second bullet and she's dead. Where's Edwards?"

"In the barn, getting ready to leave," Lisa said. "We're heading out this evening. We've got a TV studio ready for us in Wilmington."

"It's too late for that—there's a news blackout except for what Homeland Security approves for broadcast. I've got a safe house lined up for us in Richmond."

"Toby doesn't trust you—he hardly trusts us," Lisa told him. "We wanted to leave yesterday, but he refused."

"Well, we have to move now. They'll be here soon. You can't stay and you've got nowhere else to go. Listen to the radio if you don't believe me. There's a state of emergency."

"I believe you." Toby's voice startled Lisa. He had slipped around from the side of the house and was standing on the grass. In the morning he'd trimmed his hair and beard, but the rain made him look as bedraggled as before. "We just heard the news on the radio, but that doesn't mean I trust you, Mr. Dougherty."

"Why not, Toby? Why did you run? You were safe with me."

"I was never safe and you know it."

"Safer than you are now. I found out who gave the orders, Toby. When the time's right, we can bring them down. But right now we have to hide you again—wait out the state of emergency."

"How long?"

"I wish I knew. All I know is I've got to get you out of here fast. My car is parked in the woods. Let's go."

"They know your car," Lisa said. "We have a truck in the barn. It's better to take that."

As they hurried to the barn, fog was wafting into the meadow, making it hard to see the ground. Lisa stumbled once, but caught herself. Inside she introduced Dougherty to Henry and explained that they all had to leave immediately. Henry didn't want to go, but Dougherty told him he was no longer safe. The army could arrive any minute. While they finished packing the truck, Lisa stood guard by the barn door, peering through a gap between two boards. The fog was so thick it was impossible to see the drive, but she thought she heard a motor in the distance. She drew Dougherty over. "You're right," he agreed. "Everyone get in the truck."

"No, I'm going out to talk to whoever it is," Henry insisted. "I'll try to put them off, but if I can't, just take off."

Henry opened the barn door just wide enough to get out while Dougherty stood to the side, his pistol pointed at it. Wedged between Nick and Toby in the truck, Lisa counted the minutes. Maybe they're searching the house, she thought, hoping there was nothing inside that would give them away. At what point should they try to escape? Nick's hands gripped the wheel as if they were already on the road. She touched his arm and they exchanged a brief glance.

Suddenly, Dougherty gestured that someone was coming. A few minutes later she heard Henry shouting. "I told you there's nothing in there."

Another voice. "If there's nothing in there, why won't you open the door? Open it or we'll have to knock it down."

"I have a studio in there. I make stained glass."

"Sure you do, old man. Just open the fucking door."

Dougherty pressed himself against the wall as the door slid open. He let

Henry step inside before he started firing at the soldiers. They answered with a burst of automatic gunfire and then there was a loud explosion. Nick turned the key and pressed the accelerator. The truck shot forward as a propane tank caught fire, sending flames shooting up the wall. "Stop!" Dougherty yelled as they bucketed out of the barn. Two soldiers lay on the ground outside, wounded or killed, Lisa couldn't tell. "Henry's shot! We've got to get him out."

They ran back into the barn. The whole wall was on fire now. Black smoke choked their lungs as they cast around blindly for Henry. Lisa heard a moan and worked her way toward it. A flaming board fell in front of her in a shower of sparks. "Over here!" she screamed to the others as she reached the work bench. "He's over here!" Together they dragged him out and lifted him into the back of the truck. One of his pant legs was drenched with blood. Nick slashed it open with a pen knife. There was a bullet hole in Henry's wiry thigh muscle; it seemed to have gone in on an angle and missed the bone. He pulled off his shirt and wrapped Henry's leg with it. "I'll ride with him," Lisa said.

As they started up the drive, she looked through the back window. In the fog she could just make out flames creeping along the barn roof. It was raining harder now—maybe it would slow the progress of the fire. "My window," Henry whispered as he drifted into unconsciousness. "Can you save my window?"

"Yes," she lied as she stroked his forehead. With her other hand she clutched her gun, worried that a bump might thrust it out of her hand.

Nick drove fast until they reached the creek. It was swollen with rain and running fast, almost impassable, but he gunned the engine and they made it across. It grew even foggier as they passed through the swamplands, forcing them to slow down. Even so the tires slid on the muddy road, threatening to plunge the truck into a ditch. There were still a few miles to go, and even the highway wouldn't be safe.

Nick didn't see the army jeep until it was almost upon them. He swerved past it, the truck's right tires slamming into the side of the ditch where they spun, then gripped, then spun and gripped again. The jeep turned to pursue them. Lisa ducked down just as a spray of bullets shattered the back window. "Better learn how to use a gun," her father had told her. "You need to protect yourself. You need to protect Sam."

She imagined his hand on her arm, guiding her. He was helping her to aim. Aim for the tires, Lisa. She lifted her head a few inches and through a hole in the glass shot out the front right tire of the jeep.

17

At 9:00 PM on the dot Faith Jones sat down at her desk, waiting for Henry's daily call. Typically they exchanged only a few words, but it was a signal that all was OK. If he didn't call, she was supposed to leave immediately with Samira and Ali. A minute passed, then two. Henry's years working for the military had made him the most punctual person she knew. To calm her nerves, she started stacking the mail on the desk: bills on one side, catalogues on another. In the process she uncovered the initials Jackson carved into the wood when he was about Ali's age. A big, bold JJ. She wanted to punish him for it, but Paul had dissuaded her. "A boy that age needs to leave his mark," he said. Jackson had left his mark, all right, not by his life but by his death.

Another minute passed, then another. Ali and Samira were sitting in front of the TV, watching the scene the networks were playing over and over again, the First Lady holding her husband, the skirt of her pink suit splattered with blood. Maybe it was uncharitable of her, but Faith felt a lot sorrier for the librarian. She was dead after all. The President was just wounded. He should have been the one who got killed. After all, Jackson was murdered on his watch.

Lord have mercy on my soul for having such thoughts, she rebuked herself, then checked her watch again. Five after nine. "Turn off the TV and get your bags," she told Samira and Ali. "If cousin Henry doesn't call in five minutes, we're leaving."

"But Grandma…"

"It doesn't mean anything's wrong, Ali. We just have to take care. We'll come back as soon as we can."

"But I got a baseball game tomorrow."

"You think I don't know that, child?"

At ten past nine they headed out the back door just as a police car turned into the street. Keeping to the bushes and back alleyways, they walked the five blocks to Reverend Lee's house behind the church. The light was on in the kitchen and Faith peered in the window. The Reverend was sitting at the table, eating a big bowl of ice cream. Faith tapped on the window. "Reverend," she called through the screen, "please let us in."

"What the devil are you doing at my back window, Faith Jones? Don't you know I have a front door?"

"Let us in, please. I'll explain."

"What's going on?" he asked as he opened the kitchen door. "Why are you carrying those bags?"

"The police are looking for us, Reverend. We need sanctuary in the church."

"In the church?"

"Yes, in the church," she replied emphatically and then went to the window and pulled down the blind.

"But why, Faith?" The Reverend was flustered. "You have to explain first. You can't just…"

Faith glanced disapprovingly at the way his bathrobe parted over his belly, revealing his boxer shorts. Sheepishly, he turned to the side and quickly rewrapped the robe and tightened the sash. "Your wife Millie was my best friend, Reverend Lee," Faith said, meeting his eye. "She would never turn me and these children away from your door."

"I know that, Faith, but I can't break the law."

"What law do you answer to, Reverend Lee? God's law or the government's?"

"Fortunately, they usually coincide."

"I'm surprised to hear you say that, Reverend. Did they coincide when they turned the water hoses on us? It wasn't so long ago, you know. You stood on the front line, do you remember that? Millie told me it was the proudest moment of her life, to see you there, linking arms with Reverend King and the other brave men. You knew which law mattered back then."

"That was a different time."

"Well, I'm telling you that time is back again. They lynched my son, Reverend, and all I'm trying to do is to bring his killers to justice. There's nothing wrong with that, nothing against God's law. Now get the boy a bowl of ice cream, please, while Samira and I find some bedding. We'll sleep in the church basement, in the Sunday school room. You just give me the key and we'll take care of everything else."

"What if they come looking for you?"

"You lie. You tell them you don't know where we are."

"I never lie."

"Oh, is that so?" Faith stared hard at him. "Millie confided in me, Reverend. She told me a few things I wouldn't want the boy to hear."

Reverend Lee turned toward the refrigerator. "What kind of ice cream you want, son?"

The pool lights were the only ones on when Lyndon pulled into the driveway of the suburban ranch house in Vienna, Virginia, where Skip had arranged to meet him. He walked around back, entering the yard through a gate in the tall stockade fence. Skip was in the pool, swimming laps. He lifted his head to acknowledge Lyndon's arrival, but kept swimming. He had a strong but inelegant stroke with a kick that made too much of a splash. Lyndon sat in one of the deck chairs and closed his eyes. If Skip could take a moment's respite, so could he. This had been one of the longest days of his life. "Go back to Washington," Trudy told him after the President came out of surgery. "I'll manage here." He knew she would keep her part of the bargain, but could he?

Skip lifted himself out of the pool and shook off like a dog. He was wearing a skimpy bathing suit that revealed more than it hid. He grabbed a towel and wrapped it around his waist. "Sorry to keep you waiting," he said sitting next to Lyndon. "I set myself a goal of fifty laps."

"Whose house is this?"

"A friend's—he lets me use the pool when he's out of town."

"Any chance the place is bugged?"

"I checked already and it's clean." Skip leaned back, running his fingers through his hair like a comb. In the bluish glow cast by the pool he looked sallow despite his tan.

"So tell me, Skip, why the second bullet?" Lyndon began.

"It wasn't ours."

"Then whose was it?"

"Your guess is as good as mine."

"A terrorist?"

"That's what Homeland Security thinks. But it could be some crank. Dalla is full of crazies, would-be Oswalds."

"A pretty strange coincidence, wouldn't you say?"

"Yes, I would say that." Skip reached for a T-shirt and pulled it over his head "I wondered if you were behind it, Lyndon."

"Me?"

"You could have your reasons. You're screwing the man's wife, for one. And if he departs from the scene, you just might become the new candidate. We a know the VP doesn't have what it takes, upstairs or down. No brain, no balls, bad combination."

"You forget the color of my skin, Skip."

"Maybe the country's ready for a black man. It might give the party an edge on the Democrats."

"I wouldn't want to be the one to test those waters."

"Why not?"

Lyndon paused. There were so many answers to that question, answers tha Skip, or any white man for that matter, would never understand. He gave the easy one. "I prefer the role I'm in."

"Yeah, I guess you already are the president, in a manner of speaking—in bed and out."

"Let's leave Trudy out of this."

"You put her into it, Lyndon, not me."

"Fuck you, Skip."

"Fuck you, Mr. President." Their eyes met, but neither backed down. "OK truce," Skip said at last. "Just tell me what we're supposed to do now."

"Fill me in on Edwards first."

"We found him, but he got away."

"Again?"

"Bad timing. We were zeroing in, but then the guys at Fort Bragg got dis tracted when they heard about the President. They didn't notice when Dougherty gave them the slip. They caught up, but it was too late."

"What do you mean, too late?"

"Edwards and the others got away in a truck. Two of our guys got seriously hurt. Dougherty shot them. One of theirs got shot too—old black guy, one of Mohammed's relations. They took him with them."

"You've got to find them."

"You think I don't know that?" He glared at Lyndon. "You put too much on my plate, you know. Way too much. When I was in the pool, I had a fantasy that you were in there with me and I held you underwater. When I finally let you up for air, you gasped and said, 'Thank you, Skip. Thank you for all you've done for me.'"

"Is that supposed to be a threat?"

"A fantasy, like I said. A man's entitled to a few fantasies, isn't he?"

Lyndon stood up abruptly. "Get in touch as soon as you hear anything about Edwards."

"Yessir, boss."

"Don't call me boss," Lyndon said as he turned away.

"One more thing, boss. That second bullet—I did order it."

"What?" Lyndon spun around. "Why did you do that? We agreed on one—only one."

Skip shrugged. "For good measure."

"What do you mean for good measure? You killed a woman."

"I thought you should have a little more blood on your hands."

"The blood's on your hands."

"No, no, no. You've got that wrong, boss. You give the orders. I just obey."

Matt rolled over in bed to face the sunlight streaming through the window. His body was restless and twitchy, energy returning to him in fits and starts so that he felt like a sputtering engine. He'd recovered enough now that Dora and Jessie no longer had to spend the night in the hospital. It was a relief to wake up alone, to have a few minutes to himself before the nurses descended on him. Last night they hadn't been able to keep it from him that the President had been shot, and he had insisted, against everyone's advice, on watching the news. But this wasn't news, it was propaganda. A state of emergency, as defined in the second Citizen Defense Act. The President had the executive power, for a period of up to thirty days, to suspend freedom of speech with no judicial review. He reached for the phone. It was only 6:30, but he knew Fox was an early riser.

When Fox picked up, Matt could hear a broadcast in the background. "I've got the BBC on the internet," Fox told him.

"Tell me what's going on."

"Some Islamic group no one's ever heard of is claiming credit for the assassination attempt."

"Do you think it's true?"

"I don't know what to think. It's interesting that both bullets missed their mark. They're playing up the President's injury, but a bullet in the hip is not life threatening. Some of the more cynical European commentators are suggesting that it might have been staged."

"By whom?"

"The implication is that it's the President's own men."

Matt paused to absorb this. "Do you think they're right?"

"Anything's possible—even probable, given what's going on. Why else would they muzzle the press? They don't want any speculation." Now Fox paused for a moment. "The point is, Matt, we may never know who shot those bullets. But we do know the administration's going to make the most out of this. They've already declared a state of emergency. They might try to postpone the election too. We're going to have to do something."

"Have you spoken to the others?"

"I talked to Lovins last night. He wants to meet with us as soon as you're out of the hospital. I suggested we not meet at the Court. We could come to your house if it's OK with Dora."

"I'll start working on her. She knows I won't be able to sit by."

"But you do have to be careful. Your health is more important than—"

"It's funny," Matt interrupted, "but I'm feeling better today. I guess the political adrenaline's good for me. I'm looking out the window now and I want to be outside."

"That's good, Matt, but one step at a time."

"That's what they told me when I got out of bed yesterday after you left. I walked halfway down the hall, but my legs felt like rubber. They made me turn back. I'm going to do the whole hall today."

"Justice Pomeroy," Matt heard the chirpy voice of Susan, his least favorite nurse. She was too tight, too nice, with the passive-aggressive manner of a stewardess who has served too many meals. "Time to check your vitals."

"I've got to get off," he told Fox, "but I'll call you later." After he hung up, he dutifully stretched out his arm.

"It's just so sad about the President," the nurse said. "Did you see those pictures of his wife? I feel so sorry for her."

———————

Nick willed himself not to think of anything but the task before him as he and Lisa helped Henry to lie down on the kitchen table, which was covered with a sheet pulled from one of the beds in the safe house. Toby was upstairs and refused to come down. Probably for the best, Nick thought. He was barely functioning, speaking in cryptic sentences when he spoke at all. His eyes had the look of a man lost in his own private world. Getting him to talk publicly would be a major challenge now. But he shouldn't think about Toby; that task belonged to the future. All that mattered now was removing the bullet from Henry's leg. Because of the angle, the bullet wasn't lodged deep, but the wound was already starting to look inflamed. A hospital was out of the question. All the emergency rooms in the southeast would be on alert for old black men with bullet wounds. Fortunately, Dougherty had possessed the foresight to stock the house with medications and a good first-aid kit. Without them Henry's situation would be much worse than it was.

Steady your mind, Nick told himself, so you can steady your hands. He was the only one with any paramedic training—a short course during his stint in the military. But that was a long time ago. Although Henry was sedated with painkillers, he was still conscious and Nick worried about how the old man would react to the pain. Lisa was holding Henry's hand, Dougherty standing by to assist. Nick said a silent prayer as he picked up the knife. After he made the first incision, he told Dougherty to use sterile gauze to stem the flow of blood. Henry remained still until the second cut. "Lord have mercy!" he cried out. "Give me something to bite down on, will you." Lisa fetched a folded dish cloth and put it in his mouth. Dougherty handed Nick the long tweezers. As he poked around for the bullet, Henry's body began to writhe.

"Hold on," Nick told him. "If you can just stay still, it'll be over soon." Henry said something, but his voice was muffled by the cloth. "Just stay still," Nick repeated. He willed his own hands to stay steady as he trapped the bullet between the ends of the tweezers and drew it slowly out.

"Well done," Dougherty said as he pressed some fresh gauze against the wound. Nick dressed and bandaged his handiwork, and they carried Henry from the table to the living room couch. They gave him another painkiller and after a little while he fell asleep.

Leaving the others to clean up, Nick went over to the window and pulled back the curtain a few inches to look out. His hands were shaking now, and he felt chilled even though it was warm in the house. The grass outside seemed unnatural. You could still see lines between the blocks of sod. A backhoe was digging in a lot down the street, but otherwise there was no one in sight. The safe house was the first in a planned subdivision of mini McMansions on the outskirt of Richmond. No one knew about the house, Dougherty assured them. He bought it last year under an assumed name as a retreat of last resort, hidden even from his closest colleagues. The furnishings were spare, but there was a car in the garage registered in a false name.

Nick glanced at his watch. Two in the afternoon. He'd lost track of time. Probably he was hungry, but the idea of food repelled him. Lisa joined him at the window and put her arm around his waist. "What are we going to do now?" he asked her.

"I wish I knew. I wish there was an easy answer. At least you got the bullet out."

"They'll track us down here too. It's only a matter of time. We have a day or two, max."

"Do you regret what we've done?"

"What do you mean?" he asked, turning to look at her. Her face was haggard, her hair wet and stringy from the shower. Noticing blood on her shirtsleeve, he gazed down at his own arms. Blood there too—he would have to wash himself off more carefully.

"I feel like I pushed you into this."

"Well, you didn't. If anything, I made you take me along so I could share the risk. The only question I ask myself is whether that was a mistake—whether my willingness drew you into this further than you wanted to go."

She shook her head. "Don't blame yourself. It wasn't you."

"Then what was it?"

"I don't know exactly. It's hard to sort out the reasons. Senator Barrett's death maybe. I felt I owed it to her. What about you?"

"A sense of purpose, I guess. You have no idea what it's like to live without that. I wasted so much of my life." He gazed out the window again. The backhoe ad moved but otherwise the world seemed unnaturally still. If there was a wind, e wouldn't know because there were no trees, no leaves to rustle. "We need to alk to Dougherty, figure out a strategy."

"I think we need to decide on a strategy first and then present it to him."

"Why?"

"Toby trusts us more than he trusts him. We have to take charge, Nick, or e's going to bolt. I can feel it."

"I worry that he's already left."

"What do you mean?"

"He's not in his right mind. I wish I knew him better—I wish I could reach im."

"You persuaded him last time."

"I don't know if I can do it again." Nick let the curtain fall from his hands. We need a video camera so we can film him," he told her. "He may only be lucid or a few minutes, a few hours if we're lucky, and when he is, we need to record is confession. That may be our only hope."

18

Lisa leaned her head back in the sink. "Is the water too cold?" the hairdresser asked. She was a woman named Meg, in her late twenties or early thirties, with a Cleopatra haircut that looked incongruous on her round, chubby face. She had a soothing voice.

"A little too hot, actually," Lisa replied. Her scalp already burned from the peroxide in the dye.

"It's hard to get the temperature right. Is that OK?"

The water was still too hot, but Lisa didn't complain. She needed this to be over fast. She felt vulnerable with her head tipped back into a sink, but at least there wasn't a surveillance camera inside the beauty salon. She spotted three of them at the electronics store where she bought the video camera.

After she finished the wash, Meg wrapped Lisa's hair in a towel and led her back to her station for the cut. Tucked into the mirror was a photo of a kid about Sam's age, dressed in a Little League uniform and swinging a bat that looked too big for him. Next to him was picture of a little girl in a ruffled dress. Ordinarily, Lisa would have asked the hairdresser about her kids, but with Sam so far away it was too painful. When Meg was done cutting and drying her hair, Lisa took a long look at herself in the mirror. Her hair was bleached almost white, and the short, austere cut made her face look sharper and meaner. With a pair of glasses, she'd look at least ten years older. She wondered for a moment if Sam would rec-

ognize her when, or if, he saw her again. She wished she had the freedom to con
fess to the hairdresser that she had abandoned her son, but such confidence
belonged to a different time, to a world that no longer existed.

Meg was astute enough to see the regret in her face, but assumed it was dis
pleasure about her hair. "Do you like it?" she asked tentatively. "It makes you look
really professional."

"Good. I'm applying for a new job," Lisa replied.

"In what?"

She thought for a moment. "Life insurance."

"I bet that's a good business these days. Everyone's so nervous, especially after
they shot the President in Dallas. Do you think there's going to be another attack
like 9/11? Is that why they postponed the election?"

"They postponed the election?" Lisa asked in surprise.

"Didn't you know? It was on TV about an hour ago. They said the President
needs at least a month to recover from the shooting. But that's probably just an
excuse, don't you think?"

"I don't know what to think any more."

"Neither do I. My husband says they're all a bunch of liars."

"Politicians usually are."

"There, all done," Meg said as she unfastened the nylon cape around Lisa's
shoulders. Lisa gave her a nice tip, and then paid at the counter and headed out
into the crowded corridor of the mall. There was a certain safety in numbers, she
thought as she joined the flow of anonymous Saturday shoppers. In the café
square a couple of cops were standing by a faux marble fountain, their attention
directed at a group of black teenagers jostling each other in line at Taco Bell.
There was also a certain safety in being white, she told herself, but then she stared
up into the eye of another surveillance camera.

She looked at her watch: 2:50. Nick was supposed to pick her up at 3:00 in
the parking lot in front of Sears. He was driving the Toyota Dougherty had stored
in the garage. It was their first trip out, a big risk, but they had to get the camera.
She entered Sears and spent a few minutes looking through a rack of summer
shirts on sale, pretending to inspect the price tags. A saleswoman eyed her bag
and she moved on, toward the door. At 3:00 she pushed it open to a blast of hot
air. Nick wasn't there.

She waited a few minutes and then walked down a row of cars, searching for
him, the asphalt spongy under her feet. Her stomach tightened with dread

Probably he was just stuck at a traffic light, but what if they caught him? Where would she go? Richmond was close enough to Washington that they might routinely scan the footage from the mall's surveillance cameras with face recognition software. How long did she have—a few minutes, a few hours, a few days?

She heard a vehicle pulling up behind her and turned to find a mall security van. She reached into the side pocket of her purse, putting a hand on her gun. The guard lowered the window. "Lost your car?" he asked.

"No, just waiting for my husband."

"Just checking. There've been a lot of thefts around here lately. Lock up and don't leave things on the seat where they can see them. They'll break the window if they have to."

"Thanks," she said, and he pulled away. She retreated to the Sears doorway, standing in the shade of the awning. She was hot and thirsty and her hair smelled of dye. She looked at her watch again: 3:15. Where was he?

At 3:30 the security van passed through again. "Still waiting for your husband?" the guard asked.

"Afraid so."

"Better go inside. It just hit a hundred degrees. Let him find you."

From the corner of her eye she spotted the Toyota pulling into the lot, but he didn't let on. "Good advice," she told the guard. "I'll give him a couple more minutes."

It was Dougherty, not Nick, who drove up to the Sears entrance. "Get in quick," he said as he opened the door. "Was that guy questioning you?"

"He was just telling me it was too hot to be outside. Where's Nick? Why are you late?"

He checked the rearview mirror before pulling out into the line of cars. "I've got bad news. Toby's disappeared. Nick's looking for him."

"What?"

"He snuck out when Nick and you left. I should have kept an eye on him, but Henry was watching TV and called me over. They postponed the election, you know."

"I just heard."

"That's what they've been planning all along."

"Did Toby take the truck?"

"No. He's on foot. Nick searched the neighborhood, but there's no sign of him anywhere."

"I bought the camera," she said.

He looked at her dispassionately. "It won't be much use unless we find him." He checked the rearview mirror again. "Watch the right side for me, will you. If they get Toby, it won't be long before they're on to us."

Done. The election was postponed. Until the President makes a full recovery and the security situation improves enough to lift the state of emergency. Indefinitely, in other words, words Lyndon instructed the White House press secretary not to use.

He should feel relieved, he told himself as he took a breather in his office. He had been preparing for this for so long. But ever since his last encounter with Skip, he had been feeling disoriented, as if his biological clock was out of whack. He found himself looking at his watch every ten minutes to remind himself what time it was and where he was supposed to be. Even at night he woke up frequently to check the time like an anxious traveler about to embark on an early morning journey. He hoped Trudy might shake him out of it, bring the relief he was starting to crave.

But maybe relief, like the election, would also have to be postponed. There were already reports of angry demonstrations in the usual hotspots—New York, Boston, Seattle, and San Francisco. He worried little about them; the National Guard would do their job and most of the rabble-rousers were already in preventive detention. What worried him the most was Hartley. Lyndon had just received word that the Democrat was on a plane bound for Montreal, in a self imposed exile meant to protest the administration's actions. Lyndon wasn't sure whether it was better to have him out of the country or not. And then there were the other wildcards: Edwards was still missing, Pomeroy was still alive, and the President was at a private evangelical rehab center. Only he and Trudy knew he was there to dry out. Even the Vice President assumed he was doing post-surgical physical therapy. Would he dry out? That was the million-dollar question.

Lyndon looked at his watch again. It was exactly ten minutes later than the last time he checked. He slipped the watch off his wrist and into his pocket.

Trudy was waiting in the den, listening to a bluesy female vocalist. As he sat next to her on the couch, he thought back to their first kiss. It seemed ages ago, another era. She looked different tonight, more intentionally stylish and less the little girl. She had on a black velvet top he hadn't seen before, draped with a silk scarf of marbled turquoise and purple. Her hair was tied back with a gold ribbon. "So how is he?" Lyndon asked. She was just back from visiting the President.

"We shouldn't have sent him there, Lyndon."

"What do you mean?"

"He's given up, or rather he's given himself to Jesus." She curled herself into a corner of the sofa and pulled her knees to her chest. "He wants to get well, but he says he has no worldly ambition left. He says he even wants to step down from the Presidency."

"What?"

"He told Brendon and me that Jesus has told him to step down." Lyndon tried a laugh, but instead made an ugly choking sound. "You forget he takes his religion seriously, not like you and me."

"We should have never sent him to a Christian place."

"It's the only one he would go to. He's born again—again. I know, I can see it in his eyes. When he's like this, he makes up his mind and no one can change it."

"We have to change it. We have time…"

"I don't think he's going to come around, no matter what you do."

Lyndon's head felt so heavy he let it drop. He stared at his feet, noticing his socks were mismatched, one dark brown, the other black. A bad sign. That's all there were these days—bad signs. The dollar was in free fall. The news hadn't broken officially because there was no news, but word was starting to leak out that Phil Douglas was resigning as Chairman of the Federal Reserve. Bolting was a better way to describe it. Yesterday he had a shouting match with Lyndon, getting on a high horse about democracy of all things. "In case you haven't noticed, Lyndon, capitalism needs democracy, just like democracy needs capitalism."

How many others would bolt? Lyndon wondered. How many would stay loyal to a President who wasn't functioning? He felt Trudy's hand on his shoulder. "Overwhelmed?" she asked softly. He nodded, still looking at the floor. The toe of his shoe was scuffed. "Look at it as an opportunity, Lyndon. The President steps down, you step up."

"To what?"

"You're in charge."

"I've been in charge for a long time."

"But you need to own it, really own it."

"How?"

"Sit up and look at me." He acquiesced, but his head was still heavy. He felt dizzy and sweat was forming on his brow. "No, I mean really look at me," she insisted.

"I don't feel well."

"Look at me, Lyndon." She cupped her hands around his face. "Now what do you see?"

"Plain you," he said in the voice he used when they made love. "And you see plain me."

She shook her head. "No, I don't."

"What do you see then?"

"The first black president."

"Don't delude yourself."

"No, really. Just think what you could be without him. You had to do all those bad things to make up for his weakness, but if you didn't have to do that you could be strong the way you want to be. You could be a real leader. It's the same with me, Lyndon. I want to know who I am without him. I'm going to leave him once he's well enough."

"He'll never be well."

"He's in love with Jesus, not me." She paused. "Do you know how hard that is to take, day in, day out?"

"He's in love with alcohol."

"He's in love with them both. Alcohol is sin, Jesus redemption. But you're not like him, Lyndon. You don't need Jesus."

"That's because I never thought I was sinning when I drank. I thought I was weak, so power was my redemption."

"So are you redeemed?"

"Hardly. The irony is I really am a sinner now."

"Because he forced you to be one."

"No one forced me, Trudy. I did it myself. Because I wanted power—or rather, I needed it."

"Do you still need it?"

There was a tiny speck of brown pigment in her blue, blue eyes, a little imperfection he had come to love, like the mole on her right breast. She knew his imperfections too, the crooked shape of his little toes, the scar left on his arm by an encounter with a fishing hook. Did he still need power? He wasn't sure about that any more, but he knew he still needed her. But would she want him without the power? That was the real question. She must have read his mind, because she dropped her hands from his face and took his hands in hers. "All I really want is plain Lyndon. You know that."

But who was plain Lyndon? The man who was about to make love to her? The myth of the first black president? The murdering schemer Skip wanted to drown? The boy whom Professor Maxwell tried to turn into a man? The addiction itself, the genie in the bottle? Or all those things? No wonder he felt so dizzy...

She took the shimmering scarf from her neck, wrapped it around his, and pulled him toward her. Let her be in charge, he thought, let her lead the way. She kissed him and then told him to lie back. As he let her undress him, he pretended he was the girl across the river at summer camp. He made believe there was grass underneath him, a Texas sky full of stars, the Big Dipper right overhead, pouring sweet elixir into his thirsty mouth. "You're scared," he remembered the girl saying. "A little," he replied. "It's all right to be scared," she whispered, "I was too, the first time."

———

Matt sat down at his desk. He'd been home from the hospital for several days now, but Dora and the doctors forbade him to do any work. She was out at her book group now, leaving him alone for the first time, and the freedom emboldened him. He felt impelled to write in his journal, to record what had just happened. It was, at least potentially, the stuff of history.

He leaned back, surveying the room with its shelves of law books as if it were a foreign country he was revisiting after an absence of many years. Could he still speak the language, understand the culture? More to the point, did he want to? His dramatic decision this morning, was it rooted in moral choice, or did it spring from a desire to leave behind the exactions of judicial life? He decided to leave such personal thoughts aside, and just write about the visit of the four justices. That should be enough to leave for posterity. He picked up a pen and replayed the scene in his head.

They had arrived separately, laden with bouquets of flowers and baskets of fruit, ostensibly on a mission to welcome him home. Dora ushered them into the living room where the curtains were drawn against the possibility of intrusive photographers. He was reclining in his leather reading chair, taking a snooze, but he brought it upright once they were all assembled. Here we are, the unlikely majority, he thought, the liberal triumvirate of Lovins, Merritt, and Jenkins, Fox the libertarian, and himself. What word was there for his own political persuasion now? "Moderate Republican" no longer fit, for there was no such thing as moderation any more. The postponement of the election, announced this morning, had sounded its death knell.

It had been strange to see them all in informal attire, Nancy Merritt slightly ridiculous in a floral sundress that revealed flabby upper arms, and Lovins even more so in shorts that exposed pale, hairy legs. Jenkins wore a sports jacket, but the sleeves were too short. Only Fox looked dapper in one of his linen suits. He began by offering a toast to Matt's health, and Nancy followed with a toast to the majority they still formed on the Court. But then Lovins made the point that their majority was meaningless if the Court couldn't convene during the state of emergency. "The Citizen Defense Act allows them to suspend the normal operations of the government in a state of emergency," he reminded them. "We won't be able to meet to decide on the constitutionality of postponing the election. They planned it that way."

"But what does normal mean?" Nancy challenged. "What if we decide to go into special session? We might be able to get around it. And remember, if they want to suspend freedom of speech beyond thirty days, they require judicial review. Presumably, that means us."

"That's a big presumption," Jenkins weighed in. "I re-read the act yesterday—it doesn't specify at what level of the federal court system such a review would take place."

"They'll probably choose a district court stacked with their cronies," Fox added cynically.

For the next twenty minutes they debated the CDA's provisions and their impact on the Court. Matt listened patiently, but with a growing sense that the conversation was beside the point. Noticing his silence, Fox suggested they give him a chance to speak. He hadn't planned what he was going to say, but it came to him suddenly. "You're debating the wrong point," he began. "As I'm sure Justice Fox has told you, some people think I was poisoned. There's no firm evidence one way or the other, and it's true I have a weak heart. But if I was indeed poisoned, it would suggest that their intent was to change the composition of the Court. Now that they've failed to do that, they may try to prevent us from going into session. But I think it's a mistake to focus too much on that. I'm sure you'll

be surprised to hear me say this, but since they are employing extrajudicial strate-
gies, perhaps we need to too. Perhaps the situation is so dire that we need to more
fully embrace our role as public figures, role models…"

"What do you mean exactly?" Jenkins asked.

"I'm not sure, but we may need to speak out, publicly, without waiting for a
case to become before us."

"But to whom? There's no press."

"There are ways," Fox interjected. "Hartley's in Canada now, giving interviews to the international press."

"Something more dramatic than that," Matt told them. "If only we had
something concrete, some evidence…"

Fox nodded. "Like proof you were poisoned."

"I think we need to go back further than that, to the beginning, to the
Mohammed case. That's when it all began, when they stopped playing by the
rules. If we had prevailed in that case, it would have undermined both Citizen
Defense Acts. But they couldn't let that happen. They wanted the authority to
declare a state of emergency, not because of the threat of terrorism but because of
the threat of losing the election. That's why they had Mohammed killed."

"There's no proof," Jenkins objected.

"I'm sure he was killed. I'm more convinced of that than my own poisoning.
The timing of his death was too convenient. And I'm willing to say so publicly,
even if I have to go to Montreal to do it."

"But, Matt, there's no proof," Jenkins declared, his voice rising. "You're a
Supreme Court Justice. If you make such an allegation on the basis of sheer conjecture, it will diminish you, and diminish the stature of the Court…"

"Let him finish," Fox broke in.

Matt turned to Jenkins. "You're right, of course. And that's why when I speak
out, I'm going to resign."

"But Matt, you can't do that," Lovins exclaimed. "We'll lose our majority—
we'll lose everything."

"What difference does our majority make under this regime? They'll do
whatever they need to do to thwart us. Our only hope is to bring them down."

"It's a risky strategy, Matt. You can speak, but what if nobody listens?"

"I've thought of that, but I have to do it. It's one of the reasons I survived,
you see."

They had looked at him strangely then. No doubt the thought passed through their minds that the heart attack had affected his mind. But then something changed. He noticed it first on Fox's face—an expression of admiration eagerness almost. "Yes," Fox said, nodding his head slowly at first and then more vigorously, "you're right to do it, Matt. It's a courageous step." And then the others nodded in assent. He knew he had made the right decision, the only decision he could make under the circumstances.

But just thinking about it made him tired. How would he get past Dora and the doctors? He hardly had the energy to write in his journal, but he had to leave a record that would justify his actions, in case he wasn't around to defend them in the flesh. And when he was done writing, he would call Jessie. Jessie would help him, and so would Fox. Fox would know how to arrange things. There was no time to lose.

———

Lisa adjusted her pillow yet another time and turned over, envious that Nick somehow had managed to fall asleep. It might be the last time they slept together in the same bed, she thought. Toby could be in custody right now, revealing their location to the authorities. At any moment armed men could storm the house Dougherty was keeping watch downstairs, but they all knew it was pointless "They wouldn't let us out alive," he told them. "If Toby isn't back by tomorrow morning, we have to leave." But where would they go? And how would they manage with Henry? His leg was healing slowly and he could only walk a few steps at a time.

She nestled closer to Nick, wrapping an arm around his waist. He stirred slightly and she remembered what it had been like to wake early in the morning and make love before Sam got up and the day began. Those were the best times when her overactive mind was still sluggish and dreamy, willing to indulge her body and his. She tried to remember what it felt like, but it seemed so long ago. Lately, it was only comfort they sought from each other, and even that was elusive. She touched her head. Her hair was now too short for him to lace his fingers through it, but when was the last time he did that anyway?

"You can't sleep?" he whispered as he rolled over to face her.

"Sorry I woke you up."

"I was just dozing. I've forgotten what it is to really fall asleep."

"Let's pretend we're somewhere else, Nick."

"Where?"

"In the apartment, in my bed, before dawn."

"I don't know if I can."

"Please, Nick. I want to carry a memory with me, just in case. Kiss me and we'll see what happens."

At first it felt like an act of faith, an empty ritual they had to follow. But then he remembered how she conquered fear as a little girl. After she woke from a nightmare, she would lull herself back to sleep by remaking the plot so she was the heroine in charge of the ending. That's what she had to do now—recover her old powers of imagination. Jumpstart the good dream and let its logic take over. Why not? Why not a reprieve from the nightmare?

And so she imagined they were back in her own bed, Sam sound asleep down the hall, Nick waking to her touch. In her waking dream, she slips off her nightgown and kicks down the covers. She likes the pure nakedness, no fabric between his skin and hers. Let them sweat into each other's pores, bleed into each other's veins, two bodies are stronger than one. She is strong, she needs to remember that. Never mind the soft fold of her belly left from bearing Sam, she is strong enough to take Nick into her and hold him as long as he wants, as long as he needs. He cries out and that triumph is the end of the dream.

Except it wasn't. Lying in Nick's arms afterwards, she realized that making love was only a prelude. She fell asleep fantasizing about Toby's return and their escape to somewhere safe.

The sex left Nick wide awake and restless. He stared at the shadows the streetlight made on the wall and thought about Toby. Where was he now? He could have hitched a ride anywhere. Maybe he was sitting next to a trucker, flying down a highway, lying about who he was and where he was going. Yet somehow Nick couldn't imagine Toby talking to strangers. He could barely speak to people he knew. Surely Toby would want to be alone with his demons. The risk was he would let them spirit him away.

Nick understood that kind of depression all too well. He himself had contemplated suicide more than once. The closest he ever came was one evening when he was camping alone on the Maryland shore. A storm at sea had made the water too dangerous for swimming, and during the day the lifeguards shut the beaches down. His body was just starting to recover from its long illness, but with the return of his physical strength came a strange, crazy surge of will, not to live, but to die. At sunset he walked on the beach, searching for a riptide that could

carry him away. He thought he was alone, but just as he started to take off hi
clothes, he spotted a girl and her father walking about fifty yards away. He waite
for them to pass, but the girl stopped to throw a ball for their black lab. She thre
it over and over again. The repetition of her act, the dog dropping the ball obe
diently at her feet, the patience of her father... His will to die seemed so insub
stantial in comparison to their collective will to have their little moment on th
beach. They said nothing to him and never knew they saved his life.

Where was Toby? If he wanted to kill himself, he wouldn't stray far, but the
had scoured the neighborhood and found no sign of him. Where could he hid
in this wasteland of construction? Maybe it was worth searching again. Withou
waking Lisa, he slid out of bed, put on his clothes, and grabbed a flashlight
Downstairs he told Dougherty he was going to look for Toby one last time.

It was muggy outside, only a few degrees cooler than the day, and the star
were obscured by a murky orange haze. Nick walked the empty streets, assigne
the names of flowers that probably would never grow here: Ladyslippe
Columbine, Blue Bonnet. Maybe the houses wouldn't grow either. Maybe th
economy would collapse and the builders go bust and the weeds reclaim th
upturned soil. That would be all right by him. "Toby," he called, "Toby, it's Nick
I've come to talk to you." He strained his ears, but there was no reply.

He passed a lot where the foundation was completed and a stack of two-by
fours was covered with a tarp. He'd checked there in the afternoon, but maybe i
was worth looking again. As he walked toward the foundation, thick dirt clun;
to the bottom of his shoes, slowing his pace. At the foundation's edge, he shon
his flashlight on the floor joists that stretched across it. A rope was tied on one
Of course, this is how Toby would choose to kill himself, Nick thought witl
sudden clarity. The same way he killed Salim Mohammed. He hesitated
moment, summoning the strength to shine the light further down the rope to th
noose, to where he would find Toby with a broken neck.

The blow from a two-by-four came from behind, directed at the side of hi
head. He fell in the dirt and his mouth filled with blood. "Let me die," he hear
Toby's voice above him. "I don't want to hurt you, but you have to let me die.
How close was he? Close enough that Nick could grab his legs and take hin
down? Even then Toby would have the advantage. Nick's head was swimming. I
would take all his energy just to move, but he had to try. The girl and dog on th
beach. The gift of a few minutes of time.

He willed himself to go beyond the sharp pain in his head to the place in hi

nind that centered him. He pretended he was unconscious and listened through
he ground for the sound of Toby's footsteps. Once convinced Nick was out, he
vould hurry to carry through with his plan. How many steps was it to the foun-
lation? Maybe fifteen.

Toby was walking past him now. Nick lunged at his legs. Toby fell on top of
aim and they wrestled, rolling in the dirt. Nick fought hard, but the blow to his
aead slowed his reactions. Finally, Toby pinned him to the ground. Nick tasted
nore blood in his mouth. "What are you going to do with me, Toby? Kill me?"

"I don't know. I don't want to kill anyone else. I just want to die."

"Don't be a fucking coward. Dying's the easy way out. You owe it to
Mohammed's family to stay alive. You owe it to the memory of your fiancée. You
»we it to all of us. You owe it to me."

"What do you mean?"

"There's blood in my mouth just because I tried to keep you from hanging
'ourself. Do you really want to die that way? You've convinced yourself you're
;oing crazy, but you're not. I ought to know. I thought I was crazy once. I almost
Irowned myself. But I didn't do it, and you know what? After that I wasn't crazy
.ny more. My head was clearer than it had been in years. I was sad, but I wasn't
razy. Don't confuse the two, they're not the same." Toby's hold on Nick's shoul-
lers slackened, but then tightened again. Nick forced himself to keep talking.
There was this little girl with a dog on the beach…"

"What are you talking about?" Toby's hands were slackening again.

"I'm talking about how life goes on."

"Mine hasn't."

"It will, Toby, it will."

"I can't talk about this."

"Oh, yes, you can. Talk to me, Toby. Just talk." A few minutes, that's all Nick
vanted. Time enough for Toby's resolve to spend itself. They had forced him to
:ill, but he wasn't really a killer. That much he must know about himself. "Let
ne sit up," Nick urged gently. "I need to spit out this blood. And then we'll talk,
iere where no one can hear us. And then you'll have to help me back to the
iouse. I'm going to have to lean on you, Toby. My head hurts where you hit me."

"I'm sorry."

"It doesn't matter. Just help me up."

———

Faith's hips hurt so much she woke up when she rolled over in the middle of the night. The basement floor was hard and cold, and the mat she was sleeping on was too thin for an old lady. Yet she didn't want to complain because it would set a bad example for Samira and Ali. "It's better than a jail cell," she kept telling them. But the Sunday school room was starting to feel like a prison, even to her. She was desperate for light and air, for the freedom to walk out the door and down the street. Tomorrow, when the church opened for services, they would have to hide in the back closet where Marcus the janitor kept his supplies. He was the only one besides the Reverend who knew about them. He was a good man, a school friend of Jackson's, and every day he brought something for Ali to cheer the boy up. A candy bar, a basketball magazine, batteries for his Game Boy.

With difficulty Faith rose from the mat and walked down the hall to the bathroom to pee. She couldn't bear the thought of lying back down on the floor so she climbed the stairs to the sanctuary. She sat in the front row pew and stared up at Jesus on the crucifix. His face was ghostly white in the soft glow of the night light. Henry had the right idea when he made the Messiah a black man. Poor Henry. Where was he now? She bowed her head and prayed for him, prayed for them all. "Lord, we only seek to do your bidding," she said.

Soon her prayers merged into dreams. She woke with a start when she heard the door opening. Reverend Lee didn't see her until she called, "Reverend, what are you doing here in the middle of the night?"

He put his fingers to his lips and hurried down the aisle. She noticed he was barefoot and wearing his robe, this time tied more tightly around his middle. "It's almost dawn, Faith," he whispered when he reached the pew. "You have to leave right away."

"What's happened?"

"Marcus just called. He was listening to the police radio. They've got a warrant to search the church. They could come any minute. My car's out back and the key's in the ignition. Take it to Harbison's Landing. Marcus will meet you there in his brother's fishing boat."

"Where's he going to take us?"

"I don't know, and I don't want to know. Go wake the others now. I'll stay here and keep watch."

19

At Dorval Airport, Matt was met by a *Mount Royal Today* employee named Charles who whisked David and Matt into a white limo with black windows. It was 9:00 in the evening, and Montreal's glow lit up the northern sky. Charles, young and elegant in chinos and a blue silk shirt, said something in French to the driver and they sped away. "He's worried we might be followed," David translated. It was disconcerting for Matt to have his son-in-law in charge, but also a relief. David was a details man, efficient and well-organized, and his French was fluent. Jessie had insisted that he accompany Matt on the trip.

Fox had set up the interview. He'd used his connections to locate the right venue, an edgy but credible English-language TV station, a small operation, but one that Canada's national network, the CBC, was apt to give attention to, especially given the American crisis. There was to be a special live feed to the internet. Matt looked out the window. Were they being followed? They had let him out of the country easily enough. The challenge might be to get back in. The exile community in Montreal was growing rapidly. "Your health is all right?" Charles asked him politely.

"Oh yes, fine," Matt replied.

"As soon as we get to the station, you'll be taken to the make-up room. Our producer Neil McKenzie will meet you there to go over the questions."

"I hope the questions haven't changed," David said. "Justice Pomeroy ha
prepared his answers. He's not to be under too much stress."

"Yes, yes, Neil's aware of that. Just a short rehearsal, that's all."

"Bien, mais c'est très important que tout va selon le plan. Son coeur n'est pa
fort."

"Ne vous en faites pas. Tout est mis en place. Nous avons un médecin…"

Matt knew they were talking about him, but pretended not to understand
He just wanted to get the interview over with. All the worry and fuss beforehanc
had worn him down: Dora crying as if she might never see him again, Jessi
trying to calm her down, David a little superciliously assuming the role as his pro
tector. He would put them all out of his mind when he sat in front of the camera
he would pretend he was on the bench again, delivering judgment, no ordinar
mortal.

And yet he knew how mortal he was. How mortal they all were. The twin
growing inside his daughter were so small and vulnerable. He wanted to live t
see them. It was for his grandchildren he was speaking out, for the future of thei
country. And for the protesters too. According to internet reports, acts of civil dis
obedience were taking place all over the country, despite the crackdown. Th
postponement of the election had wakened people from their stupor, but for hov
long? Could they be lulled back to sleep?

He looked out the window again and had the illusion that the limo was sta
tionary and downtown Montreal was speeding toward them. He closed his eye
against the rush of bright lights, longing for a moment's rest.

He woke when they reached the studio, on a dark street near the river in
renovated warehouse. Charles offered Matt a hand to help him out. They too
the elevator to the third floor where Neil was waiting for them. He didn't loo
like a typical TV host. He was bald and his face was birdlike, but he had a com
manding voice, deep and melodic. He seemed agitated and spoke to Charles i
rapid-fire French. "I'm so sorry, I'm so very sorry," he said to Matt. "There's a b
of a crisis, you see. Come into my office, please. You do take cream and sugar i
your coffee? Charles, two double-doubles, if you please."

In the office he offered Matt and David the couch while he perched on th
edge of his desk. "It's quite astonishing really," he continued. "This has neve
happened to me in all my twenty-five years in television. They just called. I jus
got off the phone when I heard the elevator."

"Who called?" David asked.

"Mes chers amis at Radio Canada. CSIS, our Canadian security service, is seeking an injunction to block our broadcast on the grounds of national security."

"What?"

"CSIS loves to play hand-and-glove with the CIA, something that's got them into trouble a time or two. Washington's laying it on thick and heavy. So CSIS is trying to slide this right under the Cabinet's nose with excellent deniability afterwards. Wouldn't be the first time. But this time, I doubt if they'll get what they're after, and they probably doubt it too, because my techies report that we're having exceptional problems with our tower, cable, and satellite feeds. Probably not a coincidence, don't you think? But it's an old building; the wiring's co-located—with one exception, the phone line, and that's the one we're going to use." Neil chuckled. "God only knows why they thought they could control the flow of information these days. Silly buggers."

"So there won't be a broadcast tonight?" Matt asked, shaken.

"No, no, of course there'll be a broadcast—damned if I'd let them get away with stopping it. We'll simply transmit the interview over the internet. It will go round the world so fast they won't know what to do. The European stations will pick it up. But we should move swiftly. I don't know what else those silly buggers might try, but let's get this done, and now. That way my station can get back to business. We won't deviate from the script, but I would also like to ask your views on government censorship, if you don't mind, Justice Pomeroy."

"Not at all," Matt said, suddenly feeling much more energized. "In fact, I relish the opportunity."

In the studio they sat opposite each other at a small table with a checkered tablecloth. "Welcome to Montreal, Justice Pomeroy," Neil began. "So many Americans have decided to take a holiday here this August. It is a fine month in Quebec with fewer mosquitoes than in June or July. But I don't think that's why you or they are choosing to visit us. Perhaps you could tell our audience why you crossed the border and have joined us here in our studio."

Matt looked directly at the camera, imagining it as a proxy for a crowded courtroom. He leaned forward as he might on the bench and cleared his throat. "I have something to say that I no longer have the freedom to say in my own country," he began. "That's why I've come to Montreal."

It was after midnight when Lyndon drove to the suburbs to meet Skip. It was the same house, the same poolside where they met before, but this time the stakes

were much higher. Justice Pomeroy's accusation that the administration had exe-
cuted Salim Mohammed was already around the world; international news medi
were jumping on the story. Pomeroy has no proof, Lyndon reminded himself. Bu
that was hardly reassuring, with Toby Edwards still on the loose. Maybe Skip ha
news about that, maybe his boys had finally caught up with Edwards and plugge
that hole.

As he pushed open the backyard gate, he experienced a childish moment o
longing, longing for his bed, his parents, being tucked in at night instead o
roaming out here in hostile territory. He was tired of this, tired of whatever it wa
in himself that had got him involved with a man like Skip.

Skip was sitting in a deck chair by the pool. A citronella candle burned o
the table next to him. "What's up?" he asked as Lyndon took a seat opposite him

"You know what's up. Do you have Edwards yet? Without him, Pomeroy
story is just a story."

"You think stories don't matter, Lyndon? You've made up a few in your time
haven't you? This story could mean even more people out on the streets."

"That's not the point. Where's Edwards?"

"That's why I called you. A few hours ago we moved in on a house i
Richmond, but they had already left."

"Bad timing again," Lyndon said, a trace of sarcasm in his voice.

"Are you implying that I let him get away?"

"Am I?"

"Fuck you." Skip reached over and blew out the candle.

"Why did you do that?"

"I don't want to see your ugly face."

"Sorry," Lyndon said. "Let's restart this conversation."

"You damn well better be sorry. And you better get one thing straight. I'n
the one who has the most to lose if Toby Edwards talks. I gave him the order t
kill Mohammed."

"And I gave you the order. That's why we're in this together."

"Are we 'in this together' with the other killings too?"

"Of course."

"Until death do us part?"

The menace in Skip's voice reminded Lyndon of their last meeting and Skip
fantasy of holding him underwater. He didn't like it, but he couldn't afford to le

himself feel scared. Skip would notice, take it as a sign of weakness. With men like Skip you always had to act like the one in charge. "Just keep those photos to yourself, that's all I ask," Lyndon said.

"I'm afraid it's too late."

"What do you mean?"

"I've set up a website where people can view them. Everyone will know about you and the First Lady by tomorrow morning."

"You what?"

"Maybe I'm telling the truth, maybe not. Maybe I'm just telling a story." Skip stood and put a hand on the back of his chair. It wasn't clear to Lyndon whether he intended to leave or stay. He remained like that for a minute or two, staring into the pool, until he walked over and picked up a long pole skimmer. He ran it over the surface of the water, scooping a few leaves. He dumped them out and then swung the pole around and hit Lyndon on the head. Lyndon managed to duck as the pole came for him a second time.

But then Skip was on him. He grabbed him by the arms and lifted him out of the chair, pushing him towards the pool. He threw him into the water and jumped in after. "I'm going to make you beg for mercy, nigger," he snarled as he seized Lyndon's shoulders and forced him under. He held him there and then let him up. "Beg," he ordered, but before Lyndon could say a word, he pushed him under again. Up, under, up, under, no time to catch a breath.

There would be no mercy, Lyndon realized, because there never was for "niggers." Skip was holding him down harder now. He was going to kill him. With the desperation of a drowning man, Lyndon kneed him in the groin. Skip's grip loosened and Lyndon kicked him again. The rest was easy, for Skip hadn't anticipated his strength. He locked his arm around Skip's neck and held him under until his body went limp.

No mercy. None at all.

———

Lisa was exhausted, but she pushed herself to keep up. With their guide, an old hippie farmer named Daniel, she and Nick had been tramping through the northern Vermont woods for five hours without pausing to rest. It was a chilly night lit by a half moon, a hint of fall or even winter in the air. "The border patrol has started using helicopters with infrared sensors," Daniel warned them before they set out. "It used to be easy to cross, but not any longer. Soon Vermont will be as dangerous as Arizona." He was taking a circuitous route, avoiding the more traveled paths and in some places bushwhacking through brush and brambles. He was a deer hunter and he knew the territory like the back of his hand.

She thought back to that last night in Richmond when they watched Justice Pomeroy's interview on the internet. They had the smoking gun. Their video of Toby's confession was the proof he needed. They had decided to split up; she and Nick would head north by bus and try to cross over to Canada to meet with Pomeroy, while the others would head west. Nick chose Burlington for their destination. He had an old war buddy there who was now active in the peace movement. Through him they connected to a local bookstore that served as the northern station of an underground railroad that transported political activists over the border at night. So far they had been lucky.

"You can rest soon," Daniel told Lisa as if reading her mind. "From here it's only about a mile to the border where the van will meet you. We're almost in Canada." She nodded, too tired to spend energy on words. Nick was silent behind her. After his ordeal with Toby, he was bruised and even more exhausted than she was.

Daniel was the first to hear the helicopter. "Damn," he exclaimed, "this is the first time they've been out this way. Quick, we've got to hide." He shined the flashlight around them, searching for a place. "There's nothing here. We're going to have to run. There's a rock ledge a couple of hundred yards away. Leave your packs here, under the brush."

He set a fast pace and Lisa and Nick struggled to keep up. The helicopter was getting closer. The pilots would have night vision goggles, Daniel had told them—they would be looking for figures fleeing through the forest. They reached the ledge and threw themselves under. The rock above them was thick, but they were unprotected on one side and Lisa wondered if the sensors would pick up their body heat. Moments later the ground vibrated as the helicopter hovered overhead. They've got us, she thought. It's over.

She peered out as a searchlight slashed through nearby trees and undergrowth. Something was moving. A bull moose bounded out, running from the noise and light. The sound of a machine gun mixed with the whirring of the blades, and the moose fell to the ground, its body writhing as more bullets tore into it. They must have shot it fifty times before the helicopter finally circled away.

"Bastards," Nick swore. "They killed it for no reason."

"It saved our lives," she said.

They waited under the ledge for a good hour, long after the sound of the helicopter faded away. There was a hint of light at the horizon when they finally reached an old logging track that brought them to an abandoned farm over the border in Canada. An old VW van was waiting, parked next to a collapsing barn. Daniel exchanged a few words in French with the driver, a young woman with streaked orange hair in a jean jacket. "It's all set," he told them. "Monique will take you into Montreal. She supplies restaurants with fresh produce. They got word to Justice Pomeroy. He'll meet you at the lookout deck on Mount Royal at 9:00. Monique's got some new clothes for you. He'll recognize you from those."

"And what will you do?" Lisa asked.

"I'll stay here until it gets dark and then make my way back."

"What if there's another helicopter?"

He shrugged. "I'll make it. Don't worry."

Before setting off, they changed into the blue suits of salesclerks, embroidered with the monogram of a Montreal department store. They rode two hours in the back of the van, wedged between crates of tomatoes and sacks of onions. At 8:30 Monique dropped them off at the top of Peel Street and they climbed the steps up to Mount Royal.

How safe were they? Lisa wondered when they reached the top and looked out over the city to the St. Lawrence River. They were in Canada now, but what did that mean? The administration's hit men might be following Pomeroy. She thought of the moose bleeding on the trail, a plane crashing in an icy field, Richard Brown slumped against her. It wasn't just the horror of it, it was the impunity. Their violence respected no borders.

She checked her watch—almost 9:00. They walked over to a viewing machine where she slipped a quarter into the slot. As Nick bent to look through the eyehole, she felt a hand on her shoulder. "Might I have a turn?" She recognized the voice of Justice Pomeroy.

"Why, of course," she replied. As Nick made way for him, she slipped the video of Toby's confession into his jacket pocket.

"You can't imagine how long I've been waiting to see this view," the justice said. "How fortunate we are it's such a clear day. I think I can see all the way to Washington."

Faith sat on the deck of the fishing boat, staring at the dark sea. This was their fifth day on the water and her patience was wearing thin. She was seasick and homesick, but she couldn't complain, for Ali and Samira's sake. Or for the sake of Marcus. He and his brother were taking such a risk. Where did such goodness come from? Yes, they were old friends of Jackson's, but they didn't owe her anything. Yesterday, when the Coast Guard patrol boat pulled aside, the brother lied so well they didn't even bother to check in the hull where she was hiding with Samira and Ali.

They stayed below most of the day—that was the hard part. It smelled of oil and rotten fish and there was nothing to do except sleep and play cards. To amuse Ali, they played so many games of Crazy Eights that it was starting to drive her crazy. At least at night she could sit on deck and get some fresh air. They were somewhere off the coast of South Carolina. How much longer could they float out here? She thought of Henry. Was he safe, or had they captured him and the others? Were they even alive?

She stretched her legs, resting her feet on a coil of rope. The others were in the cabin listening to the shortwave radio. Every night they tuned into the BBC. She didn't join them because this was the only time she had to herself. Lord knows she needed time to run things through her head. Like what to do with the house and the fish store if they couldn't go home. She hoped no one had broken in or busted the windows.

She heard the cabin door open. "Faith, come here," Marcus called urgently. "You have to hear this."

"Coming, coming," she said as she tugged on her sandals.

Marcus made room for her at the table. "It's that man who came to the store, Grandma," Ali told her. "The man with the truck."

Ali was right. It was Toby's voice on the radio, and he was doing what he promised her—confessing to Jackson's murder. "I was ordered to go to Mohammed's cell and strangle him," he said. "They told me if I refused, they'd torture and kill my fiancée. I didn't know they had already killed her."

There was a pause and then Faith heard another man's voice, one she didn't recognize. "My name is Thomas Dougherty. I was an officer in the Central Intelligence Agency in charge of Salim Mohammed's interrogation. I never gave orders for him to be killed. In fact, I hoped the Supreme Court would decide that he should receive a fair trial as an American citizen. Can you tell us, Toby, the identity of the man who ordered you to kill Mohammed?"

"I heard him called Skip. I never heard his last name."

"Is this his photograph?"

"Yes."

"The man in question is Walter Morley, known by the nickname Skip," Dougherty continued. "He's an employee of Homeland Security who answers directly to White House advisor Lyndon Tottman."

20

As the plane took off, Matt looked down at Montreal beneath him, wondering if other exiles were also on their way home. Fox had called last night, offering to arrange a hero's welcome for him at National Airport, complete with red carpet, flashing cameras, banners and bouquets. Matt refused, pleading poor health. The real reason was that he wasn't ready to face the press and the first question they would ask: was he prepared to reconsider his resignation from the Supreme Court?

How could he? He had made a public accusation based on conjecture, not facts. The Edwards confession came later. It proved him right, but that did not exonerate his behavior. He had stepped outside the bounds of his role as Supreme Court justice. Once out, how could he possibly step back in? To do so would diminish the standing of the office.

"But, Matt, these are extraordinary times," Fox tried to convince him. "You had to do what you did. We need you back, and not just to keep our majority. You're the anchor, the only one who can bring us together to find the middle ground. The Court needs you, the country needs you. Even Chief Justice Reynolds wants you back."

"Reynolds? You're kidding?"

"No, I'm not. He needs to save face. Now that the President's resigned, all his lackeys are running around like dogs with their tails between their legs. It's a pleasure to watch, I tell you, a real pleasure."

Matt smiled at the image. Where was Scott now? he wondered. Did he have his tail between his legs too, or was he going to be one of the survivors? Matt would do everything in his power to expose him, but so much depended on finding Lyndon Tottman. The morning papers said he was missing. The body of his associate, Skip Morley, had been found in a swimming pool in Virginia. As if that weren't sordid enough, salacious photographs of Tottman and the First Lady were circulating all over the internet, trumping the real story behind the administration's collapse. Pornography instead of politics. He hoped the history books would see beyond the cheap sensationalism.

He reclined his seat. Next to him David was already asleep, worn out by his vigil in Montreal. Matt was grateful to him, but ready for a break from his company. His son-in-law was a little tiresome, too obsessive. Matt hoped fatherhood would loosen him up and push him off his linear trajectory. Children forced you to zigzag and curve, to master a new geometry.

The flight attendant came down the aisle, carrying a tray with a bottle of champagne and two glasses. Matt wondered who could stomach a drink at 9:00 in the morning. She stopped by his seat. She was middle-aged and stout, her hair pulled back in a perfunctory bun. "Justice Pomeroy?" she asked, and Matt nodded cautiously. "The Captain asked me to give you this as a token of our esteem."

"Well, thank you," Matt said, "but I couldn't possibly drink it now."

"That's OK. Take the bottle with you."

"Well, thank you," he repeated.

"No, thank you," she replied. "Thank you for your courage."

He felt the heat rising in his cheeks. How strange. It had been years since he blushed. People across the aisle were staring at him and he blushed even more. He bent down to slide the bottle under the seat. Then someone started clapping and another and another, until applause filled the cabin. David woke with a start. "What's happening?" he asked.

"I guess they recognize me."

It was even worse when they got off the plane. Fox had ignored his orders, arranging not only a red carpet, but a brass band. A crowd of reporters pressed toward him, thrusting microphones in his face. David tried to shield him, but it was futile. They shot questions at him: "Justice Pomeroy, have you reconsidered your resignation?" "Are you aware that thousands of people have gathered outside of the Supreme Court to demand your reinstatement?" "There's a rumor that you're considering running for President—is it true?"

"I'm not running for President," he replied. "That much I can tell you."

"Then you are considering rejoining the Court?"

"I didn't say that. Now please, let me pass."

He spotted Dora and Jessie on the fringe of the crowd and somehow managed to push his way through to them. Each took an arm, guiding him toward the door while David went to fetch the luggage. "Damn Fox," he said. "I told him I didn't want this kind of attention."

"It wasn't Fox," Jessie said.

"Then who was it?"

She shrugged. "I don't know. You're famous, Dad. You're just going to have to live with it."

———————

Nick parked on the side of the dirt road. "You stay here," Lisa told him. "I won't be long." She didn't really know what she'd come to find. All the wreckage would be long gone, scavenged by disaster tourists. If the plane had left marks in the earth, they were obscured by tall grasses and wildflowers and the wild berry bushes whose prickly stems reached out to slow her progress. In the center of the field stood a simple wooden cross, painted white, only its top visible.

She'd come to seek counsel, but from whom? Senator Barrett was dead. There was nothing here except an empty field, and beyond it long stretches of lonely road, broken only by occasional bars, bait shops, and substandard housing. This detour to the White Earth Indian Reservation meant a delay in seeing Sam. Did her need to come here first make her a bad mother? "Lisa, it's always a question of priorities." Weren't those Senator Barrett's last words to her?

But how do you determine priorities? That was the question she wished she could ask the senator. How do your rank them?

"You don't," the senator would probably say. "It's all done by the seat of your pants." That was an expression she'd liked to use, *by the seat of your pants.* "Political calculations never add up the way you expect, so you'd better be ready to change course at the drop of a hat." *Drop of a hat,* that was another favorite.

Well, Lisa had learned that lesson all right. These last weeks she had lived by the seat of her proverbial pants, ready to move at the drop of a hat. She supposed Senator Barrett would think that was good training, but for what?

"Politics, my dear," she could hear her say. "What else is there?"

Motherhood. Taking care of Sam.

"Oh yes, there is that too, but now you've found a man to share the burden with. Your generation is very fortunate that way."

If Lisa was going to enter politics seriously, it had to be now, when she had national name recognition and was a heroine of sorts. She'd just got word that she could stand for Senator Barrett's seat. Olsen was withdrawing after the press dredged up something about his involvement in a St. Paul real estate deal that went sour. He didn't want any more exposure. But was she ready? Senator Barrett first paid her dues in Minnesota state politics.

"People pay dues different ways," Nick advised her last night. "Don't you think you've paid yours already?" He wanted her to run for the Senate. He said he'd marry her tomorrow to make their relationship more respectable. He was too good. She didn't deserve him.

And now she'd left him sitting in the car.

She glanced in his direction. He was standing outside, leaning against the hood. She waved and he waved back. She knew he was impatient to get going. He wanted to reach the farm before nightfall.

She picked a raspberry off a bush and tasted it. It was tangy but sweet, perfect. She picked another. Tomorrow at the farm she'd take Sam out to collect raspberries and they'd make a pie and maybe he'd forgive her for abandoning him these last months. All his life he would have so much forgiving to do.

Senator Barrett once confided in her that her own son had never really forgiven her passion for politics, but he admired her, and maybe admiration was more important than forgiveness after all. "No one can be a perfect parent anyway," she said, "there's always something wrong." Then she said, out of the blue, "If you have a gift for power, Lisa, you have to use it. Otherwise it will eat you up inside. How many women have let that happen, chewed themselves up because they were afraid to acknowledge their gift for power? Either you have it or you don't. You're born with it, like a birthmark. It marks you for life."

She picked a handful of berries to take back to Nick. There was nothing new to learn here. The senator had already told her what she needed to know. She would expect Lisa, the survivor, simply to carry on.

On the way to the farm, she would make some calls on her cell phone and let them know she was ready to run.

———

"So it's you," Professor Maxwell said as he opened the door. "I thought you'd come."

"You did?"

"Yes," Maxwell replied, but he made no move to let Lyndon in.

"Can I come inside?"

The professor studied him for a moment. "I guess so. Should I call the police?"

"Not unless you want to."

"We'll see, then."

Except for a light in the den, the house was dark. It smelled musty, and a cough rose in Lyndon's throat. The weather was hot and humid, an ugly late summer night in New Jersey. The frail professor evidently didn't feel the heat, for he was wearing a wool cardigan. "Take a seat," he instructed Lyndon when they reached the den. "Can I get you something to drink?"

"Just a glass of water," Lyndon began, but then added, "Do you have Scotch by any chance?"

"I thought you didn't drink."

"I don't, but I'm making an exception tonight."

"Are you expecting me to remind you there are no exceptions for alcoholics?"

"No, I take full responsibility."

"All right, then. On the rocks?"

Lyndon nodded. Maxwell disappeared and then returned a few minutes later with two glasses of whiskey. After handing Lyndon one, he sat in the battered leather armchair. "I liked you better when you drank," he said, "perhaps because I harbored the illusion you could be saved."

"You don't have that illusion any more?"

"Am I supposed to? Is that why you've come here, hoping I'll save you?"

Lyndon shook his head. "No, I just need to talk."

"This den is not a confessional. I'm a professor, not a priest."

"I know that." Lyndon took a sip of Scotch. How long had it been—twelve years? It was single malt, expensive, he could still taste the difference. The glass felt so good in his hands, heavy and cold, a thing of substance. He swished the ice around and took another sip. "I thought you were supposed to drink single malts neat."

"An old man takes liberties. I like it with ice in the summer."

"So do I."

"Tell me, Lyndon, should I be frightened of you?"

"What do you mean?"

"You're on the run. I suppose you could take me hostage."

"I just want to talk to you—it won't take long."

"Suppose the police ask me what we talked about?"

"You can tell them. I don't care."

Maxwell leaned back, partially closing his eyes. "I'm trying to remember what we talked about in our final tutorial, when you defended your senior thesis. I dug it out the other day. I kept copies of them all, you know. My wife called me a packrat. It's probably good she died before me. Otherwise I would have left her with the burden of getting rid of all those papers." He smiled wistfully, running his fingers through a few remaining strands of hair. "I read your thesis last night. It's quite well-written for an undergraduate, but full of unsubstantiated assertions. You never had much patience for research, did you?"

"I still don't."

"A pity. You might have learned from other men's mistakes. That's why politicians should read history."

"They don't have time to read anything."

"Then someone should read it for them." The gaze Maxwell fixed on Lyndon was sharp and penetrating, all the force left in his diminished body concentrated in the eyes. "Hubris, that's it. We talked about the tragedy of hubris, or the farce, depending on the context. I wanted you to take a good, long look at yourself, but it seldom works with students. They're too young. Now that you're older, Lyndon, I imagine you've learned something about hubris?"

"That's not what I suffer from, Professor Maxwell."

"Then what is?"

"The longing to belong. You know."

"No, I'm afraid I don't."

"I don't blame it all on race…"

"Thank God for that."

"But it's a big part of it."

Maxwell shook his head. "Too simple, Lyndon. You're insulting your own intelligence, denying your own agency. You made moral choices, choices that have nothing to do with the color of your skin."

"That's not true."

Maxwell sighed. "Then explain, please."

"I only killed one man with my own hands. He called me 'nigger.' He tried to drown me, so I drowned him."

"That's not a moral choice. That's self-defense. It's the others I'm talking about—the others you arranged to have killed."

"How do you know that I did?"

"Why else would you be here?"

"I swear I had nothing to do with Senator Barrett's plane crash. That really was an accident."

"What about the others? Salim Mohammed? The ACLU lawyer?"

Lyndon looked away. The curtains were open. Someone standing on the street would be able to see inside, but his back was to the window—they wouldn't be able to see his face. He took another sip of Scotch, diluted now by melting ice. "Those were political decisions, not moral choices."

"Political decisions are moral choices. I taught you that."

"Well, I must have missed that lesson."

"Have you learned it now?"

Lyndon nodded slowly. "I'm a slow student, Professor, but I'm almost there."

"Do you feel remorse?"

"I can't feel anything. I know I should, but I can't. Maybe the whiskey will help."

"Are you going to turn yourself in?"

"I don't know. But I'll punish myself, don't worry." He paused, draining the last of the Scotch. "I should go."

"Is there anything else you want to tell me?" Maxwell asked.

Lyndon thought a moment. A full confession would last hours and he didn't have the time. And as Maxwell said, he was a professor, not a priest, a man trained to teach, not to listen. "There's just one thing," he said finally. "I wish you hadn't encouraged me to go into politics. It was the wrong path for me."

"How was I to know that, Lyndon? My job is to spot talent. I can't always anticipate the results."

"You pushed me because I was black. You wanted one of your black students to succeed, to make it big in Washington."

Maxwell knit his brow as if struggling to remember. "Maybe there's some truth to what you say, I don't know. It was a different time, there were different pressures. Mainly I saw that you had talent, and I didn't want to see it go to waste. I'm not prescient, and it appears that I'm not a very good judge of character either. I didn't foresee your capacity for evil. I wish I had."

"So do I. But I don't blame you, I blame myself. Don't worry about that."

"I don't have much worrying left in me, Lyndon. But what I have, I spend on you."

"Please don't. I don't merit it."

"It's not a question of merit. Quite the contrary, in fact."

Lyndon stood up. There was nothing else to say. The whiskey had made him dizzy and he needed some fresh air. He longed for his real father, not the old professor standing in for him, standing by as he plotted his own final act of destruction. His father would have put out a hand to restrain him, or at least to touch him one last time. "Don't get up," he told Maxwell. "I'll let myself out."

"Good-bye, then. I won't say good luck because that's not what you need."

"Good-bye, Professor." Lyndon shut the door quietly behind him. On the street he looked back through the window. Maxwell was still sitting in his chair. He wouldn't rush to call the police, Lyndon thought—in fact, chances were he would never call them. He was too private a man for that. Nevertheless, Lyndon walked the few blocks to the boathouse with haste, careful to keep his head down.

He broke the lock on the boathouse door with a rock, and from the rack he selected a single scull which he carried to the water. He climbed in, laced in his feet, secured the oars, and then pushed off from the dock. There was no wind and the water was perfectly still. He heard a dog barking in the yard of one of the houses on the lake, but other than that and the distant sound of passing cars, all was quiet. He rowed out to the middle of the lake and then north, towards the town of Kingston. Although he hadn't sculled for years, the movement returned easily and soon the oars seemed like natural extensions of his arms. This was the part of crew he'd liked—not the practices or races with the team, but being alone on the water. No winners, no losers. No coxswain shouting orders.

Their cox was a girl, small and thin but buff, with a ponytail that stuck out the back of her Princeton cap. Harriet was her name. He fancied her little breasts and made a move on her one night, but she rebuffed him. "No way, Lyndon, don't sleep with men." After that her voice grated on his nerves.

He shouldn't think of her now. He should think of the people he loved, or who had loved him. But there were so few of them. Was that why Harriet came to mind? A reminder of how little he would be missed?

He felt for the bottle of pills in his pocket. The plan was to swallow them and then flip the boat, but he wanted to feel first and he still couldn't. Maybe if he kept rowing, it would come to him, the remorse he needed to complete his manhood. He wanted to die a man, not an overgrown boy.

What if the remorse didn't come? Should he end his life anyway, or was that too easy a way out?

He stopped rowing and closed his eyes. He saw Trudy's face, the last person he had loved. Had she really loved him in return, loved plain Lyndon? He needed to know that before he died. Because if she had loved him, maybe there was something in him after all, something that would show him how to feel. He needed to see her one last time—that was all. He started rowing back to shore.

epilogue

From the ballroom stage of the Minneapolis Sheraton, Lisa looked out at the crowd of jubilant campaign workers and supporters swaying to the beat of a loud rock song. Her huge margin over her Republican opponent allowed the election to be called early. Hartley too had won by a landslide. She smiled and waved to the crowd, yet her mood was less than exuberant. This room was the last place she had seen Senator Barrett alive.

In truth, she didn't feel ready for the victory. She was worn out from the frantic weeks of campaigning. Somehow they had managed to fit in the wedding too, a small family affair at her parents' farm. She hardly knew who she was any more. In the morning she saw a politician in the mirror, but at night in bed, reflected through Nick's eyes, she saw an exhausted woman in need of comfort and confidence to face the tasks ahead. It must be worse for Hartley, she thought—he would be expected to work miracles. And if he couldn't, what then? The previous administration was history, but not the power base that supported it. So far no one had been brought to justice. Lyndon Tottman was still missing.

She sounded this somber note in the first draft of her acceptance speech, but last night Nick convinced her to change it. "People need to celebrate," he told her. "And that includes you. It's been a long time since we've had much to be happy about." Reluctantly, she took his advice and altered the tone. In a few minutes she would deliver the speech with Nick and Sam by her side. She looked over at Sam who was waving to the crowd like a pro. In the last month of the campaign he had come out of himself, or grown into himself, she wasn't sure which. He was an asset, her handlers told her. An asset. Such a cold word for a son.

The song was almost over, and the head of the state Democratic party was moving toward the podium. He would introduce her, though of course she needed no introduction. Her name and face were on banners and buttons and the front pages of newspapers all over the state. Lisa Derby was famous now. For better or worse, she had closed off all avenues of escape.

Watching Lisa deliver her victory speech, Nick thought back to the convention when she deviated from her scripted tribute to Senator Barrett and asked the questions no one else was asking. He knew she wanted to keep asking questions but it wouldn't be easy now that she was an elected official, a cog in the party machine. The strain of constant compromise already showed on her face, the lines etched deeper on her forehead, a few hairs turning gray. "Enjoy this moment, Lisa," he had reminded her as they mounted the stage. "How many times do you have like this in life?" But she wasn't enjoying it, he could tell. She was a good enough actress to fool the crowd, but not him. Beneath her words he could hear the silent fears that still stalked her.

At the point in her speech where she thanked Sam and him for their support, the three of them joined hands and raised their arms together to loud applause. "I couldn't have done it without them," Lisa shouted. She squeezed Nick's hand hard before she dropped it and moved closer to the mike. "We've been through a lot, Nick and me," she said, turning toward him. From the sudden fierce look in her eye he knew she was going to do it again—scrap the rest of the speech and say what she wanted to say. "You've have heard our story many times. But I want to tell you something he told me last night. I've been thinking about it all day long. I told him I was still afraid for myself and for this country, afraid that the nightmare we've just been through could happen again. And Nick had this wise advice for me. 'Lisa, freedom from fear is an illusion,' he said. 'It's only a question of knowing which fears are justified and which aren't, and then figuring out how to live with the ones that are.'

"My husband is right. But I don't want to just live with my fears. I want to work with them, make them work for me, and for you." She laughed. "They didn't call me the Princess of Paranoia for nothing." The crowd joined her laugher. "No, seriously, as your senator, I want to do everything in my power to ensure that we never again come so close to the death of our democracy. My fear will make me vigilant. I will defend the Constitution against its enemies with every breath of my body, with every step I take, with every vote I cast. That is my promise to you. Even in the glow of this wonderful victory, even when all feel ight again with the world, I will remain vigilant. I will be custodian of our ightful fears. Thank you. Thank you so much for believing in me."

The crowd cheered and hundreds of balloons lifted into the air. Lisa took Nick and Sam by the hands again and they walked to the front of the stage for a inal bow. More applause. More cheers. She had taken another gamble, Nick hought, but it worked again, and now she looked genuinely happy. As the con-etti rained, she stooped to shake hands. Nick looked out over the room, won-lering if there were any enemies there. To lose her to a plane crash or an assassin's bullet—that was his worst fear, and he knew it would never go away. He would ave to take his own advice and learn to live with it.

At 1:00 AM Matt was still glued in front of the television, reveling in the olling data and victory speeches. Dora had gone to bed at midnight, chastising im for staying up so late. Now that he was retired from the Court, he stayed up ast midnight almost every night and slept in late in the morning. She didn't like t; she wanted them to have breakfast together. Oh well, their marriage had sur-ived worse frictions. He picked up the phone and dialed Fox's number. He would still be up, Matt knew.

"Glory, glory, hallelujah," Fox sang into the phone. "I never thought I'd be appy about a Democratic landslide, but it's sweet, very sweet. And there's more ood news, my friend."

"What's that?" Matt asked.

"Reynolds is going to resign soon, citing health reasons."

"How do you know?"

"One of my sources."

"You and your sources."

"Have they ever been wrong?"

"No, but…"

"But what? Aren't you happy?"

"Delighted, of course."

"And you know who Hartley's going to nominate for chief justice?"

"Who?"

"You."

"What? Don't kid me now, Eric. My old heart can't take it."

"You'd better get back in shape. No more of this retirement nonsense—you're oing to have a lot of work to do."

"I don't believe it—it's just a silly rumor."

"No, it's not. You're the only man for the job and Hartley knows it. The only person who can bring the Court back together. You'll have to accept."

"I can't," Matt stated as forcefully as he could. He had said those two words many times in the last few months in response to pleas to withdraw his resignation. But this was different. There was no greater honor than to be asked to serve as chief justice. He had never let himself hope for this, never planned or plotted to go so far. He wanted it, of course he wanted it, but he would have to steel himself against the temptation.

"Don't you think you've held out long enough?"

"Believe me, Eric, I'd like to say yes, but you know why I resigned. When made an accusation without proof, I crossed a line from which there's no return I haven't changed my mind about that."

Fox sighed audibly into the phone. "Oh, get off your high horse, will you Matt? The administration forced us into the trenches. What were we supposed to do, stand there and let the cannons blow off our heads? So you got your hands little dirty. Believe me, they're a lot cleaner than Reynolds's hands ever were You're far too hard on yourself."

"I did something a justice should never do, Eric. Rejoining the bench would dishonor the Court and all it stands for."

"Don't you realize that most people don't even think what you did is problem, and that those who do have already forgiven you?"

Matt took a moment to consider the point. True, most people had forgiven him. Even top legal scholars, people he respected, had urged him to reconsider citing the extraordinary circumstances. But over the last few months he had come to believe that excessive willingness to forgive was one of the main problems with the country. "Americans forgive their leaders all too easily," he told Fox. "Look at the President, or the ex-President I should say. No one's holding him accountable Instead they blame the men around him. People actually feel sorry for him and it makes me sick."

"It makes me sick too, but your situation is hardly the same as his. At least think it over."

"I have. Holding myself accountable to the rule of law is what I want my final legacy to be."

"As chief justice, you'll leave a far greater legacy than that."

"No, I don't think so. Respecting the rule of law has gone out of fashion. I want to remind people how important it is, how our democracy can't function without it."

Fox sighed again. "You're a stubborn bastard, Matt."

"Yes, Eric, I'm afraid I am."

———

Groggily, Faith Jones reached to turn off the alarm clock. Usually she was wide awake by 6:00 AM, but last night she'd stayed up late watching the election returns. She'd turn over and go back to sleep if she hadn't promised to meet Toby Edwards for a morning walk on the beach. He'd made a special trip to see her. She rose slowly from the mattress, holding onto the bedside table to help herself up. Her hips pained her more these days, and she was thinking of cutting back her hours at the store. Soon Samira would be able to take charge and Marcus had hinted he might like to quit his job to work with them. He had his eye on Samira, she could tell, and he was good with Ali. She wondered if Jackson was jealous up in heaven, or if those things stopped mattering once you were dead.

Toby was already at the beach parking lot when she arrived, standing by his truck. He was wearing a green running suit and his shoes looked new, white with a red stripe. For once he wasn't wearing dark glasses. They shook hands solemnly and then walked to the beach in silence. The rising sun was bobbing on the water, soon to be lost in a cloud. A sandbank broke the waves a couple of hundred feet out, so they rolled in small, hardly making a sound as they hit the shore. The wind was up and she was glad she was wearing a scarf over her hair. She pulled the knot to tighten it.

"I'm glad you came back," she said as they moved closer to the water's edge. "You should be in touch with Henry too. He asked me the other day if I'd heard anything from you. His crucifixion window survived the fire, did you know that? It's a miracle. I'm trying to get my church to put it up." She waited a moment to see if he would respond, but he just nodded. "Is there something you want to tell me?" she asked. "Is that why you wanted to meet me?" He nodded again. Cat got your tongue, she wanted to say, but refrained. As if to mock his silence, a gull screeched overhead.

"I want to ask for your forgiveness again," he said, staring straight ahead.

"Well, you earned it, didn't you?"

"Did I?"

"Yes, of course you did."

"I have a hard time believing that."

"Look at me, Toby," she ordered, recalling the time she had made him take off his sunglasses. His eyes were watery today—from sadness or the salt air, she couldn't tell. "It's often harder to accept forgiveness than to give it, especially for someone with a conscience. Henry told me you tried to kill yourself."

"I almost succeeded."

"Well, you can be sure I wouldn't have forgiven you for that. You did the right thing by staying alive, by speaking out. I'm grateful for that."

"But I killed your son, Mrs. Jones."

"Don't you think I know that, boy? Every night I imagine your hands around his neck, but that doesn't mean I can't forgive you. You make it easy, don't you see? It's much harder to forgive the people who made you do it."

"Have you forgiven them too?"

She shook her head. "No, I haven't even started to try. Have you forgiven the people who killed your fiancée?"

"No."

"Well, then we're in the same boat, you and me."

"I never thought of it that way."

"Maybe it will give you some comfort."

"Yes," he said, "I believe it will. Thank you, Mrs. Jones." He bent down and picked up a flat stone which he skipped on the water. She left him there, skipping stones.

———

So little has changed, Lyndon thought, as he pulled into Camp Shawnee in the hills outside Austin. The totem pole out front was just the same, the proud eagle perched on top, the bear at the base holding the weight of all the lesser creatures. He parked the car and wandered among the empty cabins, still stained dark brown. He looked through the window of one where he had stayed, wondering if his initials were still carved into the wall above the bunk.

At the end of the playing field he found the path down to the river. It was overgrown and there was trash along its sides, liquor bottles and plastic bags left by local kids who hung out here in the off-season. When he reached the river bank, the water was running faster and deeper than he remembered, probably due to the last month's heavy rains. The girls' camp was still on the other side, though last year he heard a rumor that it might sell out to a vacation condo devel-per. Surely the wife of some rich oilman would come to the rescue. Nostalgia was big bucks in Texas.

He hoped Trudy would come this time. Three times before he had arranged to meet her, but she hadn't shown up. He didn't know how much longer he could keep on the run. His money was almost exhausted and so was his spirit. He was staying alive for her, but she didn't know that.

"Hello, Lyndon." He turned toward her voice and there she was, plain Trudy. She laughed nervously. "You look so different."

His hand went up to touch his hair. He had grown an Afro and a beard as a disguise and put on weight from the fast food he survived on. She was wearing tight jeans and a suede jacket, her hair loose and wind-blown. "You look the same—beautiful," he told her.

"I'm not the same."

"I guess it's impossible to stay the same under the circumstances."

"Yes." She moved closer to him, but not close enough for him to touch her. He wanted to—he wanted so much to hold her. "This is the river you told me about?" He nodded. "I guess I didn't expect it to be so brown and muddy."

"It's because of the rain," he explained. "All the sediment washes down."

"Would you swim it for me like you did for that girl?"

"Of course." She laughed nervously again, and this time there was something in it that reminded him of what they'd had, what they'd lost, the intimacy that had started as sex and ended up as something else, if not love exactly, then a certain confidence in each other, a faith. He wanted it back. "Did you ever love me, Trudy? Just tell me that—I need to know."

"Honestly, Lyndon, I can't remember. It seems ages ago."

"I can remember."

She acted as if she didn't hear him. "I've been so busy—it's been crazy."

"Doing what?"

"Salvaging what I can from the wreck. We need to rebuild. It's going to be hard after this defeat, but we can do it. We always do."

"And your husband?"

"He's much better."

"He is?"

"He tricked us both, Lyndon. Oh, he was drinking all right, but he made it look worse than it was. He knew he was going to lose to Hartley, and that all the dirt was going to come out. So he decided to go into hibernation. If you suc-

ceeded in keeping him in power by other means, fine. But if not, well, you would
be the one to take the fall. And it worked. You're the bad guy on the run, not him.
He's just an alcoholic, another weak man recovering in the strong arms of Jesus."

"What? I can't believe it!"

"He's cleverer than you think. He wants me to play the victim too. We're
both your victims, you see. You blackmailed me into having sex with you. If I
didn't, you were going to tell the world he was drinking. I had no choice."

"That's a lie."

"Of course it is, but when did either of you ever care about the truth?"

"I did when I was with you."

She looked down and his eyes followed, but there was nothing on the muddy
ground but a few broken twigs. "I'm sorry, Lyndon, but I have to play it this way.
Not just for me, but for what we believe in. I'm a celebrity now, you know. I've
been offered a two million dollar book contract for the inside story of you and
me, but my agent's telling me to hold out for more. I'm going to use the money
to buy my way in. This time I want my own seat at the table."

"What if I told you I don't believe in our cause any more? That I want to feel
remorse for what I did?"

"I'd tell you our ways have parted."

"Trudy, really…" He ventured a little closer. "You're making a mistake."

"Maybe, but it's worth trying. My husband's going to help from behind the
scenes. What are you going to do, Lyndon? They're going to catch up with you
eventually, you know."

"Why did you come, Trudy? If you don't love me, why did you come?" From
the look that passed over her face he suddenly knew. Somewhere hidden in the
trees was a photographer, taking shots for the cover of her book. And then they
would close in on him. That would be photographed too, Lyndon Tottman
handcuffed, pushed into the back of a police car. Trudy, the victim turned
heroine, turning him in. Trudy, the only one left with any power.

He threw off his jacket, raced to the river and jumped in. He felt remorse at
last, remorse at his own blind stupidity. There's blood on your hands, Lyndon
Tottman. He felt remorse for the killings too, but not for the time he had killed
with his own hands. He swam a few strokes and surrendered to the current, letting the cold water wash away the blood and carry him downstream to the
freedom he had finally earned.

About the author

Betsy Hartmann writes fiction and non-fiction about critical national and global issues. She has written for the *Boston Globe*, *New York Times*, the *Nation* and a variety of policy and scholarly publications. She is the author of *The Truth about Fire*, a political thriller about neo-Nazis in the American heartland, and *Reproductive Rights and Wrongs: The Global Politics of Population Control*. She is co-author of *A Quiet Violence: View from a Bangladesh Village* and co-editor of the anthology, *Making Threats: Biofears and Environmental Anxieties*. She lives in Amherst, Massachusetts where she teaches and directs the Population and Development Program at Hampshire College. She received her B.A. from Yale University and PhD from the London School of Economics and Political Science.

Learn more about Betsy Hartmann at www.BetsyHartmann.com.

Printed in the United States
204166BV00003B/274-303/P